The Tyndale New Testament Commentaries

General Editor:
THE REV. CANON LEON MORRIS, M.Sc., M.Th., Ph.D.

1 PETER

THE FIRST EPISTLE OF PETER

AN INTRODUCTION AND COMMENTARY

by

WAYNE A. GRUDEM, B.A., M.Div., Ph.D.

Associate Professor of Biblical and Systematic Theology,
Trinity Evangelical Divinity School,
Deerfield, Illinois

Inter-Varsity Press
Leicester, England

William B. Eerdmans Publishing Company
Grand Rapids, Michigan

Inter-Varsity Press
38 De Montfort Street, Leicester LE1 7GP, England

Wm. B. Eerdmans Publishing Company
255 Jefferson S.E., Grand Rapids, MI 49503

Published and sold only in the USA and Canada by Wm. B. Eerdmans Publishing Co.

British Library Cataloguing in Publication Data

Grudem, Wayne, *1948–*
 The First Epistle General of Peter.
 1. Bible. N.T. Peter, 1st – Commentaries
 I. Title. II. Series
 227'.9207

 IVP ISBN 0-85111-886-0

EERDMANS ISBN 0-8028-0407-1

Set in Palatino
Typeset in Great Britain by Parker Typesetting Service, Leicester
Printed in USA by Eerdmans Printing Company, Grand Rapids, Michigan

Inter-Varsity Press is the book-publishing division of the Universities and Colleges Christian Fellowship (formerly the Inter-Varsity Fellowship), a student movement linking Christian Unions in universities and colleges throughout the United Kingdom and the Republic of Ireland, and a member movement of the International Fellowship of Evangelical Students. For information about local and national activities write to UCCF, 38 De Montfort Street, Leicester LE1 7GP.

GENERAL PREFACE

The original *Tyndale Commentaries* aimed at providing help for the general reader of the Bible. They concentrated on the meaning of the text without going into scholarly technicalities. They sought to avoid 'the extremes of being unduly technical or unhelpfully brief'. Most who have used the books agree that there has been a fair measure of success in reaching that aim.

Times, however, change. A series that has served so well for so long is perhaps not quite as relevant as when it was first launched. New knowledge has come to light. The discussion of critical questions has moved on. Bible-reading habits have changed. When the original series was commenced it could be presumed that most readers used the Authorized Version and one could make one's comments accordingly, but this situation no longer obtains.

The decision to revise and up-date the whole series was not reached lightly, but in the end it was thought that this is what is required in the present situation. There are new needs, and they will be better served by new books or by a thorough up-dating of the old books. The aims of the original series remain. The new commentaries are neither minuscule nor unduly long. They are exegetical rather than homiletic. They do not discuss all the critical questions, but none is written without an awareness of the problems that engage the attention of New Testament scholars. Where it is felt that formal consideration should be given to such questions, they are discussed in the Introduction and sometimes in Additional Notes.

But the main thrust of these commentaries is not critical. These books are written to help the non-technical reader to

5

understand the Bible better. They do not presume a knowledge of Greek, and all Greek words discussed are transliterated; but the authors have the Greek text before them and their comments are made on the basis of the originals. The authors are free to choose their own modern translation, but are asked to bear in mind the variety of translations in current use.

The new series of *Tyndale Commentaries* goes forth, as the former series did, in the hope that God will graciously use these books to help the general reader to understand as fully and clearly as possible the meaning of the New Testament.

LEON MORRIS

CONTENTS

AUTHOR'S PREFACE

Over the last four years l have worked closely with the text of 1 Peter, both in teaching it and in writing this commentary. As I now complete the commentary I am surprised that, far from being tired of the words of this letter, I hear them speak with more directness and urgency to my own life, and I still find joy and spiritual refreshment reading them again and again. For me personally, this is yet further confirmation of the character of this letter as 'the living and abiding word of God' (1 Pet. 1:23).

I do not think that any Christian can study this letter for long without hearing in it the voice of God speaking powerfully to the needs of today's church. In only 105 verses, 1 Peter ranges over a wide field of Christian theology and ethics. Here is the great doctrine of redemption, from its conception before the foundation of the world to its consummation in our receiving an inheritance that will never fade away. Here are repeated calls to holiness and to humble trust in God for each day's needs. Here is practical counsel – for marriage, for work, for relating to the government, for witnessing to unbelievers, for using spiritual gifts, for serving as a church officer.

Here also is profound comfort in sorrow, and insight, as far as God allows, into the deep mysteries of suffering and reprobation. Here is the majestic beauty of the church as a 'spiritual temple' in which we daily offer 'spiritual sacrifices' pleasing to God. And here is Jesus – the chief Shepherd who cares for us, the example who leads us, the chosen cornerstone who establishes and unites us, and the Saviour who bore our sins in his body on the cross – the one whom, not having seen, we love. The glory of Christ shines forth from this letter into the hearts of all who read it. For churches and for individuals seeking to grow in holiness, in ·faith, and in love for Christ, God's words in 1 Peter will richly repay serious study, memorization, and meditation.

Studies in 1 Peter during this century have tended to emphasize attempts to discover sources behind 1 Peter (was it originally a baptismal sermon? a baptismal liturgy? does it depend on Paul? on James? on early catechisms? on moral codes common in a pagan society?). Other studies have focused on the setting in which it was written (official persecution? baptismal service? Easter liturgy?). But exegesis of the text itself (other than to answer those questions) has been somewhat neglected.

I have found myself largely unpersuaded by these studies regarding sources and setting, primarily because – in my own judgment at least – they almost uniformly attempt to draw conclusions based on far too little data. Perhaps it is time to admit that the requisite evidence for answering such questions is simply not available to us, and that good stewardship of the time and skills which God has given us would seem to require that we give more attention to the text itself, not primarily to determine its original setting and sources, but to ascertain its meaning for Peter and his original readers, and then its proper application to our own lives.

This commentary probably has a higher than average frequency of citations from other ancient texts, both biblical and extra-biblical, and a lower than average frequency of citations from other commentaries. This is intentional, because I think it very important for Christians to come to accept a particular interpretation of any verse *not* because some expert has given his opinion in favour of it, but because they have seen for themselves the *evidence* which supports that interpretation, and the evidence has convinced them.

Such evidence may come in the form of (1) other texts where the *same word* (or grammatical construction) is used, illustrating the meaning of the word (or grammatical construction); (2) other texts on the *same subject* in 1 Peter or in the larger context of the New Testament or the whole Bible, illustrating the teaching of Peter and of the other biblical writers elsewhere on this subject; (3) arguments from the flow of thought in the passage and the role an individual phrase plays in furthering the author's overall purpose in the passage ('the context'). In most cases all three types of evidence can be presented in such a way that even readers without knowledge of Greek can understand and evaluate the evidence for themselves. In some cases I have quoted the other texts which convinced me; in other cases I have just cited the references, expecting the interested reader to look them up.

Some readers of this series may feel that the unique authority of the Bible is somewhat compromised by the frequent citation of extra-biblical literature such as Josephus, Philo, the Apocrypha, the Rabbinic literature, the Apostolic Fathers and other early Christian writers, and even secular Greek authors. But here a distinction needs to be made. I do not think that a citation from any of these writings can prove that Peter must have held a certain doctrine or agreed with some current opinion, no matter how popular in the first-century culture, for the biblical authors frequently differ from both their Jewish background and the secular culture which surrounds them. But I do think that examples of usage of *words* from extra-biblical Jewish and Christian writers, and even from such secular writers as Strabo (writing *c.* 20 BC–AD 19), Diodorus Siculus (writing *c.* 40 BC), or Plutarch (*c.* AD 46–120) can be very useful in understanding New Testament words, especially those for which there are few examples in the New Testament itself or in the Septuagint, the Greek translation of the Old Testament. Extra-biblical sources can also provide helpful glimpses of the *historical situation* in which Peter and his readers lived, including the thought-patterns common among members of the societies which surrounded them. For these purposes the vast amount of ancient Jewish, Christian, and secular Greek literature which remains today can be seen as a blessing preserved by God's providential oversight, so that we might be able to understand his Word more accurately.

I owe much to the help of others in this work. I am thankful for the detailed comments and encouragement of Leon Morris, the editor of this series, and of David Kingdon, theological books editor at Inter-Varsity Press, whose perceptive reading has resulted in many improvements both in style and in content. I am thankful to many friends who in conversation and

1. OTHER TEXTS WHERE THE SAME WORD IS USED
2. OTHER TEXT ON SAME SUBJECT
3. ARGUMENT FROM THE FLOW OF THOUGHT IN CONTEXT

written comments have helped my understanding of the text, especially George Knight III, Murray Harris, Stanley E. Porter, C. F. D. Moule, D. A. Carson, and many students in my classes at Trinity Evangelical Divinity School. Moreover, Sherry Kull, Marie Birkinshaw, Jane Preston, and Sylvia Akhurst have helped me by accurately typing various sections along the way. I wish to thank the Board of Directors of Trinity Evangelical Divinity School for granting me a sabbatical to work on the commentary, and the Tyndale House Council for allowing me to use the excellent library facilities of Tyndale House, Cambridge, where most of this commentary was written.

I especially wish to thank my parents for generously providing the financial assistance which enabled me to complete this work. And my three boys, Elliot, Oliver, and Alexander, have been a continual source of joy and encouragement, even as they kept wondering if Daddy 'got another verse done on his commentary today'. But most of all I wish to thank my wife Margaret, who has encouraged me when the task seemed long, and who has made many sacrifices in time and effort because she was convinced that it was pleasing in the Lord's sight for me to complete this work. I dedicate this book to her, one who 'in God's sight is very precious' (1 Pet. 3:4), and in mine.

To God alone be glory.

WAYNE GRUDEM

ABBREVIATIONS

BOOKS AND JOURNALS

Alford	H. Alford, *The Greek Testament*, vol. 4 (Cambridge: Deighton, Bell, and Co., ³1866).
AV	Authorized Version (King James'), 1611.
BAGD	W. Bauer, W. F. Arndt, F. W. Gingrich, and F. W. Danker, *A Greek-English Lexicon of the New Testament and other Early Christian Literature* (Chicago: University of Chicago Press, ²1979).
BDB	F. Brown, S. R. Driver and C. A. Briggs, *Hebrew and English Lexicon of the Old Testament* (Oxford: University Press, 1906).
BDF	F. Blass, A. Debrunner, and R. W. Funk, *A Greek Grammar of the New Testament and Other Early Christian Literature* (Chicago: University of Chicago Press, 1961).
Beare	F. W. Beare, *The First Epistle of Peter* (Oxford: Blackwell, ³1970).
Best	E. Best, *1 Peter*, New Century Bible (London: Oliphants, 1971).
Bigg	C. Bigg, *A Critical and Exegetical Commentary on the Epistles of St. Peter and St. Jude*, International Critical Commentary (Edinburgh: T. & T. Clark, ²1910).
Blum	Edwin A. Blum, '1 Peter', in *The Expositor's Bible Commentary*, vol. 12, edited by Frank E. Gaebelein (Grand Rapids: Zondervan, 1981).
Calvin	J. Calvin, *Calvin's Commentaries: The Epistle of Paul*

13

	the Apostle to the Hebrews and the First and Second Epistles of St. Peter, translated by W. B. Johnston, edited by D. W. and T. F. Torrance (Grand Rapids: Eerdmans, 1963).
CBQ	*Catholic Biblical Quarterly*.
CIJ	J.–B. Frey, *Corpus Inscriptionum Iudaicarum*, 2 vols. (Rome: Pontificio Instituto di Archeologia Christiana, 1936, 1952).
Cranfield	C. E. B. Cranfield, *1 and 2 Peter and Jude*, Torch Bible Commentaries (London: SCM, 1960).
Dalton	W. J. Dalton, *Christ's Proclamation to the Spirits* (Rome: Pontifical Biblical Institute, 1965).
Deissmann	G. A. Deissmann, *Bible Studies*, translated by A. Grieve (Edinburgh: T. & T. Clark, 1901).
ExpT	*Expository Times*.
France	R. T. France, 'Exegesis in Practice: Two Samples', in *New Testament Interpretation*, edited by I. H. Marshall (Grand Rapids: Eerdmans, 1977).
Grammar	A. T. Robertson, *A Grammar of the Greek New Testament in the Light of Historical Research* (Nashville: Broadman, [4]1934).
Hart	J. H. A. Hart, 'The First Epistle General of Peter', *The Expositor's Great Testament*, vol. 5, general editor W. R. Nicoll (1910; reprinted Grand Rapids: Eerdmans, 1970).
HDB	J. Hastings, editor, *A Dictionary of the Bible*, 5 vols. (Edinburgh: T. & T. Clark, 1898–1904).
Hort	F. J. A. Hort, *The First Epistle of St. Peter 1:1–2:17* (London: Macmillan, 1898).
Huther	J. E. Huther, *The General Epistles of James, Peter, John, and Jude*, trans. P. Gloag *et al.*, Meyer's Commentary (New York: Funk and Wagnalls, [6]1884).
IB	G. A. Buttrick *et al.*, editors, *Interpreter's Bible*, 12 vols. (New York: Abingdon-Cokesbury, 1952–57).
ICC	International Critical Commentary series (Edinburgh: T. & T. Clark).
IDB	G. A. Buttrick *et al.*, editors, *The Interpreter's Dic-*

	tionary of the Bible, 4 vols. (Nashville: Abingdon Press, 1962).
JBC	*Jerome Biblical Commentary*, 2 vols., edited by Raymond Brown *et al.* (London: Chapman, 1968).
JBL	*Journal of Biblical Literature.*
JETS	*Journal of the Evangelical Theological Society.*
JTS	*Journal of Theological Studies.*
Kelly	J. N. D. Kelly, *A Commentary on the Epistles of Peter and Jude*, Black's New Testament Commentaries (London: Black, 1969).
Lampe	G. W. H. Lampe, *Patristic Greek Lexicon* (Oxford: University Press, 1961).
LCL	Loeb Classical Library.
Leaney	A. R. C. Leaney, *The Letters of Peter and Jude*, Cambridge Bible Commentary (Cambridge: University Press, 1967).
Leighton	R. Leighton (died 1684), *Commentary on First Peter* (reprinted Grand Rapids: Kregel, 1972).
Lenski	R. C. H. Lenski, *The Interpretation of the Epistles of St. Peter, St. John, and St. Jude* (Minneapolis: Augsburg, 1966).
LSJ	H. G. Liddell, R. Scott, and H. S. Jones, *Greek–English Lexicon* (Oxford: University Press, ^{9}1940).
MHT	J. H. Moulton, W. F. Howard, and N. Turner, *A Grammar of New Testament Greek*, 4 vols. (Edinburgh: T. & T. Clark, 1908–76).
MM	J. H. Moulton and G. Milligan, *The Vocabulary of the Greek Testament Illustrated from the Papyri and other Non-literary Sources* (1930; reprinted Grand Rapids: Eerdmans, 1972).
NASB	New American Standard Bible, 1963.
NEB	New English Bible: New Testament, ^{2}1970; Old Testament, Apocrypha, 1970.
NIC	New International Commentary series (Grand Rapids: Eerdmans).
NIV	The Holy Bible, New International Version: New Testament, ^{2}1978; Old Testament, 1978.

NovT	*Novum Testamentum.*
NovTSup	*Novum Testamentum*, Supplements.
NTI	D. Guthrie, *New Testament Introduction* (Leicester: Inter-Varsity Press, ³1970).
NTS	*New Testament Studies.*
OCD	N. G. L. Hammond & H. H. Scullard, editors, *The Oxford Classical Dictionary* (Oxford: University Press, ²1970).
ODCC	F. L. Cross and E. A. Livingstone, editors, *The Oxford Dictionary of the Christian Church* (Oxford: University Press, ²1974).
OTP	J. Charlesworth, editor, *The Old Testament Pseudepigrapha*, 2 vols. (Garden City, NY: Doubleday, 1983, 1985).
Phillips	J. B. Phillips, *The New Testament in Modern English*, 1958.
Reicke	B. Reicke, *The Disobedient Spirits and Christian Baptism* (Copenhagen: Munksgaard, 1946).
RSV	Revised Standard Version: New Testament, ²1971; Old Testament, 1952; Common Bible, 1973.
RTR	*Reformed Theological Review* (Australia).
SBL	Society of Biblical Literature.
Selwyn	E. G. Selwyn, *The First Epistle of St. Peter* (London: Macmillan, 1949).
Stibbs/Walls	A. M. Stibbs and A. F. Walls, *The First Epistle General of Peter*, Tyndale New Testament Commentary series (London: Tyndale, 1959).
TDNT	G. Kittel and G. Friedrich, editors, *Theological Dictionary of the New Testament*, translated by G. W. Bromiley, 10 vols. (Grand Rapids: Eerdmans, 1964–76).
TEV	Today's English Version, 1976 (= Good News Bible).
ThL	*Theologische Literaturzeitung.*
TrinJ	*Trinity Journal.*
TynB	*Tyndale Bulletin* (formerly THB).
UBS	United Bible Societies, *The Greek New Testament*, edited by K. Aland *et al.*, ³1975).

UPZ	*Urkunden der Ptolemäerzeit*, 2 vols., edited by U. Wilcken (Berlin: W. de Gruyter, 1927–57).
WTJ	*Westminster Theological Journal*.
Zahn	T. Zahn, *An Introduction to the New Testament* (ET, Edinburgh: T. & T. Clark, 1909), vol. 2.

ANCIENT EXTRA-BIBLICAL LITERATURE

Abr.	Philo, *On Abraham*.
Ant.	Josephus, *Antiquities of the Jews*.
b.R.H.	Babylonian Talmud, *Rosh Hashshana*.
b.Sanh.	Babylonian Talmud, *Sanhedrin*.
CD	*Qumran Damascus Document* (Dead Sea Scrolls).
Diod. Sic.	Diodorus Siculus.
Eccl.R.	Midrash Rabbah on Ecclesiastes.
Ecclus.	Ecclesiasticus (Apocrypha).
EH	Eusebius, *Ecclesiastical History*.
Exod.R.	Midrash Rabbah on Exodus.
Gen.R.	Midrash Rabbah on Genesis.
Moses	Philo, *Life of Moses*.
Mut.	Philo, *On the Change of Names*.
Num.R.	Midrash Rabbah on Numbers.
Q.Gen.	Philo, *Questions on Genesis*.
Sib. Or.	*Sibylline Oracles*.
SongR.	Midrash Rabbah on Song of Songs.
T.Levi	*Testament of Levi* (in *Testaments of the Twelve Patriarchs*).
T.Naph.	*Testament of Naphtali* (in *Testament of the Twelve Patriarchs*).
War	Josephus, *Jewish War*.

GENERAL ABBREVIATIONS

ET	English translation.
Fs.	Festschrift.
LXX	The Septuagint (pre-Christian Greek version of the Old Testament).

mg.	margin.
MS(S)	manuscript(s).
ns, NS	new series.
sec.	section.
v.l.	variant reading.

In citations from the LXX where the chapter/verse numbering of the English translations differs from that of the Greek text, the former is cited first and the latter is put in brackets.

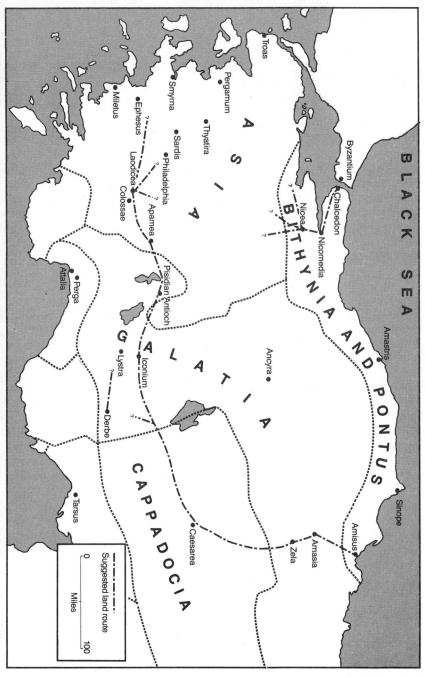

THE CIRCULATION OF 1 PETER

INTRODUCTION

I. AUTHOR

A. EVIDENCE WITHIN THE LETTER

The author identifies himself by name in the first phrase of the letter: 'Peter, an apostle of Jesus Christ.' This is consistent with the practice of other New Testament authors (*cf.* the opening phrases in the letters of Paul, James, John, and Jude; also in 2 Pet. 1:1).

Although further evidence for Petrine authorship will be given below, it should be noted at the outset that, even on historical grounds alone, this statement attests to the fact that from the earliest time the letter circulated in the church, it was known and accepted as a letter written by Peter.

1 Peter 5:1 gives additional evidence, for there the author calls himself 'a witness of the sufferings of Christ'. Such a claim fits well with Peter's presence at Jesus' trial (Mt. 26:58, 67–69; Mk 14:54; Lk. 22:54, 61). It also means that 1 Peter 2:23 may be the recollection of an eye-witness: 'When he was reviled, he did not revile in return; when he suffered, he did not threaten; but he trusted to him who judges justly.'

Finally, 1 Peter 5:13 indicates two facts which are consistent with authorship by Peter. It says, 'She who is at Babylon, who is likewise chosen, sends you greetings; and so does my son Mark.' If we understand 'Babylon' to refer to Rome (see commentary on 5:13), this verse is consistent with evidence from the early church which locates Peter in Rome during the end of his life and connects Peter with Mark (see below).

B. EVIDENCE OUTSIDE THE LETTER

Early evidence relevant to the authorship of 1 Peter is found in 2 Peter 3:1, in which the author calls his writing 'the second letter that I have written to you'.[1] This same author earlier claims to be Peter (2 Pet. 1:1, 16–18). Whether or not one thinks that Peter wrote 2 Peter,[2] 2 Peter 3:1 can still be understood as a very early testimony to the fact that an earlier letter claiming to be from Peter (and widely accepted as that) was known and was in circulation at the time 2 Peter was written.

In the present commentary, I have assumed Petrine authorship of 2 Peter (for this is my own position) and have therefore cited 2 Peter for parallel examples of themes and of word usage at several points. Yet, on any view of authorship, 2 Peter is illustrative of the use of Greek in the Christian community in the late first or early second century AD.

The earliest definite citation of 1 Peter outside the New Testament is found in Polycarp (died AD 155), *Epistle to the Philippians*. Polycarp quotes 1 Peter several times: for example, in 1.3, 'in whom, not seeing, you believe with unutterable and exalted joy' (*cf.* 1 Pet. 1:8); 2.1, 'not returning evil for evil or reviling for reviling' (*cf.* 1 Pet. 3:9); and 8.1, 'who bore our sins in his own body on the tree, who did no sin, neither was guile found in his mouth' (*cf.* 1 Pet. 2:24, 22).

Although the writings of Papias (died *c.* AD 130) have been lost, Eusebius says that Papias 'used quotations' from Peter's letter.[3]

The first extant writing which quotes Peter by name is Irenaeus, *Against Heresies* (AD 182–188):[4] 'Peter says in his

---

[1]Zahn, pp. 194–198, argues that 2 Pet. 3:1–2 cannot refer to the contents of 1 Peter, but must refer to another letter of Peter's with similar content to 2 Peter. But this view depends on too narrow an understanding of 2 Pet. 3:2, which means in general just 'to remember the Old Testament writings and the apostolic teachings' – something which could certainly describe 1 Peter, as the early church thought it did.

[2]For arguments in defence of Petrine authorship of 2 Peter see the extensive discussion in Michael Green, *2 Peter and Jude* (London: Tyndale Press, 1968), pp. 13–55; also Guthrie, *NTI*, pp. 814–863 and 671–684.

[3]*EH* 3.39.17.

[4]*Against Heresies* 4.9.2; Irenaeus also quotes Peter by name in 4.16.5. An extensive list of other citations, some certain and some merely possible (or even unlikely), is given in Bigg, pp. 7–15. The clear citations increase in frequency after Irenaeus.

epistle: Whom, not seeing, you love; in whom, though now you see him not, you have believed, you shall rejoice with joy unspeakable' (*cf.* 1 Pet. 1:8).

There seems to have been no doubt anywhere in the early church that 1 Peter was written by the apostle Peter.[1] Writing in AD 325, Eusebius includes 1 Peter among those books everywhere recognized as belonging to the New Testament.[2] Wherever it was circulated, it was accepted as genuine.

C. THE ROLE OF SILVANUS (5:12)

The question of authorship is complicated somewhat by 1 Peter 5:12, which says, 'By Silvanus, a faithful brother as I regard him, I have written briefly to you, exhorting and declaring that this is the true grace of God; stand fast in it.'

Many have concluded that this verse indicates that Silvanus was the secretary or 'amanuensis' who recorded or wrote the letter at Peter's direction (see, for example, Selwyn, pp. 11–17, and response by Beare, pp. 212–216).

However, this sentence gives little support to the view that Silvanus was involved in the actual writing of the letter. The Greek phrase meaning 'to write to someone by someone else' is nowhere else clearly seen to mean 'to dictate a letter with the help of someone else'. Kümmel notes, 'No-one has yet proved that *graphō dia tinos* can mean "to authorize someone else to compose a piece of writing"'.[3] On the other hand, there are clear cases where this same Greek construction is used to designate the messenger who carries a letter to someone: note Acts 15:23, for example (Greek text: 'through the hand of them [Judas and Silas]').[4]

---

[1] 1 Peter is not mentioned in the Muratorian Canon (*c.* AD 170), but neither are Hebrews, James, or 2 Peter, probably due to a textual corruption at this point. *Cf.* B. F. Westcott, *A General Survey of the History of the Canon of the New Testament* (London: Macmillan, ⁷1896), pp. 222–223.

[2] *EH* 3.25.2.

[3] W. G. Kümmel, *Introduction to the New Testament*, revised edition, tr. H. C. Kee (Nashville: Abingdon, 1975), p. 424.

[4] Other examples of this construction designating the messenger are Ignatius, *Rom.* 10:1; *Phil.* 11:2; *Smyr.* 12:1, and the subscripts (in the Byzantine text tradition) at the end of many

Moreover, the fact that Peter calls Silvanus *a faithful brother as I regard him*, argues strongly for Silvanus as the bearer of the letter: this expression would have no function if Silvanus were merely the secretary, but it would be very appropriate as a personal recommendation if Silvanus were the bearer (note Paul's similar commendation of the bearers of his letters in 1 Cor. 16:10–11; Eph. 6:21–22; Col. 4:7–9; Tit. 3:12–13). And though Tertius mentions himself in Rom. 16:22, no New Testament author ever explicitly mentions or commends an amanuensis elsewhere.

Therefore, the expression 'through Silvanus' or 'by means of Silvanus' (RSV, *by Silvanus*) even by itself would probably designate Silvanus as the bearer of the letter, and the commendation of him as a *faithful brother*, similar to several other commendations of messengers in New Testament letters, makes it very likely that he carried Peter's letter to its readers.

If it is admitted that 5:12 designates Silvanus as the bearer of the letter, then the amanuensis view must be seen for what it is: a theory with no hard historical data left to support it. For if 5:12 designates Silvanus as the bearer of the letter, then there is nothing in 5:12 which also designates him as the amanuensis, nor is there historical data elsewhere which would indicate this role for him.

It is best to conclude that there is no clear evidence in the letter indicating that Silvanus had any role in the composition of the letter. Authorship by Peter the apostle means simply that Peter himself wrote the letter.

D. OBJECTIONS TO PETRINE AUTHORSHIP

Although many major commentaries can be found in support of Petrine authorship of 1 Peter,[1] several objections have been

---

of Paul's letters (Rom., 1 and 2 Cor., Eph., Phil., Col., Phlm.): see subscripts in Nestle-Aland Greek text, and discussion by F. H. Chase, *HDB* 3, p. 790.

[1]Commentators supporting Petrine authorship include Hort, Bigg, Selwyn, Stibbs/Walls, Cranfield, and Blum. Kelly (pp. 32–33) is non-commital. Lengthy defences of Petrine authorship may be found in Guthrie, *NTI*, pp. 773–790, and in Stibbs/Walls, pp. 15–68. Many who support Petrine authorship allow a large role to Silvanus in the actual style of Greek used.

raised against the internal and external evidence noted above. These objections have seemed convincing enough to lead some commentators (such as Beare and Best) to deny Petrine authorship. Indeed, Beare says, 'There can be no possible doubt that "Peter" is a pseudonym' (p. 29).

The following four objections to Petrine authorship are listed in Kümmel;[1] a fuller statement of these objections can be found in the introduction to Beare's commentary (pp. 28–50) and in Best (pp. 49–63).

1. *The Greek is too good for Peter.* It is argued that the polished and rather elegant style of the letter could not have been written by a Galilean fisherman such as Peter, a man who was called 'uneducated' in Acts 4:13. And Mark is said to have been the 'interpreter' (*hermēneutēs*) of Peter in Eusebius[2] (similarly Irenaeus[3]). Someone who needed an 'interpreter', it is argued, could not have been very fluent in Greek. Beare writes of Peter, 'That he should ever become a master of Greek prose is simply unthinkable' (p. 47).

2. *1 Peter reflects a time after Peter had died*, a period of intense persecution not seen until the persecutions under Domitian (AD 95) or Trajan (c. AD 112). But Peter died under Nero during the local persecution of Christians in Rome in AD 64–68.

3. 1 Peter is said to be *too Pauline in theology* to come from the apostle Peter, and to be too dependent on Paul's writings.

4. The author of 1 Peter shows *no evidence of familiarity with the earthly life of Jesus*, and gives little if any attention to the earthly teachings of Jesus in what he writes. But this is thought to be unlikely for Peter, who accompanied Jesus throughout his earthly ministry.

These four objections may be considered in the order presented above.

1. *The Greek is too good for Peter to have written*

It is true that 1 Peter is written in very good Greek, exhibiting an extensive vocabulary and ability to use effectively a wide variety

---

[1]*Introduction to the New Testament*, pp. 423–424.   [2]*EH* 3.39.15.
[3]*Against Heresies* 3.1.1 and 3.10.6.

of verbal forms and sentence structures.¹ But the stylistic quality can be overestimated: note Nigel Turner's allegations of several areas of stylistic weakness and departure from high literary standards in 1 Peter.² The Greek may be said to be excellent, but to say it is a literary masterpiece is probably an overstatement. Yet the question remains whether Peter could have written Greek of this good quality.

a. Was Peter illiterate or in need of a translator?
The word *agrammatos*, 'unlearned', is used of the apostles Peter and John in Acts 4:13: The members of the Sanhedrin perceived 'that they were *uneducated*, common men', and were amazed at their boldness and wisdom in defending themselves. Does this mean that Peter was unable to read or write?

Although *agrammatos* can at times mean 'illiterate, unable to read or write', it can also mean 'not formally educated',³ and would readily have that nuance next to *idiotēs*, 'common man, layman, non-expert' in Acts 4:13. Moreover, the Sanhedrin would not have known from the brief verbal exchange whether or not Peter and John could read or write, nor was that the focus of their amazement. They were amazed rather that people without formal rabbinic training could hold their own in argument with the scholarly experts of the nation and, recalling how Jesus had similarly handled them in discussion, 'they recognized that they had been with Jesus' (Acts 4:13b; *cf.* Jn. 7:15). It is therefore best to conclude that Acts 4:13 means that Peter and John were 'not formally educated', apparently because they had not received formal rabbinic training.

With respect to references to Mark serving as the 'interpreter' of Peter, it should be noted that *hermēneutēs*, 'interpreter', does not always mean 'one who translates from a foreign language', but can also mean 'expounder',⁴ or 'one who explains a teaching'. The related verb *hermēneuō* takes this sense in the variant reading at Luke 24:27 (Jesus *interpreted* to them in all the Scriptures the things concerning himself); also

¹See the stylistic analysis by F. H. Chase in *HDB* 3, pp. 781–782; *cf.* MHT 2, pp. 26–27.
²MHT 4, pp. 127–130.
³See BAGD, p. 13, and references there.
⁴LSJ, p. 690 (*cf.* the entry under the alternate spelling *hermēneus*); so also Lampe, p. 549.

in Josephus[1] ('interpreting' Scripture). In Clement of Alexandria,[2] Moses is called an 'interpreter' (*hermēneus*) of sacred laws.

The sentences which have been quoted alleging Peter's need of a translator are in contexts discussing Mark's Gospel, where it would be useful to say that Mark was explaining or expounding Peter's gospel message, and that is the sense we must give those passages.

b. Could Peter have known Greek well?

Even if we conclude that Peter was not illiterate, and that he did not need a translator, the question still remains: how much Greek could he have known? A response to that question requires a knowledge of the degree to which Greek was spoken by Jews in Palestine in the first century AD.

When Alexander the Great conquered Palestine in 332 BC, a process of 'Hellenization' (the imposing of Greek language and culture on non-Greek people) began, and it continued for the next four centuries. Thus, by the time Peter wrote, there had been nearly four hundred years of Greek influence in Palestine.

There were many Greek cities, especially in and around Galilee. Joppa on the coast had been a centre of Greek influence for many years. The ten Greek cities called the 'Decapolis' were within easy travelling distance. In addition, such newer cities as Caesarea (the administrative capital of Judea), Antipatris, Sebaste (ancient Samaria), Neapolis, Tiberias (on the sea of Galilee), and Caesarea Philippi, were more or less thoroughly Greek cities, peopled mainly by non-Jews and using Greek as their everyday language.

Ancient evidence of the use of Greek in Palestine is abundant. Hundreds of Jewish ossuaries (stone 'coffins' in which the bones of dead people were placed) have been uncovered in and around Jerusalem, all dating from the first century AD or earlier. Yet, 'Of the inscriptions on ossuaries in Jerusalem mentioned by Frey, 97 are in Hebrew or Aramaic, 64 in Greek and 14 are bilingual.'[3] These ossuaries are significant because it is likely that surviving relatives writing the name of the deceased person

---

[1] *Ant.* 20.264.   [2] *Stromata* 1.22 (end).

[3] J. N. Sevenster, *Do You Know Greek? How much Greek could the first Jewish Christians have known? NovTSup* 19 (Leiden: Brill, 1968), p. 146.

on a stone coffin would write in the language most familiar to them or in the language in which the person was usually addressed.

A large plaque from the entrance to the temple in Jerusalem, unearthed in the 19th century, and dating from before AD 70, warned all non-Jews not to enter beyond that point. The inscription is written only in Greek.[1] Of course, one might argue that this inscription does not prove that the Jews spoke Greek, for it was addressed to non-Jews living in Jerusalem. This is true, but it does indicate that Greek was assumed to be the language which at least every Gentile in Jerusalem could read and understand. Therefore, if the Jews in Jerusalem spoke with Gentiles at all (which they certainly did in everyday life) they probably would have spoken frequently in Greek.

Even more remarkable is an inscription from the wall of a synagogue which was found on the Ophel, the hill south of the temple area in Jerusalem. The inscription, written only in Greek, reads:

> Theodotos, son of Vettenos, priest and archisynagogos [ruler of the synagogue], son of an archisynagogos, grandson of an archisynagogos, built the synagogue for the reading of the law and for the teaching of the commandments; furthermore, the hospice and the chambers, and the water installation for the lodging of needy strangers. The foundation stone thereof had been laid by his fathers, and the elders, and Simonides.[2]

The fact that a memorial plaque on the wall of a Jewish synagogue in Jerusalem could be written in Greek, and that it commemorated the work of the ruler of the synagogue who was both a priest (presumably in the Jerusalem temple) and the son and grandson of synagogue rulers, shows how thoroughly the use of the Greek language had penetrated even to the centre of Judaism in Palestine at or before the time of the New Testament.

All this indicates that it would not have been unusual for

---

[1] See photograph in *CIJ*, 1400 (vol. 2, p. 329).
[2] See photograph and transcription in *CIJ*, 1404 (vol. 2, p. 333); the translation here is taken from E. Sukenik, *Ancient Synagogues in Palestine and Greece* (London: British Academy, 1934), p. 70.

Peter to have used Greek regularly for over thirty years in the Jerusalem church (as well as earlier in even more thoroughly Greek-speaking Galilee), and to have become very familiar with the Greek translation of the Old Testament, the Septuagint (as the Old Testament quotations in 1 Peter indicate).

Public decrees and proclamations were also written in Greek and posted where they could be seen all.[1]

A passage in the Babylonian Talmud seems to indicate extensive knowledge of Greek in Palestine in the school of Gamaliel in the first century AD: 'Behold Rab Judah declared that Samuel said in the name of Rabban Simeon ben Gamaliel . . . there were a thousand pupils in my father's house; five hundred studied the Torah and five hundred studied Greek wisdom'.[2] Moreover, Josephus comments that in his day 'even slaves who so choose' could acquire fluency in Greek, and that it was 'common' to ordinary freemen.[3]

It seems fair to conclude that the Greek language was well known and commonly used in Palestine in the first century. This was true even in Jerusalem (although Aramaic was still the most commonly used language there). But it was even more the case in Galilee, where Peter grew up, surrounded by Greek cities and the influence of residents and visitors who spoke only Greek.

Sevenster writes:

> There were many regions of the Jewish land which bordered directly on areas where mainly or almost exclusively Greek was spoken. The obvious assumption is that the inhabitants of such regions at least understood Greek, often spoke it and were thus bilingual. This can probably be said of people from all levels of society, not merely the top social or intellectual layer.[4]

Joseph Fitzmyer similarly states:

> Greek was widely used at this time and not only in the clearly Hellenized towns, but in many others as well. Indeed, there

---

[1]See Sevenster, *op. cit.*, pp. 117–121, with discussion of a marble plaque from Nazareth.
[2]*Sotah* 49b.   [3]*Ant.* 20.263.   [4]Sevenster, *op. cit.*, p. 99.

are some indications that Palestinian Jews in some areas may have used nothing else but Greek.

He adds,

I would maintain that the most commonly used language of Palestine in the first century AD was Aramaic, but that many Palestinian Jews, not only those in Hellenistic towns, but farmers and craftsmen of less obviously Hellenized areas used Greek, at least as a second language . . . in fact, there is indication . . . that some Palestinians spoke only Greek.[1]

A. W. Argyle notes:

To suggest that a Jewish boy growing up in Galilee would not know Greek would be rather like suggesting that a Welsh boy brought up in Cardiff would not know English. If Joseph and Jesus wanted their carpentry business to prosper, they would be happy to welcome Gentile as well as Jewish customers. They would therefore need to speak Greek as well as Aramaic if they were to converse with all their customers. . . . There is greater readiness now than there was formerly to admit that Jesus and his disciples, all of whom were Galileans (Acts ii.7), were bilingual, speaking Greek as well as Aramaic.[2]

Could someone who lacked a formal education have learned to write Greek well enough to write 1 Peter? If lack of such an education was not an insuperable obstacle to John Bunyan, the Bedford tinker who wrote *Pilgrim's Progress*, can we assume that Peter could not have written the letter which bears his name?

Those who object that Greek was not Peter's first language overlook the fact that in bilingual areas, such as Wales and the French-speaking areas of Canada, a high degree of fluency in a

[1]'The Languages of Palestine in the First Century A.D.', *CBQ* 32 (1970), pp. 512, 531; *cf.* C. F. D. Moule, 'Once More, Who Were the Hellenists?', *ExpT* 70 (1958–59), pp. 100–102; R. H. Gundry, 'The Language Milieu of First-Century Palestine', *JBL* 83 (1964), pp. 404–408; also P. E. Hughes, 'The Languages Spoken by Jesus', in *New Dimensions in New Testament Study*, eds. Richard Longenecker and Merrill Tenney (Grand Rapids: Zondervan, 1974), pp. 127–143.

[2]'Greek Among the Jews of Palestine in New Testament Times', *NTS* 20 (1974), pp. 87–89.

second language is quite common. It is also possible, as the example of Joseph Conrad (1857–1924) demonstrates, to become a highly accomplished writer in a second or even third language. Conrad's first language was Polish; his second, learned as a youth, was French. He began to learn English only at the age of twenty-one when he signed on as a seaman on a British ship, yet his novel, *Lord Jim*, is acknowledged as an English literary classic. Those who deny that Peter could have written 1 Peter would probably also consider it 'unthinkable' that a Polish sailor could have acquired the elegance and fluency in English evident in Conrad's novels and short stories, particularly without benefit of formal education. (He once said, 'I've never opened an English grammar in my life.'[1]) That Conrad should have done this may be 'unthinkable'; but he did it none the less. Such an accomplishment is many times more incredible than that the leader of the early church in a thoroughly bilingual culture could have written a letter like 1 Peter. It is unthinkable only if we have not carefully examined the evidence.

2. The letter reflects a time after Peter died

This objection assumes that 1 Peter must be reflecting official persecution by the government which extended throughout the entire Roman empire. Such an assumption is hardly justified by the text itself. Indeed, Peter's specific directive regarding the government is simply to be submissive to it (1 Pet. 2:13–14) and to 'honour the emperor' (1 Pet. 2:17). And he does not specify one kind of suffering but says his readers may have to suffer grief in 'various trials' (1:6). All the other statements about suffering in 1 Peter can be understood as general statements addressed to Christians where there was a likelihood of localized persecution. This would not be unusual for the first century in Asia Minor. From the first spread of the gospel there had been hostility and even violent opposition in many places (see detailed discussion in commentary at 4:12).[2]

[1] *Encyclopaedia Britannica*, 1945 ed., vol. 6, p. 278.
[2] C. F. D. Moule, 'The Nature and Purpose of 1 Peter', *NTS* 3 (1956–57), pp.7–9, demonstrates parallels between references to persecution in 1 Peter and similar references in the rest of the New Testament.

Thus the letter cannot be said clearly to reflect a time after Peter's death, and can fit well with the situation which existed throughout Peter's lifetime.

3. 1 Peter is too Pauline to have been written by Peter

This objection assumes a necessary divergence of viewpoint or even conflict between Pauline and Petrine ideas of Christianity. Such a view has been widely criticized in many places, and it is not necessary to deal with the question in detail here.[1]

On the contrary, it would be quite surprising if a letter written near the end of Peter's life did not show several similarities in thought, and perhaps even in wording, to some of Paul's letters. If we are to trust the historical traditions reported by Eusebius and Tertullian (see below), then Peter near the end of his life was teaching with Paul in Rome. Moreover, the Silvanus whom Peter names as the messenger carrying his letter (1 Pet. 5:12), was Paul's travelling companion and assistant (also known by the name Silas) for many years. This also suggests some close association between the two apostles. Further detail may be noted if necessary (see Stibbs/Walls, pp. 39–48, for a very helpful discussion), but it is sufficient to note here that affinities to Paul's writings weigh more heavily in favour of authorship by Peter the apostle than against it.

4. 1 Peter shows no evidence of familiarity with the earthly life of Jesus

The primary weakness of this objection is a failure to give due weight to the difference between a gospel and a brief letter. Peter was writing not to recall many details of Jesus' earthly life, but rather to give instruction to his hearers regarding specific situations which they faced. With regard to the situation of persecution, Peter does certainly employ the example of Christ (2:21–23; 3:18; 4:1–2, 13; 5:1). Such repeated reminders of Christ's sufferings appropriately and specifically applied to the

---

[1]See D. A. Carson, 'Unity and Diversity in the New Testament: The Possibility of Systematic Theology' in *Scripture and Truth*, eds. D. A. Carson and J. D. Woodbridge (Grand Rapids: Zondervan; Leicester: Inter-Varsity Press, 1983), pp. 71–72, with notes to other literature.

situation of the readers; further detail was unnecessary, especially if Peter could assume that the elements of the gospel stories were well known.

In conclusion, the objections to authorship by Peter remain unpersuasive.[1] There is no compelling evidence to keep us from accepting what the early church universally believed and what the letter itself clearly states, that 1 Peter was written by Peter the apostle.

II. PLACE OF WRITING

In 1 Peter 5:13, Peter says, 'She who is at Babylon . . . sends you greetings, and so does my son Mark.' Here Peter can hardly be referring to the ancient city of Babylon in Mesopotamia, the capital of the Babylonian empire, for by the first century it was a small and obscure place. There is no evidence of a visit there by Peter or by Peter and Mark. Nor is there evidence even of a Christian church there at this time. Diodorus of Sicily (writing 56–36 BC) says:

As for the palaces and the other buildings, time has either entirely effaced them or left them in ruins; and in fact of Babylon itself but a small part is inhabited at this time, and most of the area within its walls is given over to agriculture'.[2]

Similarly, Strabo (died AD 19) writes:

The greater part of Babylon is so deserted that one would not hesitate to say . . . 'The Great City is a great desert'.[3]

---

[1]Guthrie, *NTI*, adds another significant point: If the author was using Peter's name as a pseudonym, it seems impossible to free him from the charge of intentional deception (pp. 787–788). Those who argue that pseudonymous writing was a commonly accepted literary style in the first century have failed to answer Guthrie's demonstration that this practice was not found in personal letters (pp. 671–684). He notes that if someone actually did write under 'Peter' as a pseudonym, no adequate motive can be found which does not involve the intention to deceive (p. 788).

[2]Diod. Sic. 2.9.9.

[3]*Geography* 16.1.5 (C738). In *Geography* 17.1.30 (C807), Strabo mentions another 'Babylon' near Memphis in Egypt, on the Nile River, where a Roman legion was stationed, but this city was even more obscure than Babylon in Mesopotamia, and there is no record of

But the name 'Babylon' is used elsewhere in the New Testament as a reference to Rome (see Rev. 16:19, 17:5; 18:2; and note 17:9 as an identification of the 'seven hills of' Rome). Just as in the Old Testament Babylon was the centre of worldly power and opposition to God's people, so in the time of the New Testament Rome was the earthly centre of a world-wide system of government and life which was set in opposition to the gospel. By referring to Rome as 'Babylon', Peter was carrying through the imagery of the church as the new people of God or the new Israel, which he uses throughout this letter (see commentary at 2:10).

Moreover, there is historical evidence that Peter was at Rome at the end of his life.[1] In AD 203, Tertullian wrote:

> Since, moreover, you are close upon Italy, you have Rome, from which there comes even into our own hands the very authority of apostles themselves. How happy is its church, on which apostles poured forth all their doctrine along with their blood! where Peter endures a passion like his Lord's! where Paul wins his crown in a death like John's![2]

This testimony is supplemented by that of Eusebius, writing in AD 325. Speaking of Peter and Paul, he writes:

> And that they both were martyred at the same time Dionysius, Bishop of Corinth [c. AD 170], affirms in this passage of his correspondence with the Romans: 'By so great an admonition you bound together the foundations of the Romans and Corinthians by Peter and Paul, for both of them taught together in our Corinth and were our founders, and together also taught in Italy in the same place and were martyred at the same time'.[3]

Eusebius continues his history with more details about Peter and Paul:

Christian influence there in the first century. It is highly unlikely that Peter would have meant this Babylon without further specification in the context of 1 Pet. 5:13.

[1] See the very thorough discussion concerning Peter in Rome in O. Cullmann, *Peter: Disciple, Apostle, Martyr*, tr. F. Filson (London: SCM, 1953), pp. 70–152. A more recent but much less careful analysis of the evidence is found in Carsten Thiede, *Simon Peter: From Galilee to Rome* (Exeter: Paternoster, 1986), pp. 171–194.

[2] *Against Heretics* 36.   [3] *EH* 2.25.8.

Peter seems to have preached to the Jews of the Dispersion in Pontus and Galatia and Bithynia, Cappadocia, and Asia, and at the end he came to Rome and was crucified head downwards, for so he had demanded to suffer. What need be said of Paul, who fulfilled the gospel of Christ from Jerusalem to Illyria and afterward was martyred in Rome under Nero? This is stated exactly by Origen [died *c.* AD 254] in the third volume of his commentary on Genesis.[1]

Finally, Eusebius explicitly states that Peter wrote his first letter in Rome:

The bishop of Hierapolis, named Papias [*c.* AD 60–130] . . . says that Peter mentions Mark in his first Epistle, and that he composed this in Rome itself, which they say that he himself indicates, referring to the city metaphorically as Babylon, in the words, 'the elect one in Babylon greets you, and Marcus my son'.[2]

These testimonies taken together indicate that Peter and Paul both died in the persecution under the emperor Nero. This persecution lasted from the time just after the great fire in Rome in AD 64 (which was widely thought to have been started by Nero, but for which he blamed the Christians and viciously persecuted them), until Nero's death (by suicide) on June 9th, AD 68. Thus, we may conclude that the name 'Babylon' in the letter and the external historical evidence that Peter was in Rome with Paul near the end of his life combine to indicate that 1 Peter was written from Rome.

III. DATE

A discussion of suggested dates after Peter's life has already been given above (see the section on 'Author'). But if we grant that the letter was written by Peter, when during his life did he write it?

It is highly unlikely that the generally positive view of civil

[1]*EH* 3.1.2–3.   [2]*EH* 2.15.2.

government which Peter gives in 1 Peter 2:13–17 could have been written without further qualification if the persecution under Nero had already begun in Rome. The severity of this persecution,[1] coupled with the almost unqualified positive view of the government in 2:13–17, and with the traditions about Peter's death under Nero (see section on 'Place of Writing' above), combine to indicate that the letter must have been written before AD 64.

On the other hand, when Eusebius reports that Peter was in Rome 'at the end' (*epi telei en rhōmē genomenos*),[2] he indicates that he believed Peter to have been in Rome only near the end of his life. Yet the book of Acts ends with Paul in Rome (Acts 28:30–31), with no indication that Peter was present at that time. But if we date Paul's prison letters (Ephesians, Philippians, Colossians, Philemon) between AD 60 and 62, when Paul was in prison in Rome, it is interesting that he nowhere in these four letters mentions Peter. If Peter had been there at that time, it would be hard to understand sentences like Philippians 2:20–21, referring to Timothy: 'I have no one like him, who will be genuinely anxious for your welfare. They all look after their own interests, not those of Jesus Christ.' Moreover, in Colossians 4:10–11, Paul mentions only Aristarchus, Mark the cousin of Barnabas, and Jesus who is called Justus, and then adds that 'these are the only men of the circumcision among my fellow workers for the kingdom of God, and they have been a comfort to me'. He also mentions 'Luke the beloved physician' and others in Colossians 4:2–14, but there is no mention of Peter (and it is hard to think that Paul would not consider Peter 'a fellow worker').

Similarly, one might suppose that if Paul had been in Rome at the time 1 Peter was written, Peter would have mentioned that and sent greetings from Paul, for at least some of the churches which were addressed had been founded by Paul. But in 1 Peter 5:12–13 he mentions only Silvanus and Mark.

These factors combine to suggest that 1 Peter was not written until after Paul left Rome, perhaps in AD 62 (if we accept the events narrated in 1 and 2 Timothy and Titus as referring to

---

[1]See Tacitus, *Annals* 15.44.   [2]*EH* 3.1.2.

genuine events in Paul's life after he had been released from his first imprisonment in Rome).[1]

This leaves us with a date for 1 Peter between AD 62 and 64. Moreover, if we also accept 2 Peter as having been written by Peter subsequent to 1 Peter, then time must be allowed for 2 Peter to have been written, perhaps between AD 63 and 64 (or, if Peter died later in Nero's persecution, 65 or 66).[2] That would push the date for 1 Peter back toward the beginning of the period allowed, placing it in AD 62 or 63. However, although 62 or 63 seems the most probable date for the writing of the letter, it must be remembered that the evidence used to determine AD 64 as the latest date possible is more firmly attested historical data, while many of the arguments regarding the earliest date possible are admittedly from silence.

IV. DESTINATION AND READERS

The destination of the letter is explicitly stated in the opening verse: 'exiles of the Dispersion in Pontus, Galatia, Cappadocia, Asia, and Bithynia.' Hort suggested in 1898 that these names described a travel route to be followed by the bearer of the letter as he travelled through four Roman provinces south of the Black Sea, in what is today called Asia Minor, mostly in modern Turkey.[3] This suggestion has been widely accepted,[4] although it has been penetratingly refined and corrected in detail by Colin Hemer,[5] who argues that the only feasible ports and trade routes require the messenger to follow a route beginning at Amisus (modern Samsun), then travelling through Amasia in eastern Galatia, Zela, Caesarea in Cappadocia, Iconium, Pisidian Antioch, and Laodicea, and then perhaps, if time allowed, into other churches of Asia (Colossae?, even Ephesus?), then finally to Nicea, Nicomedia and Chalcedon. From there the

---

[1]Guthrie, *NTI*, pp. 589–599.   [2]Guthrie, *NTI*, p. 850.

[3]'The Provinces of Asia Minor Included in St. Peter's Address', in Hort, *1 Peter*, pp. 154–184, especially pp. 183–184.

[4]Guthrie, *NTI*, pp. 792–793, discusses some other theories, none of which has gained much acceptance.

[5]'The Address of 1 Peter', *ExpT* 89 (1978), pp. 239–243.

messenger could board a ship in nearby Byzantium and return to Rome. (See map on p. 19.)

This circular route means that all the major centres of Christian influence in Asia Minor would be reached by the letter. Moreover, copies could have been made at each stop and distributed to the smaller churches in neighbouring cities.

But if all the churches in Asia Minor in AD 62–63 were reached by this letter and were the intended recipients of it, then the question of whether Peter is writing to Jewish Christians or Gentile Christians is already answered. By this time, over thirty years after Pentecost, the rapid growth of the church would have meant that there were both Jewish and Gentile Christians in all of these churches. Therefore, while Peter can readily use Jewish terminology to apply to his readers (note the phrase 'exiles of the Dispersion' for example in 1:1), this is simply applying to the church in the New Covenant age the language which previously had been appropriate for God's covenant people, the Jews (see commentary at 2:10, and discussion there on the theme of the church as the new people of God).

There are several indications in the letter that Peter assumed there to be a large segment of Gentile Christians among his readers. He says, 'You were ransomed from the futile ways inherited from your fathers' (1 Pet. 1:18), and, 'Once you were no people but now you are God's people' (1 Pet. 2:10) – something which he would hardly say of converted Jews. He says their lives had been filled with sin uncharacteristic of Jews: 'Let the time that is past suffice for doing what the Gentiles like to do, living in licentiousness, passions, drunkenness, revels, carousing, and lawless idolatry' (1 Pet. 4:3). Then he adds that unbelievers 'are surprised that you do not now join them in the same wild profligacy' (1 Pet. 4:4), something which would not have been surprising to unbelievers if the Christians had previously been Jews following the strict moral standards of first-century Judaism.

On the other hand, there were no doubt converted Jews in these churches, for even at Pentecost there were present residents of 'Cappadocia, Pontus and Asia' (Acts 2:9). The readers are therefore best thought to be mixed congregations of Jewish and Gentile Christians.

V. PURPOSE

Since many of the exhortations in 1 Peter concern faith and obedience, it may be suggested that the purpose of 1 Peter is to encourage the readers to grow in their trust in God and their obedience to him throughout their lives, but especially when they suffer. Peter accomplishes his purpose by pointing to what God has done for them in Christ, then applying that to the readers' lives. These themes will be seen in much detail throughout the exposition of the text, but it is sufficient here to note one verse which, perhaps better than all others in the letter, sumarizes these concerns: 'Therefore let those who suffer according to God's will do right and entrust their souls to a faithful Creator' (1 Pet. 4:19). Here are found the themes of suffering ('those who suffer') and trust in God (the suffering is 'according to God's will' and should result in continual entrusting of the readers' souls [or lives] 'to a faithful Creator'); moreover, such trust in God should also be accompanied by obedience, for they should continue to 'do right'.

At the beginning of his valuable commentary on 1 Peter, Archbishop Robert Leighton writes:

> This excellent Epistle (full of evangelical doctrine and apostolical authority) is a brief, and yet very clear summary both of the consolations and instructions needful for the encouragement and direction of a Christian in his journey to Heaven, elevating his thoughts and desires to that happiness, and strengthening him against all opposition in the way, both that of corruption within, and temptations and afflictions from without.
>
> The heads of doctrine contained in it are many, but the main that are most insisted on, are these three, *faith*, *obedience*, and *patience*; to establish them in believing, to direct them in doing and to comfort them in suffering.[1]

[1]Leighton, p. 9.

FAITH — ESTABLISH IN BELIEVING
OBEDIENCE — DIRECT IN DOING
PATIENCE — COMFORT IN SUFFERING
CORRUPTION (WITHIN)
TEMPTATION (WITHOUT)

VI. THE NATURE AND POSSIBLE SOURCES OF 1 PETER

A. A BAPTISMAL SERMON?

To say that baptism is referred to only once in 1 Peter (3:21), and there only incidentally, may seem to some like shouting, 'The emperor has no clothes!' The index to Kelly's commentary, for example, lists no fewer than forty-seven places where he discusses baptism in the course of analysing 1 Peter. And several have followed Preisker's view that 1 Peter is a liturgy read at a baptismal service (with the baptism itself occurring between 1:21 and 1:22).[1] But Professor Moule lists several decisive objections to the 'liturgy' view.[2] In brief, 1 Peter so thoroughly bears the form of a letter addressed to readers distant from any local service of worship that it is hard to imagine that it originally had such a different form and purpose. Guthrie notes: 'The many instances of "now" in the Epistle need not be regarded as evidence of a liturgy in process (as Preisker assumes), but rather the realization on the part of the Christians of the importance of the present in their eschatological outlook.'[3]

But even if 1 Peter is not a liturgy for use in a service of worship, are there frequent references to baptism in it? Consider the following statements:

1:3   we have been born anew to a living hope . . .
1:12   the things which have *now* been announced to you . . .
1:18   you were ransomed from the futile ways inherited from your fathers . . .
1:22   Having purified your souls by your obedience to the truth . . .
1:23   You have been born anew . . .
2:2   Like new-born babes, long for the pure spiritual milk . . .

---

[1]The original statement is found in H. Windisch, *Die Katholischen Briefe*, Handbuch zum Neuen Testament 15, revised by H. Preisker (Tübingen: Mohr, ³1951), pp. 156–162. An excellent statement of the arguments for a baptismal background is found in F. L. Cross, *1 Peter: A Paschal Liturgy* (Oxford: Mowbray, 1954), pp. 28–35 (Cross argues that the baptismal service occurred at a Good Friday-Easter celebration).

[2]C.F.D. Moule, 'The Nature and Purpose of 1 Peter', *NTS* 3 (1956–57), pp. 4–7; note also the objections of Walls in Stibbs/Walls, p. 61–63.

[3]*NTI*, p. 798.

(but see commentary on this verse)

2:10 *now* you have received mercy.

2:25 you were straying like sheep but have *now* returned to the Shepherd and Guardian of your souls.

3:21 Baptism, which corresponds to this, *now* saves you, not as a removal of dirt from the body but as an appeal to God for a clear conscience, through the resurrection of Jesus Christ . . .

4:3 Let the time that is past suffice for doing what the Gentiles like to do . . .

From such a list, it may be seen that Peter's language frequently refers to the new life which Christians have. It may also be understood to refer to the beginning of that new life when they first came to faith. But mention of the beginning of the Christian life does not in itself imply a reference to baptism. Moreover, while these references viewed in isolation may seem at first to refer exclusively to the *beginning* of the Christian life, on closer inspection, especially within the contexts in which they occur, not one of them would be inappropriate to apply to *all* Christians, including many who had been Christians for most of their lives. The references to their new birth in Christ were appropriate reminders of their possession of a spiritual life which had begun long before. In 1:3 Peter includes himself in those whom God has 'begotten again' (AV). Thus Walls observes, 'The act of begetting is already realized and its result enjoyed: it cannot refer to an event to take place after 1:21'.[1]

The one clear reference to baptism in 1 Peter (3:21) is only a passing one, which has a brief function but certainly is not central to the apostle's argument (see commentary on 3:21). The thesis that 1 Peter was originally a liturgy or perhaps a sermon at a baptism remains unconvincing and provides an unsatisfactory setting for the composition of the letter. It is far better to understand the letter as written by Peter to distant Christians in genuine need of its teaching and encouragement.

[1]Stibbs/Walls, p. 60.

B. POSSIBLE SOURCES OF PETER'S TEACHING

One remaining question is to what extent we can determine possible sources which Peter used in compiling his letter, either in traditional Christian teaching which was circulating in the early church, in Christian or pagan moral codes ('Haustafeln')[1] which were taken over and adapted by Peter, or perhaps in the teachings and writings of the apostle Paul, or in the letter of James.[2]

It is noteworthy that Selwyn in his commentary devotes over one hundred pages (pp. 365–466) to an analysis of the sources behind 1 Peter. He finds no direct literary dependence on other New Testament writings, but finds many indications of common catechetical patterns or forms which were used widely in the early church. These familiar forms were then modified and used, according to Selwyn, by Peter, Paul, James and others.

However, although Selwyn's detailed tables of parallel themes in Peter and other parts of the New Testament are interesting, they fall far short of demonstrating the existence of early catechetical 'forms'. Many of the supposed parallels are neither precise verbal parallels nor are they parallels conceptually. They are merely statements on related topics of general concern, often ethical matters or issues related to the nature of the Christian life. But from this data we are justified in concluding only that there were many common ideas and similar teachings in the first-century church. This can all be quite satisfactorily explained by the common background of the Old Testament, the teachings of Jesus, and the shared teachings of the apostles as they found their way into the New Testament writings. To postulate the additional existence of rather fixed catechetical forms (or the adaptation of pagan moral codes, none of which have been shown to have precise and extensive parallels to New Testament commands) is not required by the evidence,

---

[1] A clear statement of the view that New Testament moral codes depend on certain moral codes common in the pagan world is found in J. W. C. Wand, *The General Epistles of St. Peter and St. Luke* (London: Methuen, 1934), pp. 3–9 (see especially the table on p. 7 – the claimed parallels are not clear enough to be convincing).

[2] Bigg, p. 23, lists some close parallels with James, but arguments for dependence one way or another are inconclusive. We do not have enough data to make a reliable decision.

nor is it particularly helpful for understanding the writings themselves. Guthrie appropriately says, 'To what extent the catechesis can be disentangled from the writings and what precise value it would be if this could be achieved with any certainty is an open question.[1]

There have also been attempts by Bultmann and Boismard to find fragments of early hymns in 1 Peter but Guthrie correctly notes that they have been largely unpersuasive. On another matter, regarding the claim (made by Perdelwitz in 1911) that several parts of 1 Peter can be traced to elements in the teachings of pagan Greek Mystery Religions, Selwyn rightly comments: 'The claim that the author owed any of his leading ideas to the Mystery Religions must be rejected as wholly unproven.'[2]

More convincing is the effort by R. Gundry to find words of Jesus echoed in 1 Peter.[3] Though he is not able to demonstrate many exact verbal parallels of any length, he adduces a remarkable number of parallels in form and general content which, taken together, leave one persuaded that Peter was writing as one who was very familiar with the teachings of Jesus, both from personal remembrance and perhaps from early acquaintance with at least some of the gospel records.

VII. PROMINENT THEMES IN 1 PETER

Several subjects occur quite frequently in this short letter, such as holiness of life, the sufferings of Christ, suffering as a Christian, God's sovereignty in salvation and life, the grace of God, the work of the Holy Spirit, the church as the new people of God, the reality of the unseen spiritual world, and trusting in God regarding daily circumstances. These themes can only be mentioned here, because the space limitations of this commentary series, and a desire to give fuller treatment to the interpretation of several difficult passages in the text, meant that discussion of these themes could not be included in this Introduction.

[1]*NTI*, p. 807, with further notes to the literature.   [2]Selwyn, p. 311.
[3]R. Gundry, *NTS* 13 (1966–67), pp. 336–50, and (answering objections) *Biblica* 55 (1974), pp. 211–232.

ANALYSIS

I. SALUTATION: PETER THE APOSTLE TO SOJOURNERS IN GOD'S ETERNAL CARE (1:1–2)

II. GENERAL DOCTRINE: THE GREATNESS OF YOUR SALVATION (1:3 – 2:10)

A. YOU GROW AS CHRISTIANS THROUGH JOYFUL FAITH (1:3–12)
   1. *Joy in future heavenly reward (1:3–5)*
   2. *Joy in spite of suffering (1:6–7)*
   3. *Inexpressible joy in knowing Christ himself (1:8–9)*
   4. *Prophets and angels amazed at the glory of your salvation (1:10–12)*
B. APPLICATION: YOU MUST BE HOLY IN ALL YOUR CONDUCT (1:13–25)
   1. *Desire the beauty of being like a holy God (1:13–16)*
   2. *Fear the displeasure of a Father who is an impartial Judge (1:17–21)*
   3. *Love one another, now and for ever (1:22–25)*
C. HOW TO ADVANCE IN HOLINESS (2:1–10)
   1. *Be nourished by the Lord through the Word (2:1–3)*
   2. *Abide in Christ – together – as the new temple of God (2:4–6)*
      a. *Unbelievers reject Christ and stumble (2:7–8)*
      b. *But you are joined with Christ to be blessed as the true people of God (2:9–10)*

III. SPECIFIC ETHICAL TEACHINGS: HOW TO BE HOLY IN THE MIDST OF UNBELIEVERS (2:11 – 5:11)

A. GENERAL PRINCIPLES (2:11–12)
  1. *Abstain from following sinful passions* (2:11)
  2. *Maintain good conduct among the Gentiles* (2:12)
B. LIVING AS CITIZENS: BE SUBJECT TO GOVERNMENT AUTHORITIES, FOR THE LORD'S SAKE (2:13–17)
C. LIVING AS SERVANTS: BE SUBJECT TO YOUR MASTERS (2:18–25)
  1. *Even to evil ones* (2:18–20)
  2. *For Christ suffered for you, trusting God* (2:21–25)
D. LIVING AS MARRIED PERSONS (3:1–7)
  1. *Wives: Be subject to your husbands* (3:1–6)
  2. *Husbands: Live considerately with your wives* (3:7)
E. LIVING AS CHRISTIANS GENERALLY (3:8–22)
  1. *Be humble and united in spirit* (3:8)
  2. *Return blessing when evil is done to you* (3:9–12)
  3. *How to act when you suffer for righteousness* (3:13 – 4:19)
    a. *Know that you are blessed* (3:13–14a)
    b. *Trust Christ* (3:14b–15a)
    c. *Use this opportunity to witness while doing right* (3:15b–17)
      (i) *For Christ suffered in order to bring you to God* (3:18)
      (ii) *Another example: Noah witnessed when persecuted* (3:19–20)
      (iii) *God will save you (as he did Noah and Christ)* (3:21–22)
    d. *Decide that you are willing to suffer for righteousness* (4:1–6)
      (i) *For a Christian who has suffered for doing right has made a clear break with sin* (4:1–2)
      (ii) *Give no more time to sin* (4:3)
      (iii) *There is a judgment coming for Gentiles who abuse you* (4:4–5)
      (iv) *For the gospel was preached to Christians who have died to save them from eternal judgment* (4:6)
    e. *This final judgment is near, so act this way within the church . . .* (4:7–11)

45

        (i) *Pray more and love each other more* (4:7–9)

        (ii) *Glorify God in using your gifts* (4:10–11)

     f. *Do not be surprised at your trials, but rejoice* (4:12–16)

        (i) *For God's judgment is beginning from God's own house* (4:17–18)

        (ii) *Therefore do right and trust God continually* (4:19)

F. LIVING AS CHURCH MEMBERS AND OFFICERS (5:1–7)

  1. *Elders: Shepherd God's flock rightly* (5:1–4)

  2. *Younger people (and all others): Be subject to the elders* (5:5a)

  3. *All of you: Be humble toward each other* (5:5b)

    a. *Humble yourselves before God* (5:6)

    b. *Gain humility by casting your cares on God* (5:7)

G. LIVING AS CHRISTIANS IN SPIRITUAL CONFLICT (5:8–11)

  1. *Beware of the devil* (5:8)

  2. *Resist the devil with firm faith* (5:9)

  3. *God will restore you after you have suffered* (5:10–11)

IV. CLOSING GREETINGS (5:12–14)

A. I AM SENDING THIS BY FAITHFUL SILVANUS (5:12a)

B. STAND IN THE GRACE I HAVE DESCRIBED (5:12b)

C. GREETINGS FROM THE CHURCH IN ROME AND FROM MARK (5:13)

D. GREET ONE ANOTHER (5:14a)

E. PEACE TO ALL WHO ARE IN CHRIST (5:14b)

COMMENTARY

I. SALUTATION: PETER THE APOSTLE TO SOJOURNERS IN GOD'S ETERNAL CARE (1:1–2)

1. The author identifies himself as *Peter, an apostle of Jesus Christ*. The word 'apostle' (*apostolos*) was used occasionally before the New Testament and had the general meaning 'messenger'. But according to the gospels Jesus gave this term a richer meaning by designating twelve of his disciples as 'apostles' (Luke 6:13). After Pentecost, those who had been Jesus' disciples ('students') began to function as his apostles (Acts 1:25).

The supreme importance of the apostles is suggested by the fact that the phrase 'of Jesus Christ' is attached to no other New Testament office: we do not read of 'teachers of Jesus Christ' or 'prophets of Jesus Christ' or 'evangelists of Jesus Christ', only of 'apostles of Jesus Christ'. Those who held this office had authority at least equal to the Old Testament prophets, for the apostles could speak and write God's very words (Acts 5:3–4; Rom. 2:16; 1 Cor. 2:13; 14:37; 2 Cor. 13:3; Gal. 1:8–9; 1 Thes. 2:13; 4:8, 15; 2 Thes. 3:6, 14; 2 Pet. 3:2) and thus could write the words which became New Testament Scripture (1 Cor. 14:37; 2 Pet. 3:16, *cf.* Rev. 22:18–19; 1 Thes. 5:27; 2 Thes. 3:14).

The opening phrase reminds the readers, then, that Peter is writing in his role as an apostle of Jesus Christ: the words are also God's words, and we should receive them as that.

The next phrase, *To the exiles of the Dispersion*, represents a compact Greek phrase which quite literally says, 'to chosen sojourners of the Dispersion'. (RSV includes the word 'chosen' in v. 2.)

The term 'exile', *parepidēmos*, always refers to a temporary resident in a foreign place. Abraham called himself 'an alien and sojourner (*parepidēmos*)' among the Hittites (Gn. 23:4, LXX). Heb. 11:13 says that all the heroes of faith from Abel to Abraham acknowledged that they were 'aliens and sojourners (*parepidēmoi*) on the earth'. The related verb is used to report a decree from the king of Egypt ordering that visitors should not sojourn (*parepidēmeō*) more than twenty days in Alexandria, because many were becoming enamoured of luxurious life in the prosperous city and neglecting essential agricultural work in the rural areas (*Epistle of Aristeas*, 110; *cf.* 1 Clement 1:2).

These examples show that 'exiles' (RSV) is not the best rendering, for no connotation of *forced* dwelling away from one's homeland is found in the word. Likewise, the rendering 'strangers' (AV; NIV has 'strangers in the world') wrongly suggests that they were not known well by their neighbours, something which was untrue of Abraham, for example (Gn. 23:4–5), or of other Old Testament saints (Heb. 11:13). Better is the phrase 'those who reside as aliens' (NASB), which, though lengthy, captures the idea of temporary residence away from one's homeland, as does the somewhat archaic word 'sojourners'.

Nowhere else in ancient Jewish or Christian literature does a writer qualify 'sojourners' with the adjective 'elect' (*eklektos*), as Peter does here (translated 'chosen' in RSV, and moved to v. 2). The word in the New Testament (twenty-two times) always refers to persons chosen by God *from* a group of others who are not chosen, and chosen *for* inclusion among God's people, as recipients of great privilege and blessing (Mt. 20:16; 24:31; Rom. 8:33; *etc.*). Many of Peter's readers would hear in the term echoes of its use in the LXX to refer to God's 'chosen' people, Israel (Pss. 89:3(LXX 88:4); 105(LXX 104):6, 43; 106(LXX 105):5; Is. 42:1; 43:20; 45:4; 65:9, 15, 22(LXX 23), and would conclude that Peter thought of them as having a privileged status before God at least equal to that enjoyed by the chosen people whom God protected, preserved and blessed in the Old Testament (*cf.* 1 Pet. 2:4–10).

The phrase 'chosen sojourners' thus becomes a two-word sermon to Peter's readers: they are 'sojourners', not in an earthly sense (for many no doubt had lived in one city their whole lives), but spiritually: their true homeland is heaven (*cf.* Phil. 3:20) and any earthly residence therefore temporary. Yet they are 'chosen' sojourners, ones whom the King of the universe has chosen to be his own people, to benefit from his protection, and to inhabit his heavenly kingdom.

The *Dispersion* (*diaspora*) was a term used by Greek-speaking Jews to refer to Jewish people 'scattered' throughout the nations, 'dispersed' from their homeland, Israel (see Jn. 7:35). Here and in James 1:1, 'Dispersion' refers to Christians, but this does not imply that Peter was writing only to Jewish Christians (see Introduction on 'Destination and readers'). Rather, the term here has a new spiritual sense, referring to Christians 'dispersed' throughout the world and living away from their heavenly homeland (yet hoping some day to reach it). The word thus reinforces the meaning of 'sojourners' and adds the idea that they are part of a 'world-wide' scattering of Christians.

The readers lived *in Pontus, Galatia, Cappadocia, Asia, and Bithynia*, five names describing four Roman provinces south of the Black Sea, in what today is called Asia Minor, mostly in modern Turkey (see map on p. 19). ('Asia' then often meant not the continent of Asia, but a single province just east of the Aegean Sea.) While three of the names (Galatia, Cappadocia, and Asia) refer to individual Roman provinces, 'Pontus' and 'Bithynia' were two regions that comprised a single province called 'Bithynia and Pontus'. Their separation into first and last positions on Peter's list is best explained by Hort's suggestion[1] that the list describes the route to be followed by the bearer of Peter's letter (probably Silvanus, 1 Pet. 5:12; see Introduction, pp. 23f.). Hort's theory has been corrected with respect to its details by Colin Hemer (see Introduction, pp. 37f.), who argues convincingly for the following route:[2] the bearer of the letter would land at a port of *Pontus* (Hemer argues that only Amisus, modern Samsun, would have provided a feasible route inland from the coast), travel to *Galatia* (stopping at Amasia in eastern Galatia), then through Zela to Caesarea in *Cappadocia*, then westward on the great trade route which traversed south Galatia (passing

[1] See 'The Provinces of Asia Minor Included in St. Peter's Address', in Hort, pp. 154–184, especially pp. 183–184.
[2] Colin Hemer, 'The Address of 1 Peter', *ExpT* 89 (1978), pp. 239–243.

through the Pauline churches of Iconium and Pisidian Antioch), then to Laodicea in *Asia*, then perhaps into other
churches of Asia (Colossae?, even Ephesus?), and finally
through the major churches of *Bithynia* (Nicea, Nicomedia, and
Chalcedon). From Chalcedon or Byzantium on the Bosporus he
could board a ship returning directly to Rome. Thus, all the
major centres of Christian influence in Asia Minor would be
reached.

2. The word *chosen* has been discussed in connection with
verse 1, where it appears in the Greek text modifying 'sojourners' (RSV 'exiles').

And destined is the RSV rendering of *kata prognōsin*, more literally translated, 'according to the foreknowledge' (NASB, NIV,
AV). The related verb 'foreknow' can refer not just to God's
knowing a *fact* (*e.g.* that Peter's readers would be chosen
sojourners in Asia Minor), but to his knowing *people* with a
personal, loving, fatherly knowledge (Rom. 8:29; 11:2;
1 Pet. 1:20; *cf.* 'know' in Jn. 10:14; 1 Cor. 8:3; 2 Tim. 2:19). Thus
'according to the foreknowledge' suggests 'according to God's
fatherly care for you before the world was made'.

But *what* is 'according to the foreknowledge of God the
Father'? The AV, NIV, and NASB make the phrase modify
'chosen' by giving 'chosen' a verbal sense. But in the Greek
text 'chosen' is merely an adjective ('chosen sojourners'), and is
nine words distant from this phrase. Since verse 1 contains no
verb, it is most natural to let 'according to the foreknowledge
of God the Father' modify the whole situation of the readers
described in the first verse: they are 'chosen sojourners of the
Dispersion in Pontus, Galatia, *etc.*, *according to the foreknowledge
of God the Father'*. This implies that their status as sojourners,
their privileges as God's chosen people, even their hostile
environment in Pontus, Galatia, *etc.*, were all known by God
before the world began, all came about in accordance with his
foreknowledge, and thus (we may conclude) all were in accordance with his fatherly love for his own people. Such foreknowledge is laden with comfort for Peter's readers.

The same content in verse 1, namely, the entire present
status of the readers, is further modified by two more preposi-

tional phrases,[1] *sanctified by the Spirit*, and *for obedience to Jesus Christ and for sprinkling with his blood*. Just as God's foreknowledge refers to past time, 'sanctification *by the Spirit*' speaks of a present influence and 'for the purpose of *obedience . . . and . . . sprinkling*' looks forward to a continuing future activity or goal.

Furthermore, the verse mentions the three persons of the Trinity: *God the Father . . . the Spirit . . . Jesus Christ*. Peter specifies distinct actions by the different persons in the Trinity yet sees them uniting to bring about a common goal, the eternal, full salvation of these 'chosen sojourners'.

The sanctifying work of the Holy Spirit, the work whereby he gradually works in Christians to free them more and more from remaining sin and to make them increasingly like Christ in holiness, faith, and love, is in view in the phrase *and sanctified by the Spirit*. But this RSV translation puts the activity too exclusively in the past: there is no past tense verb in the phrase, which literally says, 'in sanctification of (the) Spirit'.

The NIV and NASB, having focused too narrowly on the adjective 'chosen' as the reference point for 'according to the foreknowledge of God the Father', now must continue the same pattern, giving the puzzling result, 'chosen . . . by the sanctifying work of the Spirit'. This makes little if any sense, for (1) it is hard to imagine how an activity (sanctifying work) could perform a personal action (choosing), and (2) God's choosing, according to Scripture, is in eternity past, whereas the Spirit's sanctifying work, according to the rest of Scripture, is something present: but how can something in eternity past (God's choosing) be done 'by' something that begins only in the present (the Spirit's sanctifying work)? (Kelly, p. 43, has to import an entirely new idea into the text: 'This predestining choice . . . has been made operative by the sanctifying . . . action of the Spirit.')

It is much easier, again, to see the phrase 'in sanctification of the Spirit' as referring to the entire present status of Peter's readers. This allows *en* to have its common sense 'in': Peter is saying that his readers' *whole existence* as 'chosen sojourners of

[1] So also Beare: 'This threefold phrase cannot possibly be taken exclusively with *eklektois*, "chosen". . . . It is related to the entire salutation' (p. 75).

the Dispersion . . .' is being lived 'in' the realm of the sanctifying work of the Spirit. The unseen, unheard activity of God's Holy Spirit surrounds them almost like a spiritual atmosphere 'in' which they live and breathe, turning every circumstance, every sorrow, every hardship into a tool for his patient sanctifying work (*cf.* Jn. 15:2; Rom. 8:28; 2 Cor. 4:16–18; Heb. 12:10–11; Jas. 1:2–4; 1 Pet. 4:14).

For obedience to Jesus Christ indicates God's purpose in the readers' present existence as 'chosen sojourners' in their native lands: their lives ought to be leading 'toward' (*eis*) increasing obedience to Christ (*cf.* Eph. 2:10; 1 Thes. 4:3; Jn. 14:15). What the Father plans and the Spirit empowers, Christ thus receives, as exalted Saviour and ruling Lord.

Some argue that *obedience* (*hypakoē*) here means initial (saving) obedience to the gospel, but Peter elsewhere uses *hypakoē* to refer to the daily obedience of believers (1:14 and probably 1:22; also see *hypakouō* in 3:6), as do Paul (Rom. 5:19; 6:16; 2 Cor. 7:15; 10:5–6; Phm. 21) and Hebrews (5:8). No clear examples of *hypakoē* meaning 'initial saving response to the gospel' are found (for Rom. 1:5 and 15:18 are ambiguous).

Peter's readers of course realized that their obedience in this life was always incomplete, that even the most mature Christians were painfully aware of remaining sin, and that God's purpose, 'obedience to Jesus Christ', would never be completely fulfilled in this life. So Peter adds that their lives are also leading toward (*eis*) *sprinkling with his blood*.

Sprinkled blood in the Old Testament was a visual reminder to God and to his people that a life had been given, a sacrifice had been paid. But in most Old Testament sacrifices the blood was sprinkled on the altar or on the mercy seat (Lv. 4:17; 5:9; 16:14, 15, 19; Nu. 19:4). In only three cases was blood ceremonially sprinkled on the people themselves: (1) in the covenant initiation ceremony at Mt. Sinai when Moses sprinkled half the blood from the sacrificial oxen on all the people (Ex. 24:5–8; Heb. 9:19; and perhaps Is. 52:15 [Aquila, *cf.* Theodotian]); (2) in the ceremony of ordination for Aaron and his sons as priests (Ex. 29:21; probably also Heb. 10:22); and (3) in the purification ceremony for a leper who had been healed from leprosy (Lv. 14:6–7).

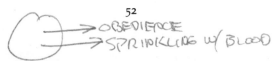

If 1 Peter 1:2 has the first in view, it means that God's purpose for the readers is that they be initiated into God's covenant and become his people, by being figuratively 'sprinkled' with the blood of Christ. The 'sprinkling' would thus refer to the *beginning* of the Christian life. But the fact that Peter lists this sprinkling after 'sanctification by the Spirit' and after 'obedience to Jesus Christ' makes this option unlikely, as does the term *eis* ('for, leading toward') in 'for . . . sprinkling'.

If the second ceremony, the ordination of priests, is in mind, it means that God's purpose for Peter's readers is that they should figuratively be ordained as priests by 'sprinkling' with the blood of Christ. But Peter already sees them as priests by virtue of their membership in the New Covenant ('you are . . . a royal priesthood', 2:9), as does Hebrews 10:22 (where the perfect tense verbs 'sprinkled' and 'washed' indicate completed events in the past), so this background is unlikely.

The third possibility, the sprinkling with blood for purification from leprosy, seems more appropriate. This passage (Lv. 14:6-7) is less obscure than we may think, for the ceremony was used for any kind of skin disease (Lv. 14:54-57) serious enough to exclude the sick person from the community: that person was to live alone and shout, 'Unclean, unclean' (Lv. 13:45-46). Thus, Leviticus 14:6-7 is an excellent passage to represent cleansing from any defilement that would disrupt fellowship with God and his people. David apparently alludes to it in Psalm 51:7: 'Purge me with hyssop, and I shall be clean' (the LXX says, 'sprinkle me with hyssop', using *rhantizō*, related to Peter's noun *rhantismos*, 'sprinkling'), here referring not to the physical defilement of leprosy but the spiritual defilement of sin. In both cases, fellowship was disrupted but membership among the covenant people of God was retained.

This 'sprinkling with blood' fits 1 Peter 1:2. Although God intended these 'chosen sojourners' to live 'for obedience to Jesus Christ', they were frequently 'defiled' by sin. Peter reminds them that their future includes continual sprinkling with the blood of Christ, that is, continual restoration of fellowship with God and his people through the sacrificial blood of Christ figuratively sprinkled over them, a continual reminder to God that their sins are forgiven and that they are welcome in God's presence and among his people (*cf.* 1 Jn. 1:7 for the idea of continual application of the blood of Christ in the Christian life).

For obedience to Jesus Christ and for sprinkling with his blood thus means that God's plan for them is not obedience marred by unforgiven sin but obedience whose failings are cleansed by the blood of Christ; it means 'for continual daily obedience and forgiveness'. F. H. Chase says Peter describes here 'a life lived in accordance with the Divine will and pattern . . . and continually cleansed from the defilement of sin by the application of the quickening blood of Christ.'[1] Here is simultaneous exhortation and comfort to bear in mind continually.

May grace and peace be multiplied to you is an expanded form of Paul's frequent 'Grace to you and peace' (Rom. 1:7; 1 Cor. 1:3; 2 Cor. 1:2; Gal. 1:3; Eph. 1:2; Phil. 1:2; Col. 1:2; 1 Thes. 1:1; 2 Thes. 1:2; Tit. 1:4; Phm. 3). Peter also couples the Old Testament blessing of God's *peace* with the New Testament blessing of *grace* (*charis*), God's freely given, undeserved favour toward his people. Peter asks that it would be *multiplied* to them; that all their moments would be filled with God's undeserved spiritual blessings.

II. GENERAL DOCTRINE: THE GREATNESS OF YOUR SALVATION (1:3 – 2:10)

A. YOU GROW AS CHRISTIANS THROUGH JOYFUL FAITH (1:3–12)

1. *Joy in future heavenly reward* (1:3–5)

3. *Blessed be the God and Father of our Lord Jesus Christ* echoes a frequent Old Testament word of praise to God (Gn. 14:20; 24:27; Ru. 4:14; 1 Sa. 25:32; 1 Ki. 1:48; Pss. 28:6; 31:21; 41:13) and changes it so as to praise God with a name he never revealed in the Old Testament, 'Father of our Lord Jesus Christ'.

The term 'Father', as applied to the first person of the Trinity, signifies not that the Father in any way created the Son or caused him to exist (for the Son has always existed and was

[1] *HDB*, vol. 3, p.796.

never created, Jn. 1:1–3; 8:58; 17:5, 24; Rev. 22:13), but that he relates to the Son as a father relates to a son normally: the Father plans and directs, the Son responds and obeys; the Father 'sends', the Son comes from the Father (Gal. 4:4; Jn. 3:16, 18; 5:19, 22, 26–27, 30). The Father creates 'through' the Son; all things come 'from' the Father 'through' the Son (Jn. 1:3; 1 Cor. 8:6; Col. 1:16; Heb. 1:2).

Peter encourages his readers to praise God, a helpful remedy for hearts weighed down with discouragement because of suffering. He then lists the reason for praise: *By his great mercy we have been born anew*. The word for 'born anew' (*anagennaō*) has a more active sense than our translation (RSV) indicates, for the root word (*gennaō*) often refers to a father's role in the birth of a child (AV, 'hath begotten us again'), either literally (Mt. 1:2–20) or figuratively, of spiritual birth (1 Cor. 4:15). 'Begot' is archaic, however, and he 'has caused us to be born again' (NASB) is probably best. In blessing God, Peter thinks first of the new spiritual life that God has given to his people.[1]

This being born anew is *by his great mercy*, a phrase with the same preposition (*kata*) as 'according to the foreknowledge' in verse 2. No foreknowledge of the fact that we would believe, no foreseeing of any desirableness or merit on our part, is mentioned here or anywhere else in Scripture when indicating God's ultimate reason for our salvation. It is simply 'according to his great mercy' that he gave us new life.

We have been born again, Peter says, *to a living hope*, or perhaps *into* (*eis*, into the sphere or realm of) 'a living hope'. This hope is the eager, confident expectation of the life to come, which Peter describes in more detail in the next verse. It is 'living' – by so describing it Peter indicates that it grows and increases in strength year by year. If such a growing hope is the

---

[1] Some commentators see this reference to new birth as an indication that this section is a hymn of thanksgiving (or a section of liturgy) which was used at baptism. This is unlikely, not only because baptism is not specifically mentioned, but also because it misses the evident fact that when Peter refers to the beginning of the Christian life he speaks not of the outward ceremony (baptism) but of the inward spiritual reality (being given new birth): note 1:3 and 23. Peter is speaking of the beginning of the Christian life here, not a ceremony which may or may not have occurred close to it in time. (See Introduction on 'Nature and possible sources of 1 Peter'.)

expected result of being born again, then perhaps the degree to which believers have an intense, confident expectation of the life to come is one useful measure of progress toward spiritual maturity. It is not surprising that such a hope is particularly evident in many older Christians as they approach death.

God brought about this new birth *through the resurrection of Jesus Christ from the dead*. Grammatically this phrase could modify the participle 'living', indicating that hope is living 'through (the power of) the resurrection' (so Kelly, p. 48), but it is unlikely that this is the correct sense: (1) such a meaning would have been more clearly expressed if Peter had used a relative clause, 'to a hope which is living through the resurrection' (*eis elpida hē zōsan di'anastaseōs*), or even 'on account of the resurrection' (*di'anastasin*); (2) a closely parallel example of God acting *through* (*dia*) some other person or thing to give us new birth is found in verse 23: 'You have been born anew ... through (*dia*) the living and abiding word of God'; and (3) there is in Peter a common pattern of persons, especially God, doing something through or by means of (*dia*) someone or something else (1 Pet. 1:5, 12, 23; 2:5, 14(?); 3:1, 21; 4:11; 5:12; 2 Pet. 1:4).

The resurrection of Christ from the dead secures for his people both new resurrection bodies and new spiritual life. Christians do not in this age receive new bodies but God does grant, on the basis of Jesus' resurrection, renewed spirits. Thus, spiritually, believers have been 'raised with Christ' (Col. 3:1; Eph. 2:6; *cf.* Rom. 6:4, 11).

4. Peter explains that the object of their 'living hope' is *an inheritance which is imperishable, undefiled, and unfading*. The New Testament regularly uses 'inheritance' (*klēronomia*) to refer not only to an earthly inheritance but also to a believer's 'share' in the heavenly kingdom, his or her future heavenly reward (Gal. 3:18; Eph. 1:14, 18; 5:5; Col. 3:24; Heb. 9:15). But the Old Testament spoke of the promised land of Canaan as Israel's 'inheritance' (Nu. 32:19; Dt. 2:12; 12:9; Jos. 11:23; Ps. 105:11; *cf.* Acts 7:5; Heb. 11:8), and frequently used 'inheritance' to refer to the portion of Canaan belonging to each tribe or family as its 'share': Nu. 26:54; 27:7–11; 36:3–12; Jos. 13:14, 23, 28, *etc*.

The contrast is striking: the readers have been born anew, not to obtain a family inheritance in the earthly land of Canaan, but to obtain an inheritance in the eternal city of God (away from which they now live as sojourners, v. 1). The 'inheritance' is thus their portion in the new creation and all its blessings.

The word 'to' (*eis*) in the phrase 'to an inheritance' often takes the sense 'into', and here may well suggest some partial present enjoyment of that heavenly inheritance 'into' which, in the spiritual realm, the readers have been born.

This heavenly inheritance is 'imperishable', meaning that it is not subject to decay, unable to be worn out with the passage of time. The New Testament uses this word only of eternal heavenly realities, such as God himself (Rom. 1:23; 1 Tim. 1:17), God's word (1 Pet. 1:23), and our resurrection bodies (1 Cor. 15:52; *cf.* 1 Cor. 9:25; 1 Pet. 3:4). All earthly possessions will ultimately decay and be destroyed (Lk. 12:33; Rom. 1:23; 2 Cor. 4:16; Col. 2:22; 1 Pet. 1:18), for the creation now is in 'bondage to decay' (Rom. 8:21).

This inheritance is also 'undefiled' (*i.e.* 'unstained by sin', Heb. 7:26; 13:4; Jas. 1:27). The LXX frequently uses the related verb 'defile' to speak of ceremonial defilement which made a person or thing unfit to come before God in worship (Ex. 20:25; Lv. 11:24, 43, 44; 13:3, 8, 11; Nu. 19:13, 20), and of moral defilement of the land by sin (Nu. 35:34; Dt. 24:4; Je. 2:7; 3:2; *cf.* Nu. 5:13–29; Dt. 21:23; Ho. 5:3; 6:10). Peter invites contemplation of a heavenly inheritance unpolluted by sin and containing nothing unworthy of God's full approval.

Furthermore, the inheritance is 'unfading'. Unlike earthly wealth (Jas. 1:11), it will never wither, grow dim, or lose its beauty or glory (*cf.* 1 Pet. 5:4).

Finally, the inheritance is *kept in heaven for you*. The form of the verb 'kept' (perfect passive participle) indicates a completed past activity (by God) with results that are still continuing in the present: God himself has 'stored up' or 'reserved' this inheritance in heaven for believers and it continues to be there, 'still reserved' for them. (Contrast the use of the same verb 'kept' in 2 Pet. 2:17; *cf.* Jude 13.)

It will never be denied to them, for Peter tells them that it has been kept '*for you*'. The surprising switch to 'you' instead of 'us' (this is the first time Peter has used the second person plural pronoun) makes the reservation of this inheritance much more personal.

The 'inheritance' of the New Covenant Christian is thus shown to be far superior to the earthly inheritance of the people of Israel in the land of Canaan. That earthly land was not 'kept' for them, but was *taken from them* in the exile, and later by Roman occupation. Even while they possessed the land, it produced rewards that *decayed*, rewards whose glory *faded* away. The beauty of the land's holiness before God was repeatedly *defiled* by sin (Nu. 35:34; Je. 2:7; 3:2).

5. Peter's readers may have been anxious about whether they would have strength to remain faithful to Christ if persecution or suffering became more intense. He assures them that they are people *who by God's power are guarded through faith for a salvation ready to be revealed in the last time*.

Guarded (*phroureō*) means 'kept safe, carefully watched', and is frequently used in military contexts: the people who agreed with the ten unfaithful spies decided that the treasures of Canaan were 'so strongly *guarded*' that they could not be taken away (Philo, *Moses* 1.235; *cf.* Judith 3:6; 1 Esdras 4:56; Wisdom 17:16). At Damascus, the governor 'guarded' the city in order to seize Paul (2 Cor. 11:32; the word is used metaphorically in Gal. 3:23; Phil. 4:7). The contexts above show that the word can mean both 'kept from escaping' and 'protected from attack', and perhaps both kinds of guarding are intended here: God is preserving believers from escaping out of his kingdom, and he is protecting them from external attacks. 'Shielded' (NIV) gives only half the sense.

The present participle which Peter uses gives the sense 'you are continually being guarded'. He stresses that this is *by God's power*. Yet God's power does not work apart from the personal faith of those being guarded, but *through* their faith. ('Faith', *pistis*, is regularly a personal activity of individual believers in Peter: 1 Pet. 1:7, 9, 21; 5:9; 2 Pet. 1:1, 5; and commonly in the New Testament.) The parallel examples of God working 'through' someone or something in Peter's writings (1 Pet. 1:3, 23; 2 Pet. 1:4, and probably also 1 Pet. 1:12; 2:14; 3:1) suggest that the believer's personal faith or trust in God is the means God uses to guard his people. Thus we might give the sense of the verse by saying that 'God is continually using his power to guard his people by means of their faith', a statement which seems to imply that God's power in fact energizes and continually sustains individual, personal faith.[1]

This guarding is not for a temporary goal but *for a salvation ready to be revealed in the last time*. *Salvation* is used here not of past justification or of present sanctification (speaking in theological categories) but of the future full possession of all the blessings of our redemption – of the final, complete fulfilment of our salvation (*cf.* Rom. 13:11; 1 Pet. 2:2). Though already 'prepared' or *ready*, it will not be *revealed* by God to mankind generally until the *last time*, the time of final judgment.

This last phrase makes it difficult if not impossible to see any end to God's guarding activity. If God's guarding has as its purpose the preservation of believers until they receive their full, heavenly salvation, then it is safe to conclude that God will accomplish that purpose and they will in fact attain that final salvation. Ultimately their attainment of final salvation depends on God's power.

Nevertheless, God's power continually works *through* their faith. Do they wish to know whether God is guarding them? If they continue to trust God through Christ, God is working and guarding them, and he should be thanked.

Additional Note: New Covenant rewards (1:4)

Peter here (v. 4) reminds his readers that in the New Covenant, God's rewards are less material, physical, earthly. There is less emphasis on present material prosperity as a reward, for God has 'chosen those who are poor in the world to be rich in faith' (Jas. 2:5, a statement which does not and could not appear in the OT). The enjoyment of physical health is also less prominent, for 'though our outer nature is wasting away our inner nature is being renewed every day' (2 Cor. 4:16). There is less emphasis

[1]Kelly's translation, 'as a result of faith', is an extremely unlikely rendering of the very common construction *dia* with genitive (the few examples of this construction meaning 'as a result of' which are suggested in BAGD, p. 180, IV, are all ambiguous, and Kelly himself gives no examples).

too on freedom from persecution, for 'if you are reproached for the name of Christ, you are blessed, because the spirit of glory and of God rests upon you' (1 Pet. 4:14). Having many children is not regarded in the New Testament as a necessary sign of God's favour, for both marriage and celibacy are his gifts (1 Cor. 7:7).

Christians should not be dismayed at this relative lack of present material rewards, however, for faith recognizes the New Covenant reward as something far greater: a present sufficiency for material needs (Phil. 4:19), a present spiritual fellowship with Christ (1 Pet. 1:8), and a future inheritance both material and eternal, which is 'imperishable, undefiled, and unfading, kept in heaven for you' (1 Pet. 1:4).

Just as God in the Old Covenant encouraged his people to look forward to the future Messiah with faith, so he now encourages us, for whom the Messiah's coming is a fact of history, to look forward to our full heavenly inheritance. Here is great comfort for every New Covenant believer. 'So we do not lose heart. . . . For this slight momentary affliction is preparing for us an eternal weight of glory beyond all comparison, because we look not to the things that are seen but to the things that are unseen; for the things that are seen are transient, but the things that are unseen are eternal' (2 Cor. 4:16–18).

2. Joy in spite of suffering (1:6–7)

6. The word *this* in the phrase *In this you rejoice* is best understood to refer to the entire future hope discussed in verses 3 to 5. It cannot refer to 'salvation', for that would require a feminine pronoun in the Greek text, whereas the pronoun in the text can only be masculine or neuter. Grammatically the word 'this' might also be translated 'whom', referring to God the Father or to Jesus Christ in verse 3. But these antecedents are too far from 'this' to be understandable to the readers without further specification. Furthermore, the flow of thought in the context makes the combination of rejoicing in hope of the future (vv. 3–5) and suffering grief in the present (vv. 6–7) a very appropriate one here.

Rejoice represents a verb (*agalliaō*) which is not used by secular Greek writers, and which always in the New Testament signifies a deep spiritual joy, a rejoicing in God or in what he has done.[1] Mary uses it in the Magnificat: 'My soul magnifies the Lord, and my spirit *rejoices* in God my Saviour' (Lk. 1:46–47). Believers who have suffered will *'rejoice* and be glad when [Christ's] glory is revealed' (1 Pet. 4:13). The Philippian jailer *'rejoiced* with all his household' that he had believed in God (Acts 16:34). This kind of joy could be called 'the joy of salvation' for it is always a spiritually prompted joy. In fact, the LXX uses a cognate noun to translate David's prayer, 'Restore to me the *joy* of your salvation' (Ps. 51:12(50:14)).[2]

Though *rejoice* could be either indicative ('in this you are rejoicing') or imperative ('rejoice in this'), it seems unlikely that Peter is commanding believers to rejoice in the great blessings mentioned in verses 3 to 5: rejoicing would be the natural response to such blessings. Furthermore, this entire section is devoted to declaring facts about the believers' lives, whereas his commands concerning the Christian life do not seem to begin until verse 13. It is better therefore to translate, 'in this you rejoice', or, bringing out more explicitly the force of the present tense, 'in this you are continually rejoicing'.

When they think about their future inheritance, the Christians to whom Peter is writing respond with intense 'salvation joy' which continues throughout their earthly lives. He thinks such rejoicing in heavenly realities to be a normal part of the ordinary Christian life.

The Christian life is not all joy, however, for Peter adds *though now for a little while you may have to suffer various trials.* The word *though* is not explicitly in the Greek text, but it is an acceptable translation of the participle 'having been grieved'. The adversative sense given by *though* seems better than any alternative because of the fundamental difference in the emotions of

---

[1]The only possible exception is Jn. 5:35, yet even here it seems to indicate a rejoicing (or willingness to rejoice) in the new work which God was doing by sending John the Baptist and thereby ending 400 years in which he had sent no prophets to his people.

[2]Other examples in the New Testament include Mt. 5:12; Lk. 10:21; Jn. 8:56; Acts 2:26; 1 Pet. 1:8; Rev. 19:7. The LXX frequently uses *agalliaō* to speak of rejoicing in the Lord (Ps. 90(89):14; Hab. 3:17–18). The related noun is used in Ps. 126(125):5–6: 'Those that sow in tears shall reap in *joy*. . . . They shall surely come with *exaltation* bringing their sheaves with them.' See also Pss. 2:11; 16:9; 32:11; 51:8; 84:2.

rejoicing and grieving.[1] These believers are rejoicing *even though* they may suffer grief.

Suffer (RSV) is better translated 'suffer grief' (NIV) or 'be grieved'. The verb (*lupeō*) always refers to the emotion of grief, not to the suffering which produces grief (note Mt. 14:9; 17:23; 18:31; 1 Thes. 4:13).

Peter makes the circumstances leading to such grief very general indeed. First, he says not that all his readers are suffering or have suffered, but that they *may have to* suffer grief in various trials (Gk. text, more literally: 'if it is necessary').[2] He does not need to specify the evident fact that he means 'necessary in God's sight', an idea which would greatly encourage his readers.

> His purpose was to show that God does not thus try His people without reason, for if God afflicted us without a cause, it would be grievous to bear. Hence Peter has taken an argument for consolation from the design of God, not because the purpose always appears to us, but because we ought to be fully persuaded that it ought to be so, because it is God's will.[3]

Peter says therefore that Christians will experience grief only as it is necessary in the light of God's great and infinitely wise purposes for them.

The phrase *various trials* should also caution us against looking for any specific kind of persecution or suffering as the historical background for this letter. Since no one kind of trial or testing is in view, Peter's words have their application to all the trials which Christians experience (*cf.* Jas. 1:2).

It is best to understand the word *now* as referring to the present existence of believers during which for a *little while*, compared with their enjoyment of eternity, they may have to

---

[1]Selwyn, p. 127, argues against translating the participle in a concessive sense ('although'), and prefers to see here rejoicing *because of* suffering. But rejoicing in the NT is not generally based on suffering itself. Rather, believers are said to rejoice because of the benefits resulting from, and the future heavenly reward that follows, suffering (Mt. 5:12).

[2]The grammatical structure here ('first class condition') does not affirm that the facts of the 'if-clause' are true (*cf.* Robertson, *Grammar*, pp. 1008–1009), but only that the speaker in this sentence is for a moment assuming them to be true in order to make his point.

[3]Calvin, p. 235.

suffer.

Though some (*e.g.* Selwyn, p. 127) understand the suffering as having been recently completed (giving the sense, 'though now for a little while you have just suffered grief in various trials'), such a translation is unlikely since it improbably assumes that all Peter's readers in many churches had just finished suffering. It is better to translate 'be grieved' (aorist participle) to indicate time simultaneous with the rejoicing,[1] for Peter's argument would lose much of its force if the grieving were already past. It is much more forceful to say that they are presently rejoicing even though they may now (from time to time) be grieving in various trials. This gives the following sense: 'In this hope of the future you are continually rejoicing, although during this life for a little time, if God deems it necessary, you are grieved in various trials.'

Peter thus shows simultaneous grief and joy to be normal in the Christian life. Grief arises because of many difficulties encountered in this fallen world, but faith looks to the unseen reality beyond this present brief existence and rejoices.

7. In verse 7 Peter gives a fuller explanation of the divine purposes behind the grief which Christians now experience. They may have to experience grief in various trials, *so that the genuineness of your faith . . . may redound to praise and glory and honour at the revelation of Jesus Christ.* The term translated *genuineness* (*dokimion*) is found outside the New Testament with the meaning 'genuine, proven';[2] here, with the definite article in front of it, the sense is 'the genuineness of your faith', or 'the proven quality of your faith'.

This word and closely related terms are frequently used of testing or refining metal (see Ps. 12:6(LXX 11:7); Pr. 27:21). Peter deliberately employs this analogy to say that situations of testing are occasions when God refines and purifies the faith of his

---

[1] Especially when an aorist participle is placed after the main verb, as it is here, it frequently refers to action simultaneous with the main verb (see, for example, Mk. 15:30; Lk. 2:16; Acts 10:33, Phil. 4:14; 1 Thes. 1:6; *cf.* Robertson, *Grammar*, p. 1113).

[2] See Deissmann, p. 260, with the quotation of a papyrus scrap which mentions gold buckles of *good* (*dokimion*) gold (*cf.* pp. 260–261; BAGD, p. 203). Thus, the NASB mg., 'genuineness', is a better translation than the NASB text, 'proof'.

people as precious metal is refined in a fire (*cf.* Is. 48:10, 'I have tried you in the furnace of affliction'). The trials burn away any impurities in the believer's faith. What is left when the trials have ended is purified, genuine faith, analogous to the pure gold or silver that emerges from the refiner's fire.

The genuine faith which emerges from trials is *more precious than gold which though perishable is tested by fire*. Though gold for centuries has been a commonly understood symbol for the most precious and lasting of material possessions, genuine faith is more precious (literally, 'much more precious') than either gold or, by implication, any other material possession.

Gold perishes even though it is refined or *tested* (*dokimazō*, from the same word group as *dokimion*, above) by fire – in fact, gold is one of the most durable of all substances. Yet Peter says that it 'perishes', because he knows that this entire creation is on its way toward final destruction (see 2 Pet. 3:7, 10–12). Genuine faith is more valuable to God than gold because he is a God who delights in being trusted. And since God's evaluation of something is the ultimate standard of meaning in the universe, Peter's readers have a secure basis for a sense of ultimate meaning and importance for their own lives.

Peter says that his readers may have to experience grief in various trials so that the genuineness of their faith *may redound to praise and glory and honour at the revelation of Jesus Christ*. He does not specify whether this praise is the praise which God gives to his people on the last day (as in Rom. 2:29; 1 Cor. 4:5; 1 Pet. 5:4), or the praise which people give to God. It seems more likely that the initial thought is of praise which God gives to his people, since in this context Peter is encouraging his readers to hope in their heavenly reward (v. 4). Furthermore, it is the genuineness of faith which is here affirmed to be more precious (in God's sight, apparently) than gold. But in this present age faith does not receive much outward or evident reward. Therefore it would appropriately receive a reward as an expression of God's approval at the day of final judgment.

By the phrase *at the revelation of Jesus Christ*, Peter is referring to the judgment of the last day when the secrets of all hearts are revealed (*cf.* 'the revelation of our Lord Jesus Christ' or similar phrases in 1 Cor. 1:7; 2 Thes. 1:17; 1 Pet. 1:13; 4:13; and the verb 'reveal' in Lk. 17:30; 1 Pet. 1:5; 5:1, *etc.*). He thus reminds Christians that God's purposes in present grief may not be fully known in a week, in a year, or even in this lifetime. Indeed, some of God's purposes will not even be known when believers die and go to be with the Lord. Some will only be discovered at the day of final judgment when the Lord reveals the secrets of all hearts and commends with special honour those who trusted him in hardship even though they could not see the reason for it: they trusted him simply because he was their God and they knew him to be worthy of trust. It is in times when the reason for hardship cannot be seen that trust in God alone seems to become most pure and precious in his sight. Such faith he will not forget, but will store up as a jewel of great value and beauty to be displayed and delighted in on the day of judgment.

3. *Inexpressible joy in knowing Christ himself* (1:8–9)

8. Peter begins with an amazing statement of the nature of the Christian life: *Without having seen him you love him.* The verb 'love' (*agapaō*) in the present tense indicates a continual or regular activity. The Christians to whom he is writing have as their normal present experience continuing love for Jesus Christ, even though they have never seen him. This implies a personal daily relationship with the ascended Lord Jesus – through prayer and worship, and no doubt also through reflection on the written words of Scripture, through which he speaks (see 1 Pet. 2:2–3, below).

The believer's present personal relationship with Jesus Christ is described more fully by Peter: *though you do not now see him you believe in him and rejoice with unutterable and exalted joy.* 'Now' here and in verse 6 indicates this present life or this present age before the Lord returns, during which we do not see Christ with our physical eyes. None the less, what Peter says of his readers is also true of all Christians during this age: we *believe* in him whom we do not see.

The verb translated 'believe' (*pisteuō*) means here to 'trust' or to 'rest one's confidence in' or to 'depend upon'. It is followed by a preposition (*eis*) which prior to the New Testament was apparently never used with this verb and which carries the surprising nuance of 'into', almost as if this personal faith were going 'into' the Lord Jesus Christ and resting or remaining there.[1] The combination of verb and preposition implies strong personal involvement in the act of believing, and carries a sense of resting oneself in Christ.

Just as the verb 'believe in' gives the sense of continual present activity (present participle), the verb 'rejoice' is also in the present tense and may be translated 'continually rejoice'. This verb (*agalliaō*) is also used in verse 6 of rejoicing in future heavenly reward. But whereas in verse 6 Peter used the word alone, here he strengthens the word by adding *with unutterable and exalted joy*. The contrast is clear: whereas in the earlier verse Peter spoke of strong rejoicing in future hope, here he says that our personal, daily fellowship with Jesus Christ himself is cause for even greater rejoicing, *unutterable and exalted joy*.

The word translated *unutterable* occurs only here in the New Testament, and describes a joy so profound as to be beyond the power of words to express. (It thus reminds us of the value of singing and other kinds of music in worship, for music often provides a vehicle for expressing the fullness of joy in a Christian's heart in a way that is much more effective than spoken words alone.)

This joy is also *exalted*. This word (*doxazō*) is the verb which corresponds to the noun 'glory' (*doxa*). These terms would quite naturally remind Peter's readers of the frequent Old Testament mention of the glory of God, that bright shining radiance which surrounded the presence of God himself. The sense of this word *exalted* (a perfect passive participle) could be given more fully by paraphrasing, 'joy that has been infused with heavenly glory and that still possesses the radiance of that glory'. It is thus joy that results from being in the presence of God himself, and joy that even now partakes of the character of heaven. It is the joy of heaven before heaven, experienced now in fellowship with the unseen Christ.

9. No new sentence begins in the Greek text at verse 9.

---

[1]See E. D. Burton, *Galatians*, ICC (Edinburgh: T. & T. Clark, 1920), pp. 480–481; MHT 1, pp. 67–68.

Rather, Peter uses a present participle, 'obtaining as the out-come of your faith the salvation of your souls ' (NASB). The NIV introduces the idea of explanation or reason with the insertion of the word 'for': 'for you are receiving the goal of your faith, the salvation of your souls'. Although such a translation of the participle is grammatically possible, it seems unwarranted by the context: it makes the reason for the believer's rejoicing to be his or her own personal spiritual growth, something worthy of joy no doubt, but certainly not worthy of the *unalterable and exalted joy* mentioned here. The NASB, however, by translating the participle in a very common sense (expressing attendant circumstances), preserves the lofty character of this passage, for it retains our present personal trust in Christ and love for him as the reason for our greatest joy.

Peter says his readers are receiving or 'obtaining' the 'goal' or *outcome* of their faith while they are believing in Christ and rejoicing in him. Once again the verb 'obtaining' is a present participle, giving verse 9 the sense of a progressive obtaining of more and more of this 'goal' or 'outcome' to which their faith leads. *Salvation* then must be used here to refer to the full possession of all the blessings of salvation (see v. 5 for the same sense). The process described in verse 9 is the entire process of growth in the Christian life, the process of appropriating in one's own life more and more of the blessings of salvation. This process happens, Peter says, as Christians continually believe in Christ and continually rejoice because of that personal trust in him. Such day by day faith and joy produces an unexpected benefit: continual growth toward Christian maturity.

4. Prophets and angels amazed at the glory of your salvation (1:10–12)

10. The purpose of this paragraph is to show Peter's readers that the spiritual blessings they now have are greater than anything that was envisaged by Old Testament prophets or even by angels. Thus Peter seeks to increase his readers' appreciation for their great salvation in Christ.

Verses 10 to 12 should be understood in connection with verse 9 because the first three Greek words in verse 10 mean

'Concerning which salvation' (that is, the 'salvation' mentioned in v. 9, the progressive obtaining by believers of more and more of the full benefits of their salvation). *The prophets who prophesied of the grace that was to be yours* are the Old Testament prophets generally,[1] with *grace* used here to refer to the New Covenant experience of salvation blessings (*cf. charis*, 'grace', used similarly in 3:7; also Acts 20:24; Rom. 5:2; 6:14; Heb. 12:15).

The prophets *searched and inquired* about this salvation. Neither term means that they merely pondered or wondered – the words both imply active effort in looking to find something. The first word, *searched* (*ekzēteō*), implies diligent searching or seeking for something, and is often used of seeking for God (Acts 15:17; Rom. 3:11; Heb. 11:6) or searching Scripture (Ps. 119(LXX 118): 22, 33, 45, 56, 94, 100, 145, 155).

The second word, *inquired* (*exeraunaō*), only occurs here in the New Testament, but thirty-two other occurrences are found in the LXX, Josephus, and Philo. Most often it refers to searching through something like a house, a tent, a city, or a country in order to find some person or thing, or else it refers to searching through Scripture (see Ps. 119:2, 34, 69, 115, 129).

11. *They inquired* does not necessarily mean that they asked questions, but that they were 'searching to find out' (*cf.* NIV, 'trying to find out'). What did they search? Since Peter does not say, we cannot be certain. Yet this word (*eraunaō*), the third 'searching' word in this sentence, is used elsewhere of searching through Scripture (see Jn. 5:39; 7:52). An excellent suggestion is therefore that they searched through earlier Scripture, and probably their own prophecies as well, to find out about the 'salvation' and the 'grace' they were predicting. Moreover, the fact that they subsequently learned that their prophecies were not for their own times but the future ('they were serving not them-

---

[1]Selwyn, pp. 259–268, argues that Peter is referring not to OT prophets but to Christian prophets of the 1st century. But he can suggest no linguistically valid sense for the phrase 'predicting the sufferings of Christ' (he must import into the text the idea that it is people, rather than sufferings, which are 'toward' [*eis*] Christ). Moreover, searching Scripture for Messianic prophecies was simply not a primary activity of NT prophets (see Wayne Grudem, *The Gift of Prophecy in 1 Corinthians* [Washington, DC: University Press of America, 1982], pp. 139–144; 181–185; 201–210; 219–222). Further objections to Selwyn on this point are in Best, pp. 83–84; see also the discussion below on v. 11, 'the sufferings of Christ'.

selves but you', v. 12) suggests that they also searched and investigated their own times and circumstances, seeking to learn if their prophecies were to be fulfilled in the events they saw in their own lifetimes. (See also Additional Note below).

The Spirit of Christ within them refers to the Holy Spirit[1] but with a title which suggests that predicting the coming Messiah (the Heb. equivalent of the Gk. term 'Christ') was the primary focus of his activity in the Old Testament prophets – so much so that Peter calls him the 'Spirit of Messiah' or the 'Spirit of Christ'.

The grammar of the Greek text requires that 'the Spirit of Christ', not the prophets, be the subject of the participle *predicting* (this is clear in the NASB and the NIV but not the RSV). *Predicting* is itself a rare word but one whose component parts give the clear sense, 'testifying or bearing witness beforehand'.

That the Holy Spirit speaking through the prophets predicted *the sufferings of Christ* is a common theme in all the New Testament proclamation about Christ (see Peter's own use of Is. 53 in 2:22–24), and the amazing accuracy of these predictions has convinced many throughout history of the divine authorship of Scripture. Yet Peter says the Holy Spirit in the prophets also predicted *the subsequent glory*. The word translated *glory* is actually plural, making 'the subsequent glories' a better translation. *Subsequent* means 'after Christ's sufferings', and the word 'glories' must refer not only to Christ's resurrection and exaltation (which are never called 'glories' [plural] in Scripture), but also to all the glories of his kingdom which come to us through his redemptive work.

Some argue that *the sufferings of Christ* refers not to Christ's own sufferings but to the sufferings of Christians as they become more like Christ.[2] But this sense of the phrase *ta eis christon pathemata* as 'the sufferings of the Christward road' (so Selwyn, p. 263) adopts a meaning which would not have been

---

[1]Kelly thinks this means 'Christ himself conceived of as divine spirit' (p. 60), but Christ is nowhere in the Bible called 'the Spirit of Christ'. Moreover, 'Spirit of Christ' in Rom. 8:9 is interchangeable with 'Spirit of God', and in Acts 16:7 'the Spirit of Jesus' must be the same person as 'the Holy Spirit' in v. 6; see also 2 Cor. 3:17; Gal. 4:6; Phil. 1:19.

[2]Selwyn, pp. 263–264; J. Dunn, *Christology in the Making* (London: SCM, 1980), p. 159; N. Hillyer, *TynB* 21 (1970), p. 66; J. W. Pryor, *RTR* 45 (1986), p. 2.

understood from the Greek phrase by first-century readers. The New Testament speaks of suffering like Christ, following after him, following in his steps, *etc.*, but it never speaks of suffering *toward* (*eis* with accusative) him – an unintelligible idea. In order to give an intelligible sense, Selwyn must import the idea that the *people* who suffer (not the *sufferings* themselves) move toward Christ, but that idea is not in the Greek text. Moreover, if the sufferings here are sufferings of Christians to whom Peter is writing, then the *meta tauta* ('after these things') glories of verse 11 must all be *after* the sufferings are completed. But this contradicts 4:14, where Peter says that glory even now rests on those who suffer. It is best therefore to understand the phrase as 'the sufferings intended for (or destined for) Christ'.

If we are to look for examples of this predicting activity, we may in fact look through the whole of the Old Testament, for the New Testament authors can sometimes speak of the whole of the Old Testament as the writings of 'the prophets' (see Lk. 24:27; also Acts 2:30 on David as a prophet). In this sense the predictions of the sufferings of the Messiah begin with the prediction of the 'seed' of the woman who would be bruised in the heel by the serpent (Gn. 3:15), and continue through much of the Old Testament writings (for, example, Pss. 22:1, 7–8, 18; 34:19–20; 69:21; Is. 50:6; 52:14–15; 53:1–12; Zc. 12:10; 13:7, *etc.*).

The Messiah's subsequent glory is predicted in Pss. 2; 16:10; 22:22; 45:7; 110:1, 4; Is. 9:6; 40:3–5, 9–11; 42:1–4; 61:1–3; Je. 33:14–15; Ezk. 34:23; Dn. 7:13–14; Mal. 3:1–3, *etc.* And the 'glories' of the Messiah's people are seen in Is. 51:11; 60:1–22; 62:2–5; Je. 31:31–34; Dn. 7:18, 27; Ho. 2:23; Joel 2:28–32; Am. 9:13–15; Hab. 2:14; Zp. 3:14–20; Zc. 14, *etc.*

Yet all these verses are only a beginning, for they do not include the 'acted-out prophecies' seen in the historical events of the Old Testament, where in the lives of people like Abraham, Isaac, Jacob, Joseph, Moses, Joshua, David, Solomon, Jonah, and often the nation of Israel generally, God brought to pass events which foreshadowed a pattern of life that would be later followed by 'one greater than Solomon', one who was David's greater Son.

Peter is saying, then, that the Old Testament prophets eagerly searched and investigated their own prophecies, other Scripture, and their own times in order to find out who or what time the Spirit of Christ was indicating when he (the Spirit in them) was predicting the sufferings of Christ and the glories of his kingdom. Since we now know the answers to 'Who?' (Jesus) and 'What time?' (Jesus' lifetime and the subsequent church age), we should read the Old Testament prophets eagerly, expecting that our hearts will often be stirred to praise when there we discover, as a central theme, the sufferings of our Saviour on our behalf and the glories of the resultant kingdom of which we even now are members.

12. *It was revealed to them* indicates a divine communication to the prophets, for the verb *apokalyptō* ('reveal'), used twenty-six times in the New Testament, and the cognate noun *apokalypsis* ('revelation'), used eighteen times, are never used to speak of human activity or communication (for that the NT generally uses another word, *gnōrizō*, 'to make known'). Rather, these terms always refer to 'revelation' given by the activity of God (Mt. 11:25; 16:17; Phil. 3:15), of Christ (Mt. 11:27; Gal. 1:12), or of the Holy Spirit (1 Cor. 2:10; Eph. 3:5), or which results from events brought about directly by them (especially Christ's return: Rom. 2:5; 8:19; 1 Pet. 1:7).

This revelation, probably specifically from the Holy Spirit working in the prophets, provided at least a partial answer to the prophets' searchings. It made known to them that their prophecies about the Messiah and his kingdom referred not to their own times but to some future generation: *they were serving not themselves but you*. The original text has another direct object for the verb, the Greek word *auta*, 'those things', a word left untranslated by the RSV. It refers to their predictions of Christ's sufferings and the glories of his kingdom. More explicitly we can translate, 'They were ministering those things not to themselves but to you.' The prophetic predictions were not without relevance for the original hearers, for they would give comfort and hope to those who looked forward in faith (*cf.* Heb. 11:13), but primarily they were given to minister to *you*, that is, to New Covenant believers. (Similar statements, affirming that other parts of the OT were written primarily for the benefit of New Covenant believers, are found in Rom. 15:4 and 1 Cor. 10:11; *cf.*

71

Lk. 24:25–27; 2 Tim. 3:16.) The word translated *serving* (*diakoneō*) is the common word in the New Testament used for ministering to or serving someone (Mk. 10:45; Lk. 10:40; Acts 6:2; 1 Tim. 3:10, 13; 1 Pet. 4:10, 11, *etc.*) – reminding us that God's great prophets are simply servants of others, as are all to whom he gives large responsibility (*cf.* Mt. 23:11), and suggesting also that we are greatly privileged as the recipients of their ancient ministry.

Those predictions are, Peter says, *the things which have now been announced to you by those who preached the good news to you* – the content of the gospel preaching which Peter's readers heard was the declaration of these prophecies and the announcement that they had found their fulfillment in Jesus Christ and in the establishment of his church. (Peter himself makes just this point in his Pentecost sermon in Acts 2:14–40.)

These things – the most significant facts in history – were *announced* or 'proclaimed' (the word usually refers to a declaration of previously unknown information which is of great import or concern to the hearers) to Peter's readers 'through those who preached the gospel to you' (NASB). The translation 'through' (NASB and also NEB) is preferable to 'by' (RSV) because this construction (*dia* with genitive) is often used by Peter to speak of the person *through* whom or thing *through* which God does something (1:3, 5, 23; 2:14; 3:1; 2 Pet. 1:3, 4; *cf.* 1 Pet. 5:12).[1] Peter thus implies, but does not state, that the proclamation actually came from God,[2] who 'proclaimed' the good news 'through' those who preached the gospel. And those who preached did so 'in (the power and character of)' or 'by means of' (both senses are possible) *the Holy Spirit sent from heaven.* This last phrase refers to the sending of the Holy Spirit from heaven in new power and fullness at Pentecost (*cf.* Lk. 24:49; Acts 1:8; 2:33).

Finally Peter adds that these facts about Christ's suffering and the subsequent glories of his kingdom are *things into which angels long to look.* The word *long* (*epithumeō*) is used in the New Testament to speak of very strong desires, both good and evil. Here

---

[1] A different construction (*hypo* with genitive) is Peter's ordinary way of speaking of an action that was done *by* someone (so 1 Pet. 2:4; 2 Pet. 1:17, 21; 3:2, *etc.*).

[2] So also Hort, p. 59.

(as in Mt. 13:17; Lk. 17:22; 22:15; *etc.*) it refers to the positive desire of sinless angels. The verb is in the present tense and cannot be restricted to a longing which the angels had before Christ came, or before the first sermon at Pentecost allowed them to hear the full Christian gospel. Peter rather says that even as he writes angels are still longing to look into these things and learn more about them. The longing must therefore include a holy curiosity to watch and delight in the glories of Christ's kingdom as they find ever fuller realization in the lives of individual Christians throughout the history of the church (*cf.* Eph. 3:8–10).

The word *parakyptō*, 'to look', is very appropriate here, for it means to peek or peep into a situation from the vantage point of an outsider, usually one who is not seen by those being watched (see Gn. 26:8, Abimelech looking out of his window; 1 Ch. 15:29, Michal watching David out of the window; the word is used of angels peering from heaven in 1 Enoch 9:1). These verses show that the word has no necessary nuance of 'stooping' to look at something (although it can be used that way) or of stealing just a quick glance, as some have assumed by looking at only one or two instances of its usage (see also Pr. 7:6; Song 2:9).

The whole paragraph carries a strong flavour of the newness and the excellence of the church age. Peter tells his readers: ancient prophets predicted the grace that would be 'yours' (v. 10); you live in the great 'time' of 'glories' (v. 11) which was long foretold; the prophets were in fact repeatedly ministering for the benefit of 'you' (v. 12a); and world-changing events have 'now' been proclaimed to 'you' through the working of the Holy Spirit 'sent' in epoch-changing new power from heaven (v. 12b). Though the world may think such Christians insignificant and worthy of pity or scorn (see 3:14–16; 4:4), angels – who see ultimate reality from God's perspective – find them to be objects of intense interest (v. 12c), for they know that these struggling believers are actually the recipients of God's greatest blessings and honoured participants in a great drama at the focal point of universal history. We too may rightly think of our Christian lives as no less privileged and no less interesting to holy angels than the lives of Peter's readers.

Additional Note: 'Time and circumstances' or 'person or time'? (1:11)

The focus of their eager interest was *what person or time* the Spirit within them was indicating. The translation of this phrase has been the subject of much discussion, but the RSV (and NASB) rendering *what person or time* is preferable to the NIV's 'the time and circumstances' or the AV's 'what, or what manner of time'.

The disputed phrase is *tina ē poion kairon*. The first word, *tina*, can mean either 'who?' or 'what?' with context being the only way to distinguish. The second word, *ē*, 'or', is not in dispute, nor is the last word, *kairon*, 'time'.

The third word, *poion*, can mean either 'what?' or 'what kind of?', and this has led to the difficulty in interpreting the verse. (It may be surprising to English-speaking readers who have learned 'what kind of?' as a brief definition of *poios*, to find that the simple meaning 'what?' is slightly more common than the meaning 'what kind of?' among the term's thirty-two NT occurrences.)

In this verse, if *poios* means 'what kind of?' the last two words mean 'what kind of time?' This allows the first word also to modify 'time' and mean simply 'what time?', giving the literal sense, 'what time or what kind of time?' (*cf.* NIV, 'the time and circumstances').

But if *poios* means just 'what?' then the last two words mean 'what time?' This requires that the first word, *tina*, must mean 'who?' (for 'what time or what time?' would be redundant). Then the literal sense would be, 'who or what time?' (*cf.* RSV 'what person or time').

Although both translations initially seem possible grammatically, an extensive examination of actual Greek usage requires that we decide in favour of the sense, 'who or what time?'

(1) All four other New Testament occurrences of *poios* with a term referring to time use *poios* in the sense 'what?' or 'which one?' not 'what kind of?': note *'which* day?' (Mt. 24:42); *'which* watch of the night?' (Mt. 24:43); *'which* hour?' (Lk. 12:39); *'which* hour?' (Rev. 3:3).

(2) Five other examples of *poios* used with expressions for

time in extra-biblical literature all follow the same pattern: *Paralipomena Jeremiou* 5:33 ('What month is this?') and 9:13 ('At *what* hour will he arise?'); *Testament of Solomon* (text D) 4:10, 'What day did he die?' (McCown,[1] p. 93, line 8); UPZ 65 [154 BC], lines 4–7 ('Send me a report, how much Peteusorpios has, and since *what* time'); and probably Philo, *Mut.* 264, '*what* season?' *The Greek Apocalypse of Ezra* 2:26 (Tischendorf,[2] p. 26, line 2) could be translated either way. (I was able to find no examples where *poios* with an expression of time meant 'what kind of time?')

(3) Even though *tis* (the lexical form of *tina*) occurs 552 times in the New Testament, it is never used to ask what time, what day, what hour, *etc.* Together with the two other groups of examples cited above where *poios* with words of time means 'what?' (not 'what sort of?'), this fact suggests that the ordinary way for a first-century speaker to ask 'what time?' was *poios kairos*, not *tis kairos*.[3]

(4) In the nature of the situation, prophecies about 'the sufferings of the Messiah and the subsequent glories' would naturally lead any prophet to seek to find out not only 'when?' but also 'who?' (*cf.* Mt. 11:3). The question 'Who is the Messiah?' would be so interesting that it is hard to imagine any Old Testament prophet not wondering about it.

These considerations combine to indicate that the translation of the RSV (and NASB), '*what person or time*', best gives the sense Peter intended and the sense in which his readers would have understood this phrase.

B. APPLICATION: YOU MUST BE HOLY IN ALL YOUR CONDUCT (1:13–25)

1. *Desire the beauty of being like a holy God (1:13–16)*

13. *Therefore* refers to the great 'salvation' blessings explained in verses 3 to 12. Because of their possession of these, Peter's readers are to think and act in certain ways.

---

[1] C. C. McCown, *The Testament of Solomon* (Leipzig: Hinrichs, 1922).

[2] C. Tischendorf, *Apocalypses Apocryphal* (Leipzig: 1966).

[3] 'In the New Testament we see a tendency for *poios* to become the adjective corresponding to the pronoun *tis*' (G. D. Kilpatrick, 'I Peter 1:11 *tina ē poion kairon*', *NovT* 28:1 (Jan. 1986), p. 92

The phrase *gird up your minds* is in Greek literally 'gird up the loins of your mind' (so AV), an almost unintelligible phrase for modern readers unfamiliar with the ancient Oriental custom of gathering up one's long robes by pulling them between the legs and then wrapping and tying them around the waist, so as to prepare for running, fast walking, or other strenuous activity (see 1 Ki. 18:46; 2 Ki. 4:29; 9:1). The NIV translation 'prepare your minds for action' conveys the general sense but obliterates the rich echoes of Old Testament background verses which would admonish readers to be ready to see God work and to respond to him with instant obedience (see Ex. 12:11; Jb. 38:3; 40:7; Je. 1:17; *cf.* Lk. 12:35). Such spiritual alertness is appropriate to life in a New Covenant age characterized by God's powerful working in people's hearts.

Be sober forbids not only physical drunkenness but also (since the phrases before and after have to do with attitudes of mind) letting the mind wander into any other kind of mental intoxication or addiction which inhibits spiritual alertness, or any laziness of mind which lulls Christians into sin through carelessness (or 'by default'). Peter uses the same word in 4:7 and 5:8 to encourage spiritual alertness for prayer and for resisting the devil. He knows how easily Christians can lose their spiritual concentration through 'mental intoxication' with the things of this world (*cf.* Mk. 4:19; Col. 3:2–3; 1 Jn. 2:15–17). We today might well consider the dangers presented by such inherently 'good' things as career, possessions, recreation, reputation, friendships, scholarship, or authority.

Set your hope fully uses the common New Testament term for 'hope', *elpizō*. This term refers to an expectation which is much stronger than the vague sense of 'wish for' or 'dream about'. Although 'hope' in the New Testament does not imply a sense of absolute certainty (see Rom. 8:24–25; 1 Tim. 3:14), it does convey a sense of confident expectation, an expectation strong enough for one to act on the basis of it (see Lk. 6:34; 23:8; Phil. 2:19, 23). The word *fully* implies a very confident and eager expectation, a very strong hope.

Such hope in great blessings when Christ returns not only encourages downcast Christians; it also prompts a reordering of priorities according to God's agenda (Mt. 6:19–21, 24) and inevitably leads to ethical changes in one's life (*cf.* 1 Jn. 3:3). Since Peter is about to launch into an extended section of moral commands (beginning at v. 14 and continuing with only a few interruptions through the rest of the letter), this exhortation to hope appropriately forms the transition point to the rest of the letter. If Peter's readers will first know the great truths about their salvation (vv. 1–12) and then begin a habit of visualizing themselves personally on a path of life leading without fail to unimaginable heavenly reward (v. 13), they will be mentally and emotionally ready to strive for a life of holiness before God (vv. 14–16, *etc.*).

The grace that is coming to you at the revelation of Jesus Christ means the further store of undeserved blessings which God will pour out on them when Christ returns. (Compare 'grace' in v. 10 and the inheritance mentioned in v. 4; for the phrase 'the revelation of Jesus Christ' see v. 7 and the passages cited there.) The present participle *pheromenēn* (literally, 'that is being carried to you') is unusual here (a future participle, as in 3:13, or a relative clause would more clearly mean 'that will come to you'). This form of the word probably should be understood to convey more vivid expectation, or even to suggest some present anticipation, of those future blessings.

The grammatical structure of the whole verse suggests a sequence of actions. The first command, *gird up*, is in a grammatical form (aorist participle preceding the main verb) which most often signifies action that occurs before the action of the main verb in the sentence (here, the verb 'hope'). The second command, *be sober*, has a form (present participle) which in this context suggests action at the same time as the main verb. We may paraphrase, 'First, gird up your minds – get ready to think on God's works and obey him at once. Then, while continuing to be spiritually alert, begin to expect eagerly and confidently that you will receive from God great blessings when Christ returns.'

14. *As obedient children* views Peter's readers as children in God's family whose lives are characterized by obedience to their heavenly Father.[1] The idea of obedience to God is prominent in

[1] The Gk. phrase is literally 'as children of obedience', a construction echoing the Heb. construct state by use of a genitive of definition (see MHT 3, pp. 440–441, and note similar phrases in Eph. 2:3 and 5:8).

Peter's mind as he writes (the same word for obedience occurs also at vv. 2 and 22 in this chapter), and Peter, having introduced the idea of obedience in the father-children relationship here, is going to maintain it in the background of the discussion until 2:3.

Do not be conformed[1] uses a word which occurs elsewhere in the New Testament only at Romans 12:2. It means 'to pattern one's actions or life after', and reminds these Christians that obedience to God and holiness of life (see v. 15) are radically different from a life that follows 'natural' (that is, non-Christian) desires wherever they lead. Doing God's will is the opposite of doing what remaining sin makes us 'feel like' doing (Rom. 6:12; Gal. 5:16–24).

Peter refers to their pre-Christian state as their *former ignorance* – ignorance of God and of his ways (*cf.* Acts 3:17; 17:30; Eph. 4:18). Then *passions* dominated their pattern of life. Although this word (*epithymia*) is used in a positive sense (Lk. 22:15; Phil. 1:23; 1 Thes. 2:17), Peter always uses it in a negative sense of sinful desires which lead people to direct disobedience to God's laws (2:11; 4:2, 3; 2 Pet. 1:4; 2:10, 18; 3:3). Christians are to recognize these desires for what they are (some are listed in Gal. 5:19–21 and 1 Jn. 2:16) and then strive not to let their lives be influenced by them. Phillips paraphrases this, 'Don't let your character be moulded by the desires of your ignorant days.' The fact that Peter could give such a command implies that he knew that such desires still remain and have some power in the hearts of true Christians. Yet he also implies that he agreed with Paul (Rom. 6:11, 14; Gal. 5:24) that the Holy Spirit's regenerating work has broken the ruling, dominating force of those desires, and that it is possible for Christians to have a significant measure of victory over them.

15. *But* signals a strong contrast with behaviour that is 'conformed to the passions of your former ignorance'. *As he who called you is holy* means 'according to the way or manner in which God is holy, you yourselves are to be holy, patterning your

---

[1] This is the first of several times where Peter uses a participle as an imperative: *cf.* 2:18; 3:1, 7–9; 4:8–10; David Daube, 'Participle and Imperative in 1 Peter', in Selwyn, pp. 467–488.

holiness after his'. *He who called you* is specifically God the Father (see 5:10; and *cf.* Rom. 8:28; 30; 1 Cor. 1:9; Phil. 3:14). By mentioning 'calling' here and four other times in the letter (2:9, 21; 3:9; 5:10; *cf.* 2 Pet. 1:3) Peter reminds his readers that it was God who initiated their salvation when the gospel came to them in power, summoning them out of darkness (2:9) into fellowship with himself. It was a powerful, effectual calling into the Christian life and all it involves – a calling to live with God and to be like him.[1]

To say that God is *holy* means that he is separated from sin and devoted to seeking his own honour.[2] Thus, things that were 'holy' in the Old Testament were both set apart from ordinary or evil use and devoted to use in glorifying God (Ex. 19:4–6; 20:11; 26:34; 29:44; Ps. 24:3; Zc. 14:20–21). God himself is the most holy one (Pss. 71:22; 78:41; 89:18; 99:9; Is. 1:4; 5:19, 24; 6:3).

The idea of holiness for God's people includes not simply a concept of 'separation' in general but a specifically moral sense of separation *from evil* and dedication *to a life of righteousness*. This is clear from the 'not . . . but' contrast in verses 14 to 15, and also from other passages where cognate nouns define 'holiness' in clear moral categories (Rom. 6:19; 2 Cor. 7:1; Heb. 12:10).

Be holy yourselves in all your conduct speaks of a pattern of life that transforms every day, every moment, every thought, every action. The word *conduct* (*anastrophē*) is frequent in Peter (eight of the thirteen NT occurrences are in 1 and 2 Peter). He uses it to refer to the evil pattern of life of unbelievers (1:18; 2 Pet. 2:7) and the good pattern of life of believers which is intended to lead to the salvation of others who observe it (2:12; 3:1, 2, 16; 2 Pet. 3:11).

To be holy 'as God is holy' includes a full and pervading holiness that reaches to every aspect of our personalities. It involves not only avoiding outward sin but also maintaining an instinctive delight in God and his holiness as an undercurrent of heart and mind throughout the day.

16. *Since* (*dioti*, meaning 'because' or 'for') introduces the reason or ground which supports the preceding statement. Why

[1] See John Murray, *Redemption Accomplished and Applied* (Edinburgh: Banner of Truth, 1961; Grand Rapids: Eerdmans, 1955), pp. 88–94.
[2] See Louis Berkhof, *Systematic Theology* (Edinburgh: Banner of Truth, ⁶1971; Grand Rapids: Eerdmans, 1939, 1941), pp. 73–74.

should Christians be holy? Because *it is written* (that is, it stands written in Scripture and remains valid today), *You shall be holy, for I am holy* (Lv. 11:44, 45; 19:2; 20:7 [LXX]; and 20:26). The holiness of God is thus in both Testaments the ground of his requirement that his people should be holy.

This is just one example of the way the New Testament repeatedly assumes that imitation of God's moral character is the ultimate basic for ethics. The final reason why some things are right and others wrong, and why there are moral absolutes in the universe, is that God delights in things that reflect his moral character (and thus reflect his excellence) and hates what is contrary to his character. Therefore, we are to imitate him (Eph. 5:1; Mt. 5:48; Lk. 6:36; Col. 3:9–10; 1 Jn. 3:2–3; 4:11, 19; *cf.* Eph. 5:2; 1 Pet. 2:21; 1 Jn. 2:6), and thereby glorify him.

Peter's reminder of the father-child theme in this context (vv. 14, 17) is appropriate, for it is the nature of children to want to imitate their parents. Christians should delight in imitating God, both because he is their Father and because his moral excellence is inherently beautiful and desirable – to be like him is the best way to be (*cf.* Pss. 34:8; 73:25).

2. *Fear the displeasure of a Father who is an impartial Judge* (1:17–21)

17. Peter now adds an additional motivation for a life of holiness: fear of God's fatherly discipline. *Invoke* is a technically correct but somewhat obscure rendering of *epikaleō* (in the middle voice), which means 'to call on for help, to appeal to' (Acts 25:11–12; Rom. 10:13; 1 Cor. 1:2; 2 Tim. 2:22). 'Address as Father' (NASB) would fit the active voice of the verb, but this is a middle, for which the meaning 'address' is not attested in the New Testament (*cf.* BAGD, p. 294). The present tense suggests regular or habitual calling to God for help – the mark of a Christian (note 1 Cor. 1:2; 2 Tim. 2:22).

And if introduces a Greek construction in which Peter assumes that the readers do pray to God regularly and know him as their Father (*cf.* NIV, 'Since . . .'). Now Peter reminds them that their Father is also the Judge of the universe. The sense is, 'If you call on a Father who is also the Judge who shows no favouritism (and will therefore show no favouritism to his friends or children), and who is continually judging and rewarding each person according to what he does, then live your life on earth in fear (that is, fear of his discipline).' Membership in God's family, great privilege though it is, must not lead to the presumption that disobedience will pass unnoticed or undisciplined.

Who judges each one impartially according to his deeds could be understood to refer to the future, final judgment in which believers will not be excluded from heaven but will be judged and rewarded according to their deeds in this life (as in Rom. 14:12; 1 Cor. 3:10–15; 2 Cor. 5:10, *etc.*). However, the phrase is better understood to refer primarily or even exclusively to present judgment and discipline in this life, because: (1) this Greek construction (*ton krinonta*, articular present participle) would naturally carry the sense 'the one who is judging'; and (2) the exhortation to 'fear' would be inappropriate to address to Christians if the subject were final judgment, for Christians need have no fear of final condemnation.

A reference to God's present discipline in this life is appropriate for Peter elsewhere recognizes God's present activity of blessing and disciplining Christians (4:14, 17 [with the cognate word *krima*]; *cf.* Heb. 12:5–11; Mt. 6:12).

Each one is a reminder that such judgment is not restricted to non-Christians only, or to Christians only, or to some Christians who lived at another time or place. It is individual, personal judgment of all people (though in this context discipline of believers is specifically in view). *Impartially* is a rare word meaning 'without showing favouritism' (similar expressions are found in Lk. 20:21; Acts 10:34; Rom. 2:11; Eph. 6:9; Col. 3:25; Jas. 2:1, 9).

Conduct yourselves with fear refers again to their whole pattern of life – *anastrephō*, 'conduct', is the cognate verb to the noun *anastrophē*, 'conduct', in verse 15. *Fear* in this context means primarily 'fear of God's discipline'. (The translation 'reverent fear' (NIV) is too comfortable for modern readers, for it suggests mainly the idea of awe during worship and allows readers to avoid the concept 'fear of discipline'.)

Although many today dismiss fear of God as an Old Testament concept which has no place in the New Covenant, they do so to the neglect of many New Testament passages and to the impoverishment of their spiritual lives. *Fear* (*phobos*) of God's discipline is a good and proper attitude, the sign of a New Testament church growing in maturity and experiencing God's blessing (Acts 5:5, 11; 9:31; 2 Cor. 7:11, 15; Col. 3:22; 1 Tim. 5:20; 1 Pet. 2:17; and probably also 1 Pet. 2:18; 3:2; 3:15). Moreover, fear of God is connected with growth in holiness elsewhere in the New Testament (2 Cor. 7:1; Phil. 2:12; *cf.* Rom. 3:18).

Fear of God is not inconsistent with loving him or knowing that he loves us.[1] If it were, we would have to say that Old Testament believers who feared God could not also have loved him – which is clearly false – or that God did not love them – which is also clearly false. Rather, fear of displeasing our Father is the obverse side of loving him.

> The fear here recommended is . . . a holy self-suspicion and fear of offending God, which may not only consist with assured hope of salvation, and with faith, and love, and spiritual joy, but is their inseparable companion. . . . This fear is not cowardice: it doth not debase, but elevates the mind; for it drowns all lower fears, and begets true fortitude and courage to encounter all dangers, for the sake of a good conscience and the obeying of God.[2]

The time of your exile refers to this present life, during which Peter's readers are 'temporary residents' on earth. The word translated 'exile', *paroikia*, is used elsewhere in the New Testament only at Acts 13:17 (of the 'sojourn' in Egypt), but it is similar in sense to *parepidēmos*, 'exile', in 1:1 – note the comments there on translation and Peter's purpose in using such terms.

18. *You know that* begins a new sentence in the RSV, but the Greek text actually continues the same sentence with a participial phrase, 'knowing that . . .', which can be translated in a

---

[1] Note that 1 Jn. 4:18, 'perfect love casts out fear', refers in context to eternal judgment: see v. 17, and the term *kolasis*, 'divine retribution, punishment' in v. 18. 'Perfect love' casts out all fear of eternal punishment, but it does not banish that godly fear which is essential to holiness (*cf.* Rev. 11:18; 15:4; 19:5).

[2] Leighton, pp. 85, 87.

variety of ways, depending on the sense of the context. Though it is not made explicit by Peter, the sense seems to be, 'Conduct your lives with fear of God's discipline (v. 17), *because* you know that God redeemed you out of a sinful manner of life at great cost – with the precious blood of Christ (vv. 18–19).' (Therefore, Peter implies, God will not be pleased if you casually disregard the ethical purposes of his redemption.)

You were ransomed is a helpful English translation of the verb *lutroō*, for this verb has the distinctive sense 'to purchase some-one's freedom by paying a ransom', and was used in secular contexts of purchasing freedom for a slave or a hostage held by an enemy.[1] The word 'redeemed' (NIV, NASB) also means this (especially as a technical term in systematic theology), yet it should be noted that the Greek term is much more specific than the vague general sense (roughly equal to 'saved') which often attaches to the word 'redeemed' today.

The realm from which the readers were ransomed is *from the futile ways inherited from your fathers. From* (*ek*) is not simply 'away from' but 'out of', giving the vivid image of people being physically removed from one 'place' (the sphere of sinful patterns of life) to another (the sphere of obedience to God). *Ways* is once again *anastrophē*, 'pattern of life' (see notes at v. 15). This pattern of life was *futile* – empty, worthless, having no meaningful or lasting results (compare this word in 1 Cor. 15:17; Tit. 3:9; and the cognate noun thirteen times in the LXX of Ec. 1 – 2). The remark-able change brought about by conversion to Christ is seen in the fact that these abandoned sinful patterns of life had been *inherited from your fathers*, an influence made weighty by the accumulation of generations of tradition in a society that valued such ancestral wisdom. 'The ancient tradition of home and nation is broken . . . because of the work of Jesus Christ who had set them free.'[2] A

[1]See the thorough discussion of *lutroō* by Leon Morris, *The Apostolic Preaching of the Cross* (London: Tyndale Press, [3]1965), pp. 11–27, 39; and on the concept of 'redemption' generally, see *ibid.*, pp. 11–64, and, in somewhat more popular format, his *The Atonement* (Leicester: IVP, 1983), pp. 106–131. Beare, p. 104, objects that if payment of a price were in view Peter would have used the genitive of price rather than the instrumental dative, but this objection is unpersuasive: instrumental dative of a price paid is found in Ex. 34:20; 1 Ch. 21:24; Rev. 5:9.

[2]W. C. van Unnik, summarizing a detailed survey of *patroparadotos* in extra-biblical literature in his article, 'The Critique of Paganism in 1 Pet. 1:18', *Neotestamentica et Semitica* (Fs. M. Black), eds. E. Ellis and M. Wilcox (Edinburgh: T. & T. Clark, 1969), p. 141.

similar purpose for redemption is affirmed in Ephesians 2:10; Titus 2:14. The hereditary chain of sin is broken by Christ (*cf.* Ex. 20:5, 6).

Peter once again shows the surpassing value of spiritual realities by calling the most precious and abiding metals *perishable things such as silver or gold*. 'Perishable', *phthartos*, is always used in the New Testament of things which will decay or wear out (Rom. 1:23; 1 Cor. 9:25; 15:53–54; 1 Pet. 1:23) because they belong to this world or this age (see notes on 'imperishable', *aphthartos*, in v. 4).

19. *But with the precious blood of Christ* affirms Christ's blood to be much more 'precious' or 'valuable' (*timios* is used of precious gems in 1 Cor. 3:12; *cf.* 'precious fruit' in Jas. 5:7) than gold or silver – apparently meaning precious in God's sight and therefore inherently valuable.

The *blood of Christ* is the clear outward evidence that his lifeblood was poured out when he died a sacrificial death as the price of our redemption – 'the blood of Christ' means his death in its saving aspects.[1] Although we might think that Christ's blood as evidence that his life had been given would have exclusive reference to the removal of our judicial guilt before God – for this is its primary reference – the New Testament authors also attribute to it several other effects. By the blood of Christ our consciences are cleansed (Heb. 9:14), we gain bold access to God in worship and prayer (Heb. 10:19), are progressively cleansed from more and more sin (1 Jn. 1:7; *cf.* Rev. 1:5b), are able to conquer the accuser of the brethren (Rev. 12:11), and are rescued out of a sinful way of life (1 Pet. 1:19). We would do well to recover this New Testament emphasis in our preaching today.

Coupled with the idea of the payment of a ransom is the idea of Christ as a substitutionary sacrifice who bore our penalty (*cf.* 1 Pet. 2:24). This is emphasized in the phrase *like that of a lamb without blemish or spot*. While it could be argued that the primary reference is to the spotless lamb of the Passover in Exodus 12:5 (see Hort, p. 77), it is more likely that the allusion is to the frequent requirement of a 'lamb without blemish' for many Old

[1] So Leon Morris, *The Apostolic Preaching of the Cross*, pp. 112–126.

Testament sacrifices (Nu. 6:14; 28:3, 9; *etc.*),[1] and then to the Christian understanding of Jesus as the perfect 'Lamb of God, who takes away the sin of the world' (Jn. 1:31; *cf.* 1 Cor. 5:7; Heb. 9:14; Rev. 5:6, 12; Is. 53:7). So precious in God's sight is this death and the blood which represents it that it should never be lightly esteemed by us. Nor may we underestimate its value: Christ's blood alone could pay the price of our redemption.

20. *He was destined* as a translation for *proginōskō* follows the RSV's translation of the cognate noun *prognōsis* as 'destined' in verse 2. Although the word in ordinary usage simply means 'known beforehand' (see its use in Acts 26:5 and 2 Pet. 3:17), here in verse 20 most versions translate it with some word implying predestination: 'foreordained' (AV); 'predestined' (NEB); 'chosen' (NIV). This is because of (1) a sense that when God knows something beforehand it is certain that that event will occur, and assuming the event to be therefore ordained by God seems to be the only alternative to the non-Christian idea of a certainty of events brought about by impersonal, mechanistic fate; (2) the fact that the use of the word when applied to God is found in contexts that suggest predestination (Acts 2:23; Rom. 8:29; 11:2); (3) a realization that in this context it would make little sense for Peter merely to say that God the Father *knew* Christ before the foundation of the world. Rather, the immediately preceding context with its emphasis on Christ's redeeming death suggests that it is *as a suffering saviour* that God 'foreknew' or thought of the Son before the foundation of the world. These considerations combine to indicate that the 'foreknowledge' was really an act of God in eternity past whereby he determined that his Son would come as the Saviour of mankind.

The foundation of the world is a New Testament phrase for 'the creation of the world' (note its use in Mt. 25:34; Lk. 11:50; Jn. 17:24; Eph. 1:4; Heb. 4:3; 9:26; Rev. 13:8; 17:8). Peter once again emphasizes the central place New Covenant Christians

---

[1]For the expression 'the Lamb of God' in Jn. 1:29 Leon Morris examines several possible backgrounds (*John*, NIC [Grand Rapids: Eerdmans, 1971], pp. 143–148) and concludes, 'All that the ancient sacrifices foreshadowed was perfectly fulfilled in the sacrifice of Christ' (p. 148).

occupy in the history of redemption by noting that this eternal plan of God to send his Son remained unfulfilled until *he was made manifest* (or revealed) *at the end of the times*, that is, at the end of the ages of history of the unredeemed creation, the 'ages' or 'times' (*cf.* Acts 17:30; Rom. 16:25) which preceded this present final age of redemption. This long-awaited appearance of the Messiah was *for your sake*, Peter tells his readers (*cf.* the note on the readers' position in the history of redemption in v. 12, above).[1]

21. Yet Peter continues beyond the specification of the readers' privilege to add that it is *through him* (*i.e.* through Christ) that *you have confidence in God*, here referring to God the Father (as is most common with the term *theos*, 'God', in the New Testament). The God who planned their redemption is now the object of their trust.

The word translated *have confidence* (*pistos*) can also mean 'faithful, trustworthy', but it cannot take that sense here, because at the end of the sentence Peter summarizes this confidence as reliance on God: *so that your faith and hope are in God*. When Peter says that it is 'through' Christ that they trust God he rules out any idea that Christians should 'fear God but trust Christ'. Rather, as Christians trust in Christ they are also *through Christ* trusting in God.

The phrase *who raised him from the dead and gave him glory*, refers to Christ's resurrection, his ascension into heaven, and reception of honour and glory from the Father (*cf.* Phil. 2:9; Eph. 1:20–23).

So that your faith and hope are in God brings Peter to the conclusion and also the main point of verses 20 to 21.[2] After telling

[1] This verse is one of several which some claim to be excerpts from an early hymn or creedal statement. But the evidence for this claim is unpersuasive: admittedly the Greek sentence is balanced and stylistically elegant – but that is not surprising, since the entire letter is well-written.

[2] The RSV mg., 'so that your faith is hope in God' (so R. Bultmann, *TDNT* 6, p. 208) might seem possible grammatically but a survey of actual usage shows how unlikely it is that any first-century reader would take it that way: a search of all 656 NT instances of adverbial *kai* (which were listed on the GRAMCORD data base at Trinity Evangelical Divinity School, Deerfield, Illinois) yielded no other examples of the sequence *kai* with predicate nominative with *eimi* or *ginomai*. This sense is also conceptually improbable, for 'faith' and 'hope', while related, are not equated in the NT (*cf.* Heb. 11:1).

his readers to live holy lives (vv. 14–16) and to fear God's discipline and displeasure if they disobey (v. 17) – for God redeemed them from sin at great cost (vv. 18–19) – he concludes by reminding them that the God whom they are to fear as Judge is also the God whom they trust as Saviour: he planned their redemption in the counsels of eternity (v. 20a), he sent forth his Son for their sake (v. 20b), he is the one whom they even now depend on (v. 21a), he raised Christ from the dead and glorified him (v. 21b), and thus he is the one in whom they place all their trust and hope (v. 21c). The God whom Christians fear is also the God whom they trust for ever, the God who has planned and done for them only good from all eternity.

3. *Love one another, now and for ever* (1:22–25)

22. *Having purified your souls by your obedience to the truth* might be understood to refer either to conversion (where 'obedience to the truth' would mean 'believing the gospel') or to growth in moral purity subsequent to conversion (where 'obedience to the truth' would mean 'obedience to God's commands in daily living').

Having purified (*hēgnikotes*, perfect participle) could refer to initial conversion as a completed event in the past with continuing effects, but since Peter elsewhere uses the perfect tense of events in the process of sanctification (4:1; 2 Pet. 1:12), we cannot be certain that this is in view.

More persuasive are arguments in favour of the view that Peter has post-conversion growth in moral purity in mind: (1) *obedience* (*hypakoē*) occurs fifteen times in the New Testament, and never clearly means initial saving faith';[1] (2) Peter uses *obedience* (*hypakoē*) in verses 2 and 14 of obedience in conduct; (3) *purify* (*hagnizō*) when employed figuratively elsewhere in the New Testament is used of moral cleansing subsequent to conversion (Jas. 4:8, 1 Jn. 3:3);[2] (4) the context is the apostle's call

---

[1]Rom. 1:5 and 16:26 are ambiguous, but see BAGD, p. 837; *cf.* also the comments at 1:2 above.

[2]Beare (p. 110), Stibbs/Walls (p. 93), and Mounce (p. 22) claim that the perfect participle must refer to a particular past act, not a process. However, the perfect participle can refer to a completed past process: note Heb. 4:15 (we have a high priest who 'in every respect *has been*

to holiness in 1:15, which suggests that the purifying obedience he has in view results from an active response to that call; (5) this 'purification'is something the readers have themselves done ('having purified your souls'), but Christians are never in the New Testament said to be active agents in God's initial cleansing of their souls at conversion. On the other hand, they are said to be active in the progressive work of sanctification (*cf.* 2 Cor. 7:1; Jas. 4:8; 1 Jn. 3:3).

This 'purification' then signifies some clear progress in gaining more purity from the moral pollution of sin, a concept very similar to that of James 4:8 and 1 John 3:3.

Your souls emphasizes the inward, spiritual nature of this purification. Though 'soul' (*psychē*) is used of the whole person (*e.g.* 3:20; 2 Pet. 2:14), had Peter meant this he would have most probably used *heatous* 'yourselves' (as in 1 Jn. 3:3). *Psychē* can also mean 'inward spiritual nature' (Mt. 10:28; 2 Pet. 2:8; *cf.* BAGD, p. 893, c.). That this is how it should be understood here is suggested by its proximity to a call to love 'from the heart'.

By your obedience to the truth might also be translated 'in [your] obedience to the truth' (NASB) – both 'by' and 'in' (NASB and also AV) are linguistically acceptable and theologically true. But 'by' is preferable here since it is by means of a process of active obedience that a Christian 'purifies' his or her soul. ('The truth' here carries a sense of the true way pleasing to God, including not merely the gospel message but the whole of Christian teaching on doctrine and life – *cf.* 2 Jn. 4; 3 Jn. 3, 4; 2 Pet. 1:12; 2:2.)

This 'purification' is not likely to be a completed stage in the sanctification process, for the New Testament knows of no such unique stage in growth, nor could Peter assume that any one level of holiness had been attained by so many Christians in several different churches.

It is better to understand the phrase as the next logical step in the development of Peter's argument. *Obedience* would then mean 'obedience to the exhortations just mentioned'. We could paraphrase, 'Then, having purified your souls by your obedience to these true commands to holiness . . . love one another

---

tempted as we are'); 5:14 (solid food is for those whose faculties *have been trained* by practice to distinguish good from evil); 12:3, 11; Jas. 5:15; 1 Pet. 4:3; 2 Pet. 3:2; Jude 17; *etc.*

earnestly.' Peter thus expects that growth in holiness will lead to deeper love among Christians. (Indeed, this conclusion would be true no matter which interpretation one adopted for the phrase 'having purified your souls'.)

A sincere love of the brethren means love that is genuine, not simply an outward appearance or profession of love. This 'love of the brethren' (*philadelphia*) is probably seen by Peter as somewhat less intense than *agapē* (note the progression in this verse, and the discussion of *agapaō* in the next phrase; *cf.* also 2 Pet. 1:17, which suggests some distinction).

By translating this phrase *for a sincere love of the brethren*, the RSV understands it to indicate purpose. But love for fellow Christians is seen in the New Testament more as a component or a result of sanctification than its goal. So it is preferable to understand this construction (*eis* with accusative) to indicate result (so NIV, NEB, Phillips; *cf.* 1:3; 2:9, 21 for the same construction used this way): 'Until you feel sincere affection towards your brother Christians' (NEB).

Love one another earnestly from the heart commands something which goes beyond the sincere brotherly affection of the previous phrase. Peter switches from a *phileō-* root ('affection, love') in the previous phrase to *agapaō* ('love, especially strong, deep love') here.[1] He adds *ektenōs*, 'earnestly', a term used elsewhere of strong, deeply felt, even fervent, emotions or desires (LXX, Joel 1:14 and Jon. 3:8; also Acts 12:5; 26:7).

From a *'pure* heart' (AV, NIV mg.; *cf.* NASB mg.) seems to be a better reading, since most of the earliest and best Greek manuscripts include the adjective *katharos*, 'pure, clean', and since it is natural in a sentence that earlier speaks of inward purification.

The sense of the verse is therefore, 'Once you have begun to grow in holiness so that you have a genuine affection for one another, make your love for each other earnest, deep, and strong.' This is Peter's first specific application of the general commands to holiness in verses 13 to 21. It is a reminder that one of the first marks of genuine growth in holiness in individuals

---

[1]However, there is considerable overlap in meaning between the two word groups, and the popular conception of *agapē* as pure God-like love is not entirely justified by the way in which *agapaō* is sometimes used (see 2 Pet. 2:15; Jn. 3:19). Moreover, *phileō* is also used of God's love (see Jn. 5:20; 11:3; 36; 16:27; 20:2; Rev. 3:19).

and in churches is earnest love for fellow Christians. It also gives encouragement that human personalities, far from being immutably fixed early in life, can be dramatically and permanently changed through the power of the gospel.

23. Though the RSV begins a new sentence here, *You have been born anew . . .*, the Greek text continues the sentence of verse 22 with a participle, 'having been born anew', which probably gives a reason or ground for the previous verse: 'for you have been born again . . .' (NASB). This 'new birth' initiates new spiritual life (see Jn. 3:3–15; *cf.* Jn. 1:12–13; Eph. 2:1, 5; Col. 2:13; Tit. 3:5; Jas. 1:18; 1 Pet. 1:3).[1] Here Peter uses the same verb (*anagennaō*) as in 1:3 (see notes there). The verb form here (perfect participle) emphasizes the continuing results of that previous new birth.

Not of perishable seed but of imperishable affirms the permanent, even indestructible character of the 'seed' that started this new life within the readers. (See notes on the words *perishable* and *imperishable* at 1:4.) 'Seed' (*spora*) can mean either 'sowing' (the activity) or 'seed' (the thing planted or sown; see 1 Macc. 10:30; Josephus, *Ant.* 2.306; BAGD, p. 763), but 'seed' is much more likely here, since it makes little sense to speak of an activity as 'imperishable' (*cf.* 1 Jn. 3:9).

The living and abiding word of God[2] is either the spoken word of God (in gospel proclamation) or the written word of God (in the Bible), or both, since the quotation from Isaiah 40:6–8 in the following verse refers to the words of God spoken and/or written through the Old Testament prophets. We should probably not try to distinguish too sharply here, for the Isaiah passage is a statement about the character of God's words generally, without reference to any particular form in which they occur.

Was the 'imperishable seed' the word of God (*cf.* Lk. 8:11)? Or did Peter mean that the 'seed' was the working of the Holy

---

[1] Here again many assume a reference to baptism, but with insufficient warrant (see v. 3 above, p. 55, n. 1).

[2] NEB mg., 'through the word of the living and enduring God', is grammatically possible but ruled out by contextual considerations: Peter's point is to emphasize the permanency of God's word (see E. A. LaVerdiere, 'A Grammatical Ambiguity in 1 Pet. 1:23', *CBQ* 36 (1974), pp. 89–94).

Spirit with and through the word of God? He says they have been born again 'of' (*ek*, 'out of, from') imperishable seed 'through' (*dia*, 'through, by means of') the living and abiding word of God. The change of prepositions may indicate a change in nuance, but the distinction is not of great significance theologically, for in any case the Holy Spirit is active in causing regeneration (*cf.* Jn. 3:5–8; Tit. 3:5), and the word of God is the means God uses to awaken new life in an unbeliever (*cf.* Rom. 10:17; Jas. 1:18). Yet in this text there is no explicit mention of the Holy Spirit. Moreover, Peter's emphasis on the fact that the word of God is *living* (*cf.* Heb 4:12) suggests its power – unlike any merely human words – to awaken new life. And the fact that it is *abiding* (*cf.* Mk. 13:31) reinforces the idea of the permanence of the new life generated by it. Finally, verses 24 to 25 continue to hammer home the theme of the permanence of God's word, which would be irrelevant if the permanence of the regenerating work of the Holy Spirit were the point of verse 23, but not if the permanence of the effect of the life-giving word of God is meant. While we should never try to separate the word of God from God who speaks that word, these considerations indicate that Peter is thinking specifically of the word of God as the life-giving 'seed'. The implications for evangelism are obvious: ultimately it is neither our arguments nor our life example that will bring new life to an unbeliever, but the powerful words of God himself – words which we still have preserved today in Scripture. It is in reading or hearing these words that people are given new life.

The argument is therefore:

(1) *love one another earnestly* (v. 22)
(2) because *you have been born anew of imperishable seed* (v. 23)

But how does verse 23 provide a ground for verse 22? Perhaps Peter is affirming that their new birth gives them power to love one another. But that would not explain his emphasis on the 'imperishable' and 'abiding' nature of God's word. Moreover, while power to love might serve as a convincing reason for an affirmation that they are *able* to love (*e.g.* 'You are able to love one another, for you have been born anew'), it is much less a convincing reason for what verse 22 actually contains, namely, a command to love.

A correct understanding of verse 23 must explain its function in a way that accounts for Peter's stress on the permanent nature of the new life given through the word of God. This emphasis makes it most likely that Peter is stressing the eternal nature of the fellowship which his readers have come to share – 'Love one another (v. 22), for you have all been born anew into a fellowship of God's people which will last eternally (v. 23).'[1] Christian growth cannot be self-centred and individualistic, for it occurs in the context of fellowship, a fellowship which must deepen and remain for all eternity.

24–25. The permanency of the word of God, mentioned in verse 23, is emphasized in these two verses. Peter quotes Isaiah 40:6–8 to contrast the frailty of human nature with the permanence of God's words. *All flesh* means 'all natural human existence' or perhaps 'every person'[2] – the sense is nearly the same. *Grass* is a general word for grass (Mt. 6:30; 14:19) or hay (1 Cor. 3:12) which lasts for a season and is gone. *All its glory* refers to all human beauty, splendour, or fame. As the *grass withers* and the *flower* fades and dies, so man's glory and greatness quickly disappear (*cf.* Jas. 1:10–11). What then can give hope of permanence or significance? *The word* (*rhēma*, the actual spoken or written word) *of the Lord abides for ever*, and it is *that word* which Peter's readers have heard and believed. That word – apparently including Old Testament Scriptures, New Testament apostolic proclamation, and the presentation of both in the message of first-century evangelists – is the word which quickened new life within them. Therefore, in contrast to the temporality of the withering grass and the fading flower, believers have an eternally abiding nature (*cf.* 1 Jn. 2:17). (Peter

---

[1] So also Beare: 'Precisely because the new life is immortal in its essence, it must find expression in the love of the brethren with whom we share it' (p. 111).

[2] The Greek *pasa sarx*, which is the LXX translation of the Hebrew phrase *kōl-baśar*, is found with the sense 'every person' at Lk. 3:6; Jn. 17:12; Acts 2:17. Yet Peter's insertion of 'its' (*autēs*) instead of the LXX 'man's' in the phrase 'all its glory' makes a reference to 'every person' difficult, and 'all natural human existence' therefore more likely.

here uses *rhēma*, 'word', to refer to the same thing as *logos*, 'word', in v. 23, suggesting that he saw little difference between them in meaning.)

These verses intensify the idea of the permanence of God's word by contrasting it with the fading glory of human achievement. Strength, power, wealth, beauty, fame – all the 'glory' of man – will quickly fade. Christians who have been 'born anew' (v. 23) will live with God for ever.

C. HOW TO ADVANCE IN HOLINESS (2:1–10)

1. Be nourished by the Lord through the Word (2:1–3)

1. *So put away* resumes the line of argument which was interrupted by verses 23 to 25. The word *so*, or 'therefore', refers back to the command 'love one another' in verse 22. This verse explains in more detail what is involved in loving one another 'earnestly': one must *put away* (give up, get rid of) attitudes and habits which are harmful to others. This same verb (*apotithēmi*) is used of taking off clothing (Acts 7:58),[1] but also metaphorically to exhort Christians to 'put off' wrongful practices (Rom. 13:12; Eph. 4:22, 25; Col. 3:8; Heb. 12:1; Jas. 1:21). It makes little difference whether the verb, which is a participle in Greek, is translated as an imperative (RSV, NIV) or as a participle dependent on the command 'long for' in verse 2 (NASB), for in both cases the force of a command is expressed.

Genuine love requires ridding one's life of *all malice* (the Gk. term *kakia* is broader, nearer to English 'evil' or 'wickedness', including not only ill intent but also any actions harmful to others), *all guile* (*i.e.* deceitfulness that harms others through trickery or falsehood), *insincerity* (or hypocrisy, the masking of inward evil by an outward show of righteousness – note this

---

[1]Kelly, p. 84, sees another reference to baptism here, which, he claims, involved 'undressing completely' in the early church. However, the earliest evidence for this (in Cyril of Jerusalem) is around AD 350, and there is insufficient evidence to say that the practice was widespread. No evidence exists for such practice at the time of the NT, nor is there good reason for thinking that the command 'put away all malice . . .' would suggest baptism to Peter's readers.

word in Mt. 23:28; Mk. 12:15; Gal. 2:13), *envy* (the opposite of thankfulness for good which comes to others), and *all slander* (any speech which harms or is intended to harm another person's status, reputation, *etc.* – the related verb is used in 2:12; 3:16; Jas. 4:11). All these sins aim at harming other people, whereas love seeks the good of others.

2. No new sentence begins here in the Greek text, and the connection Peter intended is probably best preserved by the NASB: 'Therefore, putting aside (v. 1) . . . long for the pure milk . . . (v. 2).' Peter implies that 'putting away' unloving practices (v. 1) is necessary for spiritual growth (v. 2), for the two verses are part of one long command. Someone who is practising 'deceit' or 'envy' or 'slander' will not be able truly to long for 'pure spiritual milk'.

Like newborn babes does not imply that Peter thought of his readers as young or immature Christians, for some of them had been Christians for thirty years (see Introduction, p. 38).[1] It only says that they are to long for spiritual milk in the same way that new babies long for milk (eagerly, frequently) – a metaphor easily understood by any parent whose sleep has been interrupted by the crying of a young baby hungry for milk. *Milk* in this context does not represent elementary Christian teaching (as it does in a different metaphor in 1 Cor. 3:2 and Heb. 5:12–13, where milk is contrasted with meat or solid food), but rather something to be eagerly desired for nourishment.

The readers are to *long for* this pure spiritual milk. The verb suggests an intense personal desire (note its use in

[1] To say that this verse views the readers as new Christians (so Beare, p. 114; Kelly, p. 84) would be similar to saying that the author of Psalm 42 thinks himself to be a hart or deer when he exclaims, 'As a hart longs for flowing streams, so longs my soul for thee, O God' (Ps. 42:1). The point of comparison is merely the intensity of the longing. (Selwyn, p. 154, notes the similar phrase, 'as a roaring lion' (5:8), which does not imply that the devil is a lion.)

Newborn does not imply 'just now baptized' (as some have claimed), for (1) it must be said again that here as elsewhere Peter speaks of new 'birth', not 'baptism'; and (2) the commands to 'put away' and 'long for' as they now stand in the text are addressed to all Peter's readers in many different churches, even those who had been believers for as long as thirty years. Moreover, (3) 'therefore' or 'so' in v. 1 refers back to 1:22, 'love one another'; thus, 2:1–2 must be addressed to the same persons as are addressed by this command in 1:22 – all the members of the churches to which he is writing.

Ps. 42:1(LXX 41:2), of longing for God; Ps. 84:2(LXX 83:3), of longing for the courts of the Lord; also Phil. 1:8; 2:26; 2 Tim. 1:4).

Pure (adolos) when applied to objects like wheat or wine has the sense 'pure, unadulterated' (MM, p. 10, gives several examples from Greek papyri), so the spiritual milk in view here is free from all impurities. (If this 'pure milk' is the written word of God – as is argued below – then this adjective implies that Scripture is free from impurity or imperfection, that it will not deceive or lead astray its readers, and that it affirms no falsehood.)

Spiritual (logikos) though often used with the sense of 'reasonable, rational' can mean 'mental, in idea only, *i.e.* figurative, not literal' (*cf. T.Levi* 3:6 and *Corpus Hermeticum* 1.31, which speak of 'spiritual' [not literal] sacrifices or offerings). This seems to be the force of *logikos* in Romans 12:1, its only other New Testament occurrence – 'your *spiritual* worship'. So here it seems to mean 'long for pure figurative (not literal) milk'.[1]

But what is this pure spiritual milk? Several contextual considerations favour a reference to the written Word of God, the Scriptures (whether read or listened to, *cf.* Col. 4:16; 1 Tim. 4:13): (1) the word of God has just been mentioned extensively in the previous three verses (vv. 23–25), thus, no new idea needs to be introduced into the context; (2) the fact that the word of God is said to be 'living' (v. 23) suits not only the idea that it is life-generating (v. 23) but also the idea that it is life-giving and capable of nourishing and sustaining life, enabling Christians to 'grow up to salvation' (v. 2); (3) the idea that the word of God is spiritually nourishing is consistent with statements elsewhere in Scripture which would be familiar to Peter and his readers (Dt. 8:3; Mt. 4:4); (4) the purity of God's word is an Old Testament concept which would also be familiar to them (Ps. 12:6; 18:8; 119:96), and would fit the imagery of 'pure' milk better than any other option; (5) the idea of 'longing' for God's word is also an Old Testament concept, and one which is twice expressed with the same verb (*epipotheō*) used by Peter (Ps. 119(LXX 118):20, 131); (6) reading or listening to God's word

---

[1]The translation 'the pure milk of the word' (NASB, *cf.* AV) does not seem to be supported by known uses of *logikos*, and is apparently based on a mistaken assumption of similarity in sense to the related word *logos*, 'word'.

involves a process of taking information into oneself, a process more readily represented by a metaphor of drinking milk (taking it 'into' one's body) than some other activities – such as prayer or worship – which more clearly involve 'giving out' words of prayer or praise.[1]

By taking in pure spiritual milk, those whom Peter addresses will *grow up to salvation*, *i.e.* grow towards Christian maturity ('salvation' is used in a similar sense in 1:5; see note there). *Grow up* is used elsewhere both of physical (Lk. 1:80; 2:40) and spiritual growth (Eph. 4:15; Col. 1:10; 2 Pet. 3:18).

3. *For[2] you have tasted the kindness of the Lord* gives an additional reason for the command to long for pure spiritual milk. The statement 'the kindness of the Lord' is in Greek more literally, 'that the Lord is good', an exact quotation from the LXX of Psalm 34:8 (LXX 33:9), 'O taste and see that the Lord is good.' (Peter also uses the same verb for 'taste', but in a different tense; in both cases the word is used as a forceful metaphor for 'come to know by experience'; *cf.* Mt. 16:28; Jn. 8:52; Heb. 2:9; 6:4.)[3] The context of the Psalm encourages delight in the Lord for the fact that he daily provides for all the needs of those who trust him, and the fact that the Lord is 'good' or 'kind' (*chrestos*, used also in Lk. 5:39; 6:35; Rom. 2:4; Eph. 4:32) emphasizes his habit of bringing all sorts of good blessings to the lives of his people.

But how can the goodness of the Lord (v. 3) be a reason to long for the words of Scripture (v. 2)? The connection is more natural than it first appears. Peter is assuming that the words of Scripture are the words of the Lord, so to read or listen to

---

[1]Beare, p. 116, says the 'pure spiritual milk' may be the eucharist (the Lord's supper), but more probably it refers to Christ himself, because of v. 3. He rightly dismisses 'of the word' as a translation of *logikos*, but does not consider the possibility that 'pure spiritual milk' is a metaphorical description of Scripture without actually naming it as 'the word'. (See below for an alternative view of the relationship to v 3.)

[2]The Greek word is *ei*, often translated 'if', but here (as in 1:17) the indicative mood of the verb shows that Peter is assuming the following fact to be true; thus, *since* is an appropriate translation (*cf.* BAGD, p. 219, I.1.a; also III).

[3]Kelly, p.87, sees a reference to partaking in the Lord's supper here, because Ps. 34:8 was used in communion services later in church history. But that in no way implies that Ps. 34:8 had to be used this way, or that Peter was using it this way: certainly it could not have meant this in the original Psalm.

Stibbs/Walls rightly notes Peter's 'explicit reference to the word, and the absence of any reference to the sacrament, as the proper means of spiritual nourishment' (p. 96).

Scripture is to hear the Lord speak, to take his good and nourishing words into one's heart. To drink the milk of the Word is to 'taste' again and again what he is like, for in the hearing of the Lord's words believers experience the joy of personal fellowship with the Lord himself. Moreover, those words give direction into his 'good' paths for life (*cf.* Ps. 34:12–16, quoted in 1 Pet. 3:10–12) and give promises of his continued 'goodness' in time of need (*cf.* Ps. 34:7–10 and 2 Pet. 1:4). It is significant that the 'Lord' of Psalm 34:8 is here seen to be the one to whom believers come in faith and worship (v. 4), the 'living stone' (v. 4), the Lord Jesus Christ (v. 5): thus, the Lord who is the source of spiritual delight for Old Testament saints is now in the New Covenant seen to be the Lord Jesus Christ, in whom our soul delights.

2. *Abide in Christ – together – as the new temple of God* (2:4–6)

4. This verse begins a new section (vv. 4–10) in which Peter uses extensive Old Testament imagery to show that New Testament believers (both Jew and Gentile) are in fact a new 'people of God' who have come to possess all the blessings of Old Testament Israel but in far greater measure.

Come to him employs a verb (*proserchomai*) frequently used in the LXX of 'drawing near' to God, either to hear him speak (Lv. 9:5; Dt. 4:11; 5:27) or to come into his presence in the tabernacle to offer sacrifices (Ex. 12:48; 16:9; Lv. 9:7–8; 10:4–5; *etc.*). It is also used in Hebrews as a specialized term for 'drawing near' to God in worship (Heb. 4:16; 7:25; 10:1, 22; 11:6; 12:18, 22). Peter's choice of the term here may have been suggested by its use in Psalm 34:5 (LXX: 'Draw near to him'). By this expression Peter hints, in a theme to be made explicit later in the sentence, that all believers now enjoy the great privilege, reserved only for priests in the Old Testament, of 'drawing near' to God in worship. But rather than coming to the altar or even to the holy place in the Jerusalem temple, they now come 'to him' in whom 'the whole fulness of deity dwells bodily' (Col. 2:9).

Though the RSV opts for an imperative, 'Come to him', the verbal form is actually a participle, and its relation to the main verb in verse 5 must be determined from the context. Because the verb in verse 5 is best taken as indicative ('you are being built'; see discussion below), the relation between verses 4 and 5 is well expressed by the NASB, 'And coming to Him . . . you . . . are being built' (*cf.* NIV, 'As you come to him . . . you . . . are being built', which catches the simultaneous nature of the 'coming' and 'being built', but misses the continuous sense of the present participle). This gives the sense, 'As you continually come to Christ (in initial faith, then in worship and prayer) you are yourselves being built into a spiritual house.' The verb 'being built' has the sense 'being built up, growing' when it refers to the building up of the church: Acts 9:31; 1 Cor. 8:1; 10:23; 14:4, 17; 1 Thes. 5:11. Personal devotion to Christ through the Word also increases corporate integration into the church.

Christ is called a *living stone* – a daring metaphor (for stones do not live), but one already suggested by Jesus' own application of Psalm 118:22 ('the stone which the builders rejected has become the head of the corner') to himself (Mt. 21:42; Mk. 12:10; Lk. 20:17; *cf.* Peter's own statement in Acts 4:11). Peter is about to quote three Old Testament 'stone' prophecies and apply them to Christ (Is. 28:16 in v. 6; Ps. 118:22 in v. 7; Is. 8:14 in v. 8), and his imagery here must be understood in the light of those verses.[1] The fact that Christ is the *living* stone shows at once his superiority to an Old Testament temple made of dead stones, and reminds Christians that there can be no longing for that old way of approach to God, for this way is far better.

Though *rejected by men*, Christ is *in God's sight chosen and precious*. 'Rejected', 'chosen', and 'precious' are all taken from the vocabulary of the LXX (Ps. 118:22 and Is. 28:16). The sentence contrasts the world's estimate of Christ with God's estimate, and warns the readers that while coming to Christ is to side with God, it will mean being opposed by 'men' (Peter appropriately speaks of 'men' generally here, allowing a wider application in these churches in the Gentile world, whereas Jesus had made specific application to unbelieving Jews: Mt. 21:45). The term *chosen* echoes Peter's use of the same term to apply to Christians

---

[1] N. Hillyer, ' "Rock-Stone" Imagery in 1 Peter', *TynB* 22 (1971), pp. 58–81, gives extensive discussion of OT and extra-biblical Jewish background to this imagery. C. F. D. Moule, 'Some Reflections on the "Stone Testimonia" in Relation to the Name Peter', *NTS* 2 (1955–56), pp. 56–59, suggests that the theme here has a possible connection to the name Peter ('rock') itself.

in 1:1 (see note there). *Precious* means 'highly valued or esteemed', an apt term to describe God's evaluation of his Son and also to suggest how believers should always esteem their Lord.

5. *And like living stones* extends the 'stone' imagery in a remarkable way to Peter's readers, now portraying not only Christ but also Christians as 'stones' that live (*cf.* Eph. 2:19–22; 1 Cor. 3:10–15; Heb. 3:2–6; and Mt. 16:18, all of which in various ways liken the church to a building). The Greek text begins this verse with two words meaning 'even you yourselves' (. . . like living stones are being built into a spiritual house), further emphasizing the amazing fact that these humble believers also, like Christ, have become living stones precious to God.

These 'people-stones' are being built *into a spiritual house*. The word 'house' (*oikos*) is often used to refer to God's house, the Jerusalem temple (1 Ki. 5:5; Is. 56:7; Mt. 12:4; 21:13; Mk. 2:26; Lk. 11:51; Jn. 2:16), and the mentioning of priesthood, sacrifices, and 'coming near' (to God in worship; see note on v. 4), all in this sentence, make it almost certain that Peter has in mind the house where God dwells, the temple of God (*cf.* also 1 Tim. 3:15). Thus the NEB rightly translates this phrase, 'built . . . into a spiritual temple' (*cf.* Phillips, 'into a spiritual House of God'). (See also Additional Note below.)

Thus Peter encourages Christians to think of themselves as the *living stones* of God's new temple. But what is the appropriate visual image corresponding to this metaphor? We might try picturing ourselves as changed, thinking of ourselves as block-like but animated stones, being fitted into the shape of a large rectangular temple. But that image makes it difficult to understand how Christians can be both the stones of the temple and the priests who *offer . . . sacrifices*. It is better to change our visual image of a temple, so that we no longer think of a rectangular building made of stones but of an amorphous 'building' that continually takes on the changing dimensions of God's assembled people. The beauty of this new and living 'temple made of people' should no longer be expensive gold and precious jewels, but the imperishable beauty of holiness and faith in Christians' lives, qualities which much more effectively reflect the glory of God (*cf.* 1 Pet. 3:4; 2 Cor. 3:18).

Spiritual (*pneumatikos*) when applied to 'house' and 'sacrifices' does not mean 'immaterial' (for the believers are not 'immaterial' persons!), but rather 'influenced or dominated by the Holy Spirit; sharing the character of the Holy Spirit' (Rom. 1:11; 1 Cor. 2:13, 15; 12:1; Gal. 6:1; Col. 3:16). Christians are a new temple of God under the influence and power of the Holy Spirit.

The main verb of this sentence could be either imperative ('be built', so RSV and NEB) or indicative ('you . . . are being built', so NIV, NASB, AV). Since the verb forms would be exactly the same in both cases, the sense must be decided from the context. The indicative is preferable here for two reasons: (1) It is difficult to gain a coherent idea of what Peter might have meant people to do in response to a command to 'be built'.[1] But the statement of fact, 'you are being built', makes good sense and would encourage the readers to appreciate their spiritual status as 'living stones'. (2) Both NEB and RSV, in order to make sense of what they take to be the command 'be built', must shift the main imperatival force back to the participle in verse 4 and translate it, 'Come to him'. But if Peter's main command was to come to Christ (and thus be built up), it would have been much more clearly conveyed by making the verb 'come' an imperative. (Note the contrast with vv. 1–2, where the main force is not in the participle 'putting away' but in the imperative 'long for'.)

There is encouragement in these verses, then, in this sense: 'As you (keep on) coming to Christ (in worship, in prayer and praise), you are (continually) being built up into a spiritual temple, a place in which God more and more fully dwells.'

They are also functioning as *a holy priesthood*, a phrase which combines two words from the LXX of Ex. 19:6, where God had promised that if his people were faithful they would be to him 'a royal priesthood and a holy nation' (*cf.* Ex. 23:22; Is. 61:6).

As priests, believers offer not the animal sacrifices of the Old

---

[1]The verb *oikodomeisthe* has a form that could be either passive or middle. Even if middle it would hardly take the sense 'build yourselves up' (NASB mg.) for which a reflexive pronoun would be required for clarity (see 1 Cor. 14:4; 1 Thes. 5:11), but rather 'build up for your own benefit or with your own intensive involvement', a sense scarcely distinguishable from the active voice. (No clear middle of this verb occurs in the NT.)

Covenant, but *spiritual sacrifices*, which the New Testament else-where identifies as the offering of our bodies to God for his service (Rom. 12:1), the giving of gifts to enable the spread of the gospel (Phil. 4:18), the singing of praise (Heb. 13:15), and the doing of good and sharing our possessions (Heb. 13:16). These varied examples encourage us to think that *anything* we do in service to God can be thought of as a 'spiritual sacrifice' *acceptable to God*, a continual sweet aroma that ascends to his throne and brings him delight. With this New Testament perspective on 'sacrifice', all the Old Testament passages about sacrifices can be read in a new light.

'Spiritual sacrifices' must be offered *through Jesus Christ*, for only through him are Christians qualified to be priests to God – or to do anything pleasing in God's sight.

This verse thus gives explicit statement to the doctrine of the 'priesthood of believers'.[1] Since all who come to Christ are now a *holy priesthood*, able continually to 'draw near' to God's very presence and offer *spiritual sacrifices acceptable to God through Jesus Christ*, there can no longer be an elite priesthood with claims of special access to God, or special privileges in worship or in fellowship with God. To try to perpetuate such a 'priesthood' distinct from the rest of believers is to attempt to maintain an Old Testament institution which Christ has abolished once for all. Every single Christian can now 'with confidence draw near to the throne of grace' (Heb. 4:16), and corporate worship among Christians should always be a wonderful entrance into the very presence of God.

6. Peter now supports his affirmation in verses 4 and 5 with several Old Testament quotations. He says, *For it stands in scripture*, indicating that what the Old Testament said was conclusive evidence in an argument, able to be trusted completely. *Scripture* translates the word *graphē*, which was used as a technical term by the New Testament authors to refer to the writings of our present canonical Old Testament (all fifty-one of its New Testa-

---

[1] J. H. Elliott, *The Elect and the Holy*, NovTSup 12 (Leiden: Brill, 1966), labours long (but unpersuasively) to deny that this passage teaches a universal priesthood of believers, arguing that the ideas of election and holiness are sufficient by themselves to account for the 'priestly' themes in 2:4–10.

ment occurrences refer to the Old Testament scriptures, and never once is it used to refer to any writings of the Apocrypha or any other writings outside the Bible; however, in 1 Tim. 5:18 and 2 Pet. 3:16, some New Testament writings are included along with the Old Testament under this term.[1]

The first quotation is from Isaiah 28:16, where God promises that he will reject the rebellious leaders in Jerusalem and establish as a 'sure foundation' a *cornerstone chosen and precious*. The fact that it would be the *cornerstone*, the first stone laid as the corner of the 'foundation' (Is. 28:16), indicates that the original prophecy was a prediction of the beginning of a new work by God which would stand in opposition to the leaders rejected by him (Is. 28:14–15, 17–22). The fact that the stone is laid as a foundation stone *in Zion*, the location of the Jerusalem temple, hints at the idea that this new work would in fact replace the Jerusalem temple, something Peter has already made explicit in verses 4 and 5. (On the words *chosen* and *precious*, see the notes at v. 4.)

Peter follows the LXX text (most manuscripts) but not the Hebrew text in including *in him* after *he who believes*, but once this 'stone' is understood to be a person the idea is not foreign to the context. Paul also includes 'in him' in quoting the same passage in Rom. 9:33 and 10:11, and similarly applying it to Christ.

The fact that 'he who believes in him' *will not be put to shame* indicates that there will be no ultimate disappointment or embarrassment (at having one's faith shown to have been in vain) for those who trust in this sure cornerstone, Christ himself.

Additional Note: The dwelling place of God (2:5)

The long history of God's dwelling place among his people finds New Testament fulfillment in the people of God themselves.

---

[1]Selwyn argues (p. 163) that the phrase *en graphē* here must mean 'in writing' rather than 'in Scripture', because the NT authors use the definite article ('the') before *graphē* when they want to refer to Scripture. But Selwyn's argument is incorrectly based: *graphē* without the definite article means 'Scripture' in Jn. 19:37; Rom. 1:2; 16:26; 2 Tim. 3:16; 2 Pet. 1:20. Moreover, the uniform meaning of *graphē* as 'Scripture' fifty other times in the NT means that any other sense would need extremely strong contrary evidence from the context – but here the

The glory of God, the visible evidence of his presence among his people, had led the people out of Egypt as a pillar of cloud by day and a pillar of fire by night (Ex. 13:21–22). God's glory had filled the tabernacle under Moses (Ex. 33:8–13; 40:34–38), and had later filled Solomon's temple (1 Ki. 8:10–11). But it had departed from the temple, in the time of Ezekiel, because of the sins of the people (Ezk. 10:4, 18–19; 11:23). Of the temple built after the return from exile God promised that 'The latter glory of this house shall be greater than the former' (Hg. 2:9), but his glory had never descended to fill it as it had filled the temple under Solomon. The faithful in Israel then waited over 400 years for the fulfillment of Malachi's prophecy, 'The Lord whom you seek will suddenly come to his temple' (Mal. 3:1).

The fulfillment of this prophecy was witnessed by righteous Simeon and Anna when Mary and Joseph brought to the Jerusalem temple the infant Jesus (Lk. 2:22–38), the Saviour who was 'the Messiah, the Lord' (Lk. 2:11, NASB mg. and NIV mg.). His presence was the greater glory of that temple (Lk. 19:47–48), but he also brought its judgment and word of its destruction (Jn. 2:13–17; Lk. 21:5–6), for his own body was the greater and more perfect temple of God (Jn. 2:19–21), the one in whom 'all the fulness of God was pleased to dwell' (Col. 1:19). Thus, John could say of Jesus' life, 'The Word became flesh and dwelt [literally, 'tented' or 'tabernacled'] among us, full of grace and truth; we have beheld his glory, glory as of the only Son from the Father' (Jn. 1:14). In the New Testament Jesus himself is the new and better temple of God, the dwelling place of God among men.

However, after Pentecost, the dwelling place of God is not only Jesus himself, but also his people. He promises to be 'in the midst' of them (Mt. 18:20), to be with them always (Mt. 28:20), and says that he himself, together with the Father and Holy Spirit, will dwell within his people (Jn. 14:17, 23). So now in the church age the people of God are the true temple of God, the place where God dwells.

When Christ returns and there are new heavens and a new

---

immediately following quotations are clearly from OT 'Scripture', not just from some other 'writing'. Finally, the article is often omitted in common or fixed prepositional phrases (BDF, sec. 255).

earth, the temple of God will be the whole earth, for, shining forth from the throne of God in the new Jerusalem, the glory of God will fill the whole earth, and all the nations shall walk by the light of God's glory (Rev. 21:11, 23–25; 22:5; Ps. 72:19). Then God will be King over all the earth (Zc. 14:9) and the whole earth shall come to worship before God (Is. 66:23). In anticipation of that great culmination of all history, the church even now is given the task of declaring God's glory among all the nations (1 Pet. 1:9; *cf.* Ps. 96:13; 108:5; Mt. 5:14–16).

a. Unbelievers reject Christ and stumble (2:7–8)

7. Peter puts his readers in the category of those 'who believe in him' (v. 6) and concludes that *therefore* they 'will not be put to shame' but will rather share in the 'chosen and precious' status of the cornerstone in whom they trust; in other words *to you . . . who believe* is not shame but 'honour'. This contrast suggests that the first clause of verse 7 is best translated, 'To you therefore who believe is honour'.

The RSV translation *To you therefore who believe, he is precious* (based on the AV and followed, surprisingly, by the NIV, and apparently NASB), is an extremely unlikely understanding of the Greek text and is criticized by almost every major commentator.[1] The Greek sentence contains no verb and rather literally says, 'Therefore the honour to you, the believers.' It is quite natural to understand the verb 'to be' (as commonly in Gk. sentences), so that the sentence reads, 'Therefore the honour *is* to you, the believers.' But the RSV translation depends on taking *timē* as 'the *thought* of honour or preciousness', giving the sense, 'Therefore the thought of preciousness (for Christ) is for you, the believers.' Yet the word *timē* never takes this sense in any of its forty-one New Testament occurrences (*e.g.* see Jn. 4:44; Rom. 2:10; 9:21; 13:7; 1 Cor. 12:23; 2 Tim. 2:20; 1 Pet. 3:7; 2 Pet. 1:17; and Bigg, p. 131, says the sense 'preciousness' 'gives to *timē* a sense which it cannot bear').[2] On the other hand, the

---

[1] Beare, for example, says the understanding of the word *humin*, 'you', required by the translation 'to you he is precious' 'is impossible' (p. 124); *cf.* Bigg, p. 131; Selwyn, p. 164; Huther, p. 249; Blum, p. 230.

[2] It is even more unjustifiable to take *timē* as a predicate and supply the subject 'he', again resulting in the sense, 'he is precious'. If *timē* were meant to be the predicate, it would not

translation, 'To you who believe is (the) honour' provides a contrast which might appropriately be expected to follow the fact that believers 'will not be put to shame'. A possible motivation for the RSV translation might be the supposed inappropriateness of giving honour to Christians rather than to Christ, but such a concept is not foreign to this context (where the honourable status which God gives believers is contrasted with the dishonour and shame meted out to hostile unbelievers, vv. 8–9, 15, 20; *cf.* the discussion on 'praise' at 1 Pet. 1:7; note also 1 Pet. 3:16; 4:5, 13–16, 18; 5:6, 10).

By contrast, *for those who do not believe*, Christ is, as Psalm 118:22 and Isaiah 8:14 predicted, *The very stone which the builders rejected*, and (v. 8) 'A stone that will make men stumble, a rock that will make them fall'. In Matthew 21:42 and Acts 4:11 the 'builders' were the Jewish leaders who rejected Christ, but now Peter writes more broadly of all who reject Christ.

There is no necessity to see a mixing or changing of metaphors in Peter's phrase, *the head of the corner*, for *kephalē*, 'head', can mean 'end point, furthest extremity' as well as 'top'.[1] This fits the context well since it gives it the same sense as 'cornerstone' (of the foundation) in the previous quotation from Isaiah 28:16, and it means that the translation 'capstone' (NIV) is certainly not required here. Moreover, the stone over which men will 'stumble' and 'fall' in the next verse cannot be high in the air, but must be a foundation stone on the ground.

The point of the quotation is to show that those who rejected Christ have been proved exactly wrong by God's exaltation of him to the place of greatest prominence, *the head of the corner*.

8. Peter now quotes Isaiah 8:14, which says not only that the Lord himself will become 'a sanctuary' for those who follow him, but also that he will prove to be 'a stone of offence, and a rock of stumbling' to the disobedient of 'both houses of Israel'.

---

have had the definite article in front of it, and the subject 'he' would have needed to be expressed.

[1] *E.g.*, see 1 Ki. 8:8; 2 Ch. 5:9 for this sense of both Gk. *kephalē* and Heb. *rō'sh*, the words used in Ps. 118:22, which Peter is quoting; *cf.* also W. Grudem, 'Does *kephalē* ("Head") Mean "Source" or "Authority Over" in Greek Literature? A Survey of 2,336 Examples', *TrinJ* 6, NS (1985), pp. 43–45, 51.

Since the Lord himself is said to be the stone in Isaiah 8, this verse is another instance of how readily the early Christians applied to Christ many Old Testament passages which spoke of 'the Lord' (Yahweh or Jehovah).

Peter then adds, *they stumble because they disobey the word, as they were destined to do.* Peter's purpose in making this comment is to comfort his readers. He has shown that the rejection of Christ and even the hostile unbelief which confronted these Christians on every side were predicted by God long ago in the Old Testament (vv. 7–8a). Now he says that they were not only predicted but also planned by God (v. 8b) and are therefore within the scope of his sovereign and wise plan for the world. Hostile unbelief should not terrify Christians against whom it is directed, for God their Father holds it all under his control, and will bring it to an end when he deems it best. Amazing as it may seem, even the stumbling and disobedience of unbelievers have been *destined* by God.

Stumble can mean literally tripping over something and falling (Jn. 11:9–10), but here it has a more figurative sense, 'take offence at and reject' (BAGD, p. 716), or perhaps 'fall and miss God's way' (*cf.* the same word in Rom. 9:32; 14:21; and the related noun in Rom. 14:13; 1 Cor. 8:9).

Though *disobey* (*apeitheō*) often means simply 'not obey', it sometimes has the connotation of active or entrenched opposition to God's word (*cf.* Acts 14:2; 19:9; Rom. 2:8; 10:21; 11:30–31; 15:31; Heb. 3:18; 1 Pet. 3:20; 4:17; also Hort, p. 122, who says, 'On the whole . . . the biblical use is best expressed by "rebel" or "be rebellious" '). Although some have argued that this term can mean simply 'disbelieve, be an unbeliever' (especially in Jn. 3:36), such a sense is not required in any of the word's occurrences.[1] Thus, *because they disobey the word* means not just that they refuse to believe the gospel – though it certainly

---

[1] BAGD accepts the sense 'disbelieve' in Jn. 3:36; Acts 14:2; 19:9; Rom. 15:31, but adds that this meaning is 'greatly disputed' and 'is not found outside our literature' (p. 82). Moreover, it must be noted that to 'disobey the gospel' in the NT can mean not just to 'disbelieve' it but actually to 'disobey' it: *i.e.* to refuse to respond to its command to repent and believe in Christ (note *hypakouō*, 'obey', in this sense in 2 Thes. 1:8; also Acts 6:7; Rom. 10:16). Jn. 3:36, 'he who does not obey the Son', is easily understandable in this sense, especially in light of John's tendency to view obedience as evidence of true faith and disobedience as evidence of lack of faith (1 Jn. 2:4–6, 9; 3:6–10; 4:8, 20–21; 5:18).

includes that – but that they are living lives of disobedience and rebellion against God generally. (This wider sense of 'disobey the word' fits the context of the Old Testament quotations best as well.)

The relationship between 'stumbling' and 'disobeying the word' must be gathered from the sense of the passage, for *disobey* is a present participle, which allows for several possible logical relationships. The translation which simply states the two events as going on at the same time ('they stumble while they are disobeying the word') is not wrong, and it no doubt gives part of the sense (it is common for present participles to speak of action which occurs at the same time as the verb they modify). Yet since Peter is probably affirming more here than just the two facts, the RSV translation, *they stumble because they disobey the word*, seems best (so also NIV, NASB). It indicates that many who reject Christ do so because of moral disobedience to God in their lives.

The phrase *as they were destined to do* is more literally rendered, 'unto which also they were destined'. The word 'which' (*ho*) could refer to the stumbling, the disobedience, or both. Since the actions are interconnected, and since it is not an action but the people ('they') who were 'destined', it makes little difference to the force of the passage which one of these we choose. Nevertheless, this neuter singular relative pronoun (*ho*), without further qualification and without any specific neuter noun which it could claim as an antecedent, is most naturally taken as referring to the whole preceding idea – stumbling because of disobeying the word. (Several commentators assume that 'which' must refer to the main verb, 'stumble', rather than the modifying participle, 'disobeying', but nothing in Gk. grammar requires this.)

The word *destined* is *tithēmi*, a term which elsewhere is also used to speak of God's *appointing* or *predestining* a particular event or situation long before it happens (Acts 1:7; Rom. 4:17; 1 Thes. 5:9; Heb. 1:2; probably also Jn. 15:16; Acts 13:47), or of God's *establishing* someone in a certain situation not long beforehand but at a certain point in time (*cf.* Mt. 22:44; 20:28; Rom. 9:33; 1 Cor. 12:18, 28). It is used in a passive form here ('were destined') without mentioning God specifically, but it clearly speaks of God's activity (as it does similarly in 1 Tim. 2:7; 2 Tim. 1:11; and Heb. 10:13). Here Peter uses it in direct contrast to its use in verse 6: there, God *established* (RSV: 'I am *laying*') Christ as a chosen cornerstone in Zion, but here, by contrast, God has *established* (or 'destined') the rebellious to stumbling and disobedience.

The RSV (with all major Eng. translations) correctly represents this appointment to disobedience as a completed event in the past (*they were destined*), for that is the force of the aorist indicative here. It is impossible exegetically to say that God appointed not *persons* but the *fact* of stumbling as the penalty for disobedience (so Bigg, p. 133) for the verb is plural ('*they* were appointed'), and the subject must be the *persons* who are disbelieving (v. 7) and stumbling and disobeying (v. 8). The time of such destining is not specified, but elsewhere in Scripture related passages about predestination view it as occurring before creation, or 'before the foundation of the world' (Eph. 1:4; *cf.* 2 Pet. 2:3; Jude 4; Acts 13:48; Rom. 8:29–30; 9:14–24).

The force of the text then is to say that those who are rejecting Christ and disobeying God's word were also *destined* by God to such action. It is never easy for us to hear this taught in Scripture, but the following note may help somewhat in understanding the issue.

Additional Note: Election and reprobation in Scripture (2:8)

(1) This text leaves open the possibility of repentance and saving faith in Christ for the unbelievers it talks about. The three key verbs are all in the present tense and may be rather literally rendered, 'But for those who are *presently* not believing . . . who are *presently* stumbling because they are *presently* disobeying the word, unto which also they were destined.' This does not of course imply that they will come to saving faith, but it does stop short of saying that their eternal condemnation is already ordained. It rather affirms that their *present* rebellion and disobedience has been ordained by God, and does not indicate whether it will continue throughout life or not. Indeed it could not indicate this, for Peter explicitly affirms the hope that many of these same unbelievers will come to faith (2:12;

3:1, 15; 2 Pet. 3:9).

(2) None the less the text does not allow us to conclude that all people everywhere will ultimately be saved.[1] Peter quite clearly recognizes that there will be final condemnation for all who persist in unbelief (4:5, 17; 2 Pet. 2:1, 3, 4, 6, 9, 12, 17, 20–21; 3:7, 16).

(3) It does not seem possible to escape the conclusion that what the text does affirm (the 'destining' of *present* disobedience of unbelievers) implies also that all disobedience which tragically does persist to the end of life (and thus into eternity) has been 'destined' by God (*cf*. Acts 4:27–28; Jude 4; Gn. 45:5 with 50:20; Ex. 10:20 with 8:15; 2 Sa. 16:11; Acts 2:23; Rom. 9:17–23; 11:7; 2 Thes. 2:11).

(4) We may object that this does not seem to us morally right for God, even though it seems to be the inescapable meaning of the text before us. To this objection the only answer that Scripture gives is not to answer all our questions regarding 'how' or 'why', but only to indicate that ultimately even the condemnation of unbelievers will result in greater glory to God, in the praise of his justice, and power, and mercy to those to whom he shows mercy (Rom. 9:14–25). Thus God can ordain something that is in itself displeasing to him because he knows that finally it will accomplish a greater good (the death of Christ is the ultimate example of this). When we cannot fully understand how this can be, it is for us simply to be silent before our Creator and wait for fuller understanding in eternity (Rom. 9:19–20; Jb. 38:1 – 42:6).

(5) We must note that while Scripture is willing to affirm God's ultimate 'destining' of wrongful actions (see Bible references in point (3) above), the *blame* for these actions is always given to the moral creatures (men and angels) who *willingly* choose to do wrong; the blame is never given to God (*cf*. Jb. 1:22). If we ask how God can 'destine' that something happen through the wilful choice of his creatures, yet himself

[1]Hort (p. 124) draws this conclusion: 'If it was an overwhelming thought that God Himself had appointed them unto stumbling, it was at last the only satisfying thought, for so it was made sure that they were in His hands and His keeping for ever.' This is to affirm almost exactly the opposite of what Peter says: He speaks in this verse of 'destining' to disobedience, not of predestining to final salvation.

remain free from blame (and not be the 'author' of sin in the sense of actually doing wrong himself), then we approach Paul's questions in Romans 9:19, 'Why does he still find fault? For who can resist his will?' Yet here Scripture gives us no answer except to say, 'But who are you, a man, to answer back to God?' (Rom. 9:20).[1]

Therefore, if our understanding of the text ever leads us to begin to *blame* God rather than ourselves for evil (something Scripture never does) or to engage in 'vain discussion' (1 Tim. 1:6) which is unedifying, then we may be sure that our understanding or our application of the text is contrary to its original intent.

(6) Election of some to eternal life and the passing over of others is never viewed in the same way in Scripture. Election to salvation is viewed as a cause for rejoicing and praise to God, who is worthy of praise and receives all the credit for our salvation (note 1 Pet. 1:1–3; Eph. 1:3–6). God is viewed as actively choosing us for salvation, and doing so with delight. But 'reprobation' (the passing over of those who are not chosen, and justly leaving them in their rebellion) is viewed as something which brings God sorrow, not delight (note Ezk. 33:11, and *cf.* Paul's sorrow in Rom. 9:1–2), and in which the blame is always put on the men or angels who rebel, not on God (Jn. 3:18–19; 5:40).

(7) Peter intended this text as a comfort for Christians in the midst of persecution by hostile unbelievers (see above). It can best be applied that way today also (even as Rom. 8:28 and 1 Pet. 1:7) by any Christian facing any kind of abuse from non-Christians (note David's response to Shimei's cursing in 2 Sa. 16:10–12).

---

[1]Note the very helpful discussion in John Calvin, *Institutes of the Christian Religion*, Book 1, Chapter 18, entitled 'God So Uses the Works of the Ungodly, and So Bends Their Minds to Carry Out His Judgments, that He Remains Pure from Every Stain' (vol. 1, pp. 228–237 in the translation by F. L. Battles, Philadelphia: Westminster, 1960), with discussion of many more scriptural examples.

On Rom. 9:1–23 see John Piper, *The Justification of God: An Exegetical and Theological Study of Romans 9:1–23* (Grand Rapids: Baker, 1983).

b. But you are joined with Christ to be blessed as the true people of God (2:9–10)

9. Peter now returns to his elaboration of the blessings which belong to his readers. *But you* – in contrast to those who disobey – *are a chosen race*. The word *chosen* by itself would suggest a sharing in the blessings of God's 'chosen' people in the Old Testament (see discussion of this word at 1:1), as well as a sharing in the privileged status of Christ, the 'chosen' rock (1 Pet. 2:4, 6). But when 'chosen' is placed in the fuller phrase *chosen race*, the allusion to Israel, the race God had chosen as his own, is inescapable (see Is. 43:20, where both these words are used). God has chosen a new race of people, Christians, who have obtained membership in this new 'chosen race' not by physical descent from Abraham but by coming to Christ (v. 4) and believing in him (vv. 6–7).

They are also *a royal priesthood*,[1] and *a holy nation*, two phrases quoted exactly from the LXX of Exodus 19:6 (and 23:22), where God promises this status to all in Israel who keep his covenant. (See note at 2:5 on this priestly status of believers.) Just as believers are a new spiritual race and a new spiritual priesthood, so they are a new spiritual *nation* which is based now neither on ethnic identity nor geographical boundaries but rather on allegiance to their heavenly King, Jesus Christ, who is truly King of kings and Lord of lords (Rev. 19:16).

The next phrase, *God's own people*, is more literally 'a people for possession' (with 'his' being implied). This exact expression is not found in the Old Testament, but quite similar language is found in Exodus 19:5; Isaiah 43:21; and Malachi 3:17. The Isaiah context is probably foremost in Peter's mind, since the next phrase, *that you may declare the wonderful deeds*, also contains an echo of Isaiah 43:21, 'to tell forth my praises' (Isaiah's word 'praises', *aretas* (LXX), is the same as Peter's word translated 'wonderful deeds'). The context is appropriate, for it promises redemption from captivity in Babylon (Is. 43:14) and repeatedly emphasizes that God forgives and redeems his people for his own sake, that his glory might be proclaimed (Is. 42:8, 12; 43:7;

---

[1] Peter quotes the LXX with the phrase 'royal priesthood', rather than the Heb. text, which has 'a kingdom of priests'. The difference is not one of great significance, for in either case kingly and priestly privileges are connected, as they are in Rev. 1:6; 5:10; 20:6.

43:25; 44:23). Similarly, God has redeemed Christians not out of Babylon but *out of darkness* and has called them to himself, taking them not back to Jerusalem but *into his marvellous light*. (*Cf.* 2 Cor. 4:6; Eph. 5:8; Col. 1:12–13; 1 Thes. 5:4–5; 1 Jn. 2:8–11.)

The word *aretas* has been translated 'wonderful deeds' (so RSV) or 'praises' (so NIV, AV) or *'excellencies'* (so NASB). In its other New Testament uses, *aretē* means 'excellence, worthiness of approval and praise' (Phil. 4:8, 'if there is any excellence; 2 Pet. 1:3, 5), and such a meaning is certainly suitable to this context: it is right for God's own people to declare all his excellencies – the perfections of his being.[1]

In fact, God's purpose in redeeming us is not simply our own enjoyment but that we might glorify him, as Peter indicates by the word 'that' in the phrase *that you may declare* (*cf.* Is. 43:7, 25; 48:9–11; Rev. 4:11). Seeking our own eternal well-being – right though that is – could never provide a truly satisfying goal for life. The answer to our search for ultimate meaning lies in 'declaring the excellencies' of God, for he alone is infinitely worthy of glory. Redemption is ultimately not man-centred but God-centred.

To *declare* God's excellencies is to speak of all he is and has done. Peter's word for 'declare' is not used elsewhere in the New Testament, but is used several times in the Psalms to speak of praising God (Pss. 9:14; 71:15; 73:28; 79:13; 107:22; 119:13, 26). This purpose of redemption is too often thwarted by our silence or self-congratulatory pride, but even brief association with a Christian whose speech fulfills this purpose invariably refreshes our spirits.

---

[1] 'Excellence' is by far the most common meaning of the word (BAGD, p.105, says its 'usual meaning' is 'moral excellence, virtue'; *cf.* LSJ, p. 238, 'goodness, excellence, of any kind'; also Hort, p. 129). It takes this sense several hundred times in Philo and Josephus. The meaning 'praise' is found in the LXX (Est. 4:17, end; Is 42:8; Zc. 6:13), and is possible here, but *epainos* (1 Pet. 1:7; 2:14) or perhaps *ainesis* (Heb. 13:15) would have been the expected word if Peter had meant to say 'praise'. Moreover, the sense 'excellence' seems to be the meaning of the Heb. *tĕhillāh* which underlies *aretē* in Is. 43:21 and 42:12 (see BDB, p. 240). The sense 'manifestation of divine power, miracle' is claimed for several instances in the papyri (see BAGD, p. 105, 3), but many of them are ambiguous, and there is no clear example of this meaning in the five collections of literature closest to the language of the New Testament (the NT itself, the LXX, Philo, Josephus, and the Apostolic Fathers). Thus,

10. Peter concludes with ideas and words borrowed from Hosea (1:6, 9; 2:1, 23), which show yet fuller aspects of his readers' great benefits. Like Israel when rejected by God, these Christians had at one time been *no people* and *had not received mercy* – they were under sentence of condemnation for sin. But now they have been granted the highest privilege in the universe: *now you are God's people* – not by any merit of their own, for they were deserving only of judgment. All the foregoing privileges are to be traced only to the undeserved favour of God: *now you have received mercy.*

So in verses 4 to 10 Peter says that God has bestowed on the church almost all the blessings promised to Israel in the Old Testament. The dwelling place of God is no longer the Jerusalem temple, for Christians are the new 'temple' of God (see notes on v. 5). The priesthood able to offer acceptable sacrifices to God is no longer descended from Aaron, for Christians are now the true 'royal priesthood' with access before God's throne (vv. 4–5, 9). God's chosen people are no longer said to be those physically descended from Abraham, for Christians are now the true 'chosen race' (v. 9). The nation blessed by God is no longer the nation of Israel, for Christians are now God's true 'holy nation' (v. 9). The people of Israel are no longer said to be the people of God, for Christians – both Jewish Christians and Gentile Christians – are now 'God's people' (v. 10a) and those who have 'received mercy' (v. 10b). Moreover, Peter takes these quotations from contexts which repeatedly warn that God will reject his people who persist in rebellion against him, who reject the precious 'cornerstone' which he has established. What more could be needed in order to say with assurance that the church has now become the true Israel of God?[1]

'excellencies' (NASB) is the most likely sense, 'praises' (NIV, AV) is possible but less likely, and 'wonderful deeds' (RSV) is quite unlikely.

[1]Blum, p. 231, says that these privileges given to the church do not imply that the church is Israel or that it replaces Israel, and that Rom. 11:13–16, 23–24 guards against such an idea. Certainly we can agree that Rom. 9 – 11 affirms God's continuing concern for ethnic Israel and predicts for the Jewish people a great future time of blessing when many will be joined to the church ('grafted back into their own olive tree', Rom. 11:24). Peter's statements do not

III. SPECIFIC ETHICAL TEACHINGS: HOW TO BE HOLY IN THE MIDST OF UNBELIEVERS (2:11 – 5:11)

A. GENERAL PRINCIPLES (2:11–12)

1. *Abstain from following sinful passions* (2:11)

11. Here Peter begins what is structurally the second half of the letter. Whereas the first part is primarily theological in focus with occasional application to life, this part is generally practical in emphasis with shorter theological statements included at many important points. Whereas the first half contains general exhortations to holiness (1:15), love (1:22), and trust in God (related to hope in 1:13, and implied in 1:5, 7–9, 21; 2:7), this half gives very specific instructions showing how believers are to practice holiness and trust in God in actual life situations. Though it is an oversimplification, it may be said that 2:11 – 5:11 gives specific application to the general teaching of 1:1 – 2:10.

By using the word *beloved* Peter reminds his readers that though he exhorts them as an apostle he also cares for them as beloved brothers and sisters in the Lord's family. Although 'beloved' is a rather archaic word today, 'dear friends' (NIV) seems too weak. The Phillips paraphrase is probably best: 'I beg you, as those whom I love'.

I *beseech you* is archaic language again, but 'I urge you' (NIV, NASB) is not forceful enough. The word (*parakaleō*) has the sense 'I strongly urge you, I strongly appeal to you'.

Peter speaks to them *as aliens and exiles*, using two words (found together in both Gn. 23:4 and Ps. 39:12) which emphasize the Christian's status as a temporary resident in a world that is not his home, for his true homeland is in heaven. For the word *exiles* and Peter's reason for using it, see the notes at 1:1. The term *alien* (*paroikos*) is a close synonym which means 'one who lives in a place that is not his true home' (note its use in Acts 7:6, 29; Eph. 2:19; and the related noun 'sojourning' in

---

nullify that promise. But 1 Pet. 2:4–10 does affirm that God's covenant blessings are presently enjoyed only by those who are in Christ, just as Rom. 9 – 11 affirms that future enjoyment of covenant blessings will come only through being joined to Christ.

1 Pet. 1:17). The knowledge that Christians have no true home here on earth has been of comfort especially to those who spend years and even lifetimes away from their earthly homes in the service of Christ.

Because they are 'aliens and exiles' they should *abstain from the passions of the flesh*. These 'passions' or strong desires (see note on this word, *epithumia*, at 1:14) which are characteristic of the sinful nature are not appropriate to a Christian's heavenly homeland. Examples of such desires are found in Galatians 5:19–21 and 1 John 2:16 (the discussion of 'the flesh' as the sinful nature in Gal. 5:13–25 is a good commentary on this phrase), but in fact any desires for things contrary to God's will are prohibited here. Peter has already told his readers not to let their lives be moulded by such desires (1:14); here he says they should not even let such desires be active in their lives. The verb translated *abstain* means 'to keep away from, avoid' (note its use in Acts 15:29; 1 Thes. 4:3; 1 Tim. 4:3), and its present tense[1] gives the sense '*continually* keep away from sinful desires, do not let yourself indulge in them at any time'. Such a command implies that inward desires are not uncontrollable but can be consciously nurtured or restrained – a needed rebuke to our modern society which takes feelings as a morally neutral 'given' and disparages any who would say that some feelings and desires are wrong.

These sinful desires *wage war*, a word (*strateuō*) which means 'to serve as a soldier' (see 1 Cor. 9:7; 2 Tim. 2:4; and, in a similar passage, Jas. 4:1). Here the present tense verb gives the meaning, 'which are continually waging war' *against your soul*. Though *soul* (*psychē*) can mean 'person' (as in 3:20), here it means 'the non-physical, spiritual part of a person' (see note at 1:22). To entertain such desires may appear momentarily attractive and entirely harmless, since the desires do not usually break forth into wrongful actions, but they are in reality enemies which inflict harm on the Christian's 'soul', making him spiritually weak and ineffective. To be unaware of this spiritual damage indicates a low level of spiritual perception.

[1] The UBS Greek text ([3]1975) has a present infinitive but the present imperative *apechesthe* has several excellent MSS supporting it (p[72] A C L P 33 81 Cyprian) and may be the better reading. Both readings would carry continuing imperatival force.

2. *Maintain good conduct among the Gentiles* (2:12)

12. No new sentence begins here in the Greek text, for this verse is the positive counterpart to verse 11: not only are the readers to abstain from sinful desires (v. 11), they are also to continue to *'Maintain good conduct among the Gentiles'*. *Conduct* here refers to a day-by-day pattern of life (see note on this word at 1:15). Peter calls unbelievers *Gentiles*, not because he thinks that his readers were all Jewish Christians, but because he once again assumes that Christians (both literal Jews and literal Gentiles within the body of Christ) are the 'true Israel'. Therefore all who are not Christians (both literal Jews and literal Gentiles) are truly 'Gentiles' (*cf.* 4:3).

Before these unbelievers, Christians are to maintain 'good conduct', *so that in case they speak against you as wrongdoers, they may see your good deeds and glorify God on the day of visitation*. A Christian's good life even in the face of continuing slander and false accusation may still result in the unbeliever's salvation.

On the day of visitation (RSV; similarly NASB, NIV, AV, NEB) is misleading because the definite article 'the' suggests the one last day of 'visitation' by God, the final judgment. But there is no definite article in the Greek text and 'on a day of visitation' is certainly a legitimate translation (unless 'visitation' could be shown conclusively to mean the final judgment).[1] Commentators have been overly influenced by a supposed background in Isaiah 10:3, which in the LXX speaks of *'the* day of *the* visitation'* (using two definite articles which Peter does not have) as a time of judgment by God. But Peter's phrase is neither similar enough nor long enough to prove a convincing allusion to Isaiah 10:3. *Visitation* (*episkopē*) can refer either to a time when God visits to judge (Jb. 7:18; Is. 10:3; 29:6) or to bring blessing or deliverance (Gn. 50:24–25; Ex. 13:19; Is. 23:17; Wisdom 3:7; significantly, in Lk. 19:44 it refers to 'a visitation to offer

---

[1]Peter does not use the definite article in the phrase *hēmera kriseōs* (day of judgment) in 2 Pet. 2:9; 3:7, but does use it in the phrase *tēs tou theou hēmeras* ('the day of God') in 2 Pet. 3:12; *cf.* 1 Jn. 4:17. It seems that no firm conclusions can be drawn from the use or non-use of the article alone, and the sense must be gained from the other words in the phrase.

salvation'). Peter's exact phrase (*en hēmera episkopēs*) does not appear anywhere else in the Old or New Testament, so it is unwise to assume it is a technical phrase for judgment: it is better to understand it simply to mean 'on a day when God visits' (whether to bring blessing or judgment must be determined from the remaining context).

On this *day of visitation* the unbelievers who are currently slandering Christians will *glorify God*. This glorification is almost certainly the voluntary praise of people who have been converted, and not (as Hort apparently claims, pp. 137–138) the forced acknowledgement by unbelievers that God has been right. (The verb *doxazō*, 'glorify', occurs sixty-one times in the New Testament but it is never used to speak of unbelievers who are forced unwillingly to admit that God or his people have been in the right – indeed, Rev. 16:9 says they refuse to do this.)[1] They are converted and glorify God because of seeing *your good deeds*[2] (*cf.* Mt. 5:16; 1 Pet. 3:15–16). Peter gives a specific example of this in 3:1–2, where he says that husbands may be converted when they see the good conduct of their Christian wives. (The unusual word for 'see', *epopteuō*, 'look upon, watch' occurs in the New Testament only here and in 3:2. The word for 'conduct' is also the same here and in 3:2.)[3]

Thus verses 11 to 12 form a brief prologue to the second half of the letter and in fact state in summary form what Peter will explain in detail in 2:13 – 5:11: Christians living in an unbelieving society must avoid sinful desires and continually maintain exemplary patterns of life, so that unbelievers will be saved and God glorified. There is no reason to doubt that such a strategy for evangelism would still work today.

---

[1] The forced acknowledgement of Christ's Lordship which then results in God's glory, in Phil. 2:11, is different from the active glorifying of God indicated by *doxazō*.

[2] The Gk. phrase is 'by means of your good deeds', and modifies the verb 'they may glorify'. Similar examples of *ek* with genitive used to designate the instrument or means by which something is done are found in Rom. 3:20; 4:2; Jas. 2:18, 21, 3:13; 1 Pet. 4:11, *etc.*.

[3] Beare, p. 138, unjustifiably assumes that 'in a day of visitation' refers to the final judgment and says that the verse gives the 'attractive thought' that unbelievers may change their minds at the last judgment – an idea not in this text or elsewhere in Scripture. Even if the

B. LIVING AS CITIZENS: BE SUBJECT TO GOVERNMENT AUTHORITIES, FOR THE LORD'S SAKE (2:13–17)

13. *Be subject* means to be submissive to an authority, and this usually implies obedience to that authority (note this word in Lk. 2:51; 10:17; Rom. 13:1; 1 Cor. 15:28; Eph. 5:24; Tit. 2:9; Jas. 4:7; 1 Pet. 2:18; 3:1, 5, 22; and see discussion at 1 Pet. 3:1, below). But there are occasions recorded in Scripture when God's people have disobeyed a human government and have been approved by God for so doing (Ex. 1:17; Dn. 3:13–18; 6:10–24; Acts 4:18–20; 5:27–29; Heb. 11:23). The principle to be drawn from these passages is 'obey except when commanded to sin'. This is the Christian's responsibility toward all forms of rightful human authority, whether the individual Christian agrees with all the policies of that authority or not.

The phrase *to every human institution* gives the verse broader application than just to civil government. (This is true whether we adopt this translation or the RSV mg., 'every institution ordained for men'.) In fact, Peter goes on to explain this general statement by applying it not only to civil government (vv. 13b–14), but also to encourage servants to be subject to their masters (2:18) and wives to their husbands (3:1). In all three cases he uses the same verb (*hypotassō*) to express the idea of 'being subject to'. Thus he also sees the master-servant relationship and the marriage relationship as 'human institutions' in which subjection to an authority is required 'for the Lord's sake'.

The inclusiveness of the word *every* makes it appropriate to apply this statement therefore to other legitimate human authorities (parents/children, church officers/members, and authority structures in businesses, educational institutions, voluntary organizations, *etc.*). God has established such patterns of authority for the orderly functioning of human life, and it both pleases and honours him when we subject ourselves to them. Nor should we think that the need for authority is only due to sin, for there is authority among sinless angels (1 Thes. 4:16; Jude 9), the redeemed in heaven (Lk. 19:17, 19; *cf.*

phrase is understood to refer to final judgment, it would have to refer to those who had become believers beforehand and then glorified God for his grace on the day of judgment (*cf.* a similar idea in Lk. 16:9).

1 Cor. 6:3), and even the members of the Trinity for all eternity
(1 Cor. 11:3; 15:28).

The word translated *institution* is *ktisis*, which usually means
'creature, thing created'. The context (vv. 13b–14, 18–20, 3:1–6)
makes it clear, however, that it is not every human being in the
world to whom we are to be subject (a meaning that the verb
hypotassō could not bear in any case, since it refers to subjection
to an authority), but rather to every 'institution' or
'establishment of authority'. This sense for *ktisis* would not be
puzzling to Peter's readers, for the word is used frequently in
extra-biblical literature to refer to the act of creating a governmental body or founding a city. Josephus uses *ktisis* to refer to
'settlements' which the Jews established after leaving Babylon
(*Ant.* 18.373); Plutarch (*c.* AD 50–120), *Moralia* 435D, says the
Delphic Oracle brought many benefits to the Greeks 'both in
wars and in the founding of cities' (*ktisesi poleōn); cf.* BAGD,
p. 456, 2; also the helpful discussion in Hort, pp. 139–140).[1]

For the Lord's sake or 'on account of the Lord' gives a theological basis for this submission. Our submission to authority
should imitate and thus glorify God the Son (Peter makes this
latter point explicit in 2:21–23). Moreover, since God has
established these structures of authority (*cf.* Rom. 13:1–7) he is
pleased for us to submit to them.

Whether it be to the emperor as supreme applies the general
command to a specific office. The Roman emperor at the time
Peter wrote was Nero (reigned AD 54–68), under whose persecution Peter himself would later be put to death (see Introduction,
pp. 34–37). God expects Christians to be subject even to human
authorities who are neither believers nor morally upright.

The word here translated *emperor* (*basileus*) usually means
'king' (so NIV, NASB), but the contrast with 'governors' (v. 14)
and the designation as 'supreme, in high authority', make
'emperor' more likely. There are other examples of *basileus* used

[1]Against Kelly, pp. 108–109, and J. Jeremias, *TDNT* 1, p. 366, who want the verse to teach
subjection to every human creature, but with no evidence that *hypotassō* could ever take
such a broad meaning, and without adequate treatment of Hort's discussion of the use of
ktisis to refer to governmental bodies. Other examples of *ktisis* used in this sense are Diod.
Sic. 13.59.4; 13.90.3; Polybius 10.21.3; *cf.* the verb *ktizō* used of founding not only cities but
also a temple (Polybius 9.27.7); also of 'colonizing' a country (Herodotus 1.149; 2.44).

of a Roman emperor (BAGD, p. 136). Yet whichever sense is adopted, the force of the passage is the same: Be subject to higher and lower civil authorities.

14. *Or to governors as sent by him* makes the application to rulers over Roman provinces: this title 'governor' (*hēgemōn*) is used of Pilate (Mt. 27:2) and Felix (Acts 23:24), for example. The phrase *by him* seems in the RSV text to refer to the emperor who sent the governors. But a more likely translation is 'through him' (NASB mg.), implying that governors are in the position of 'having been sent (by God) through the emperor'[1] to punish wrongdoers and praise those who do right.

The purpose of civil government is briefly defined as *to punish those who do wrong and to praise those who do right*. The word *ekdikēsis* ('punishment') has the connotation of taking vengeance, making a wrongdoer pay a penalty for the wrong done (note the word in Rom. 12:19; 2 Thes. 1:8; Heb. 10:30). Though some theories of criminal punishment maintain that reforming the criminal and protecting society from further crimes are the only legitimate purposes of punishment, Peter here includes retribution, the inflicting of just desert on the one who has harmed others, as a legitimate purpose (note the similar statement in Rom. 13:4: the civil authority is 'the servant of God to execute his wrath on the wrongdoer'). However, what Peter expects governments to do is forbidden to people acting not as representatives of governments but as individuals: they must not inflict retribution for wrong done to them (vv. 19–23; *cf.* Rom. 12:19–21; Mt. 5:38–48). By contrast, governments that fail to punish wrongdoers disobey God's purpose for their existence.

Governments are also *to praise those who do right* as a reward for good conduct and an example and incentive to others. Moral behaviour, not economic status or political favouritism, is to be the criterion. To prevent abuses of God's purpose for government it is right for Christians to pray and work for governments that act according to God's will (1 Tim. 2:1–4; *cf.* Ps. 82:1–4; 125:3).

[1]Peter often uses the same Gk. construction found in the phrase 'through him' (*dia* with genitive) to speak of the person or thing *through which* God does something (1:3, 5, 23; 2:14; 3:1; 2 Pet. 1:3, 4; *cf.* 1 Pet. 5:12). 'The king appears here not as the source of the governor's authority, but as the channel by which Divine authority is conveyed to him' (Hort, p. 141).

15. When unbelievers falsely accuse Christians of wrong-doing (*cf.* v. 12), such slander is irrational, for it springs from the *ignorance* of those who may think themselves wise but are actually *foolish men*. Yet it should be stopped, for it dishonours God. God's way of stopping it, *God's will*, is through exemplary conduct by Christians: *doing right*.[1] Since this sentence is the reason for verses 13 to 14, the specific kind of 'doing right' Peter has in mind is submission to human authorities – such a submission to authority will ultimately be used by God to silence slander.

16. Because his readers might think such extensive submission to authority would be oppressively restrictive, Peter explains that true freedom is consistent with obedience to God's will. He assures them that they are able to *live as free men*.[2] The kind of freedom meant is not specified, but certainly the great freedoms of the Christian life are freedom from the impossible obligation to earn merit before God by perfect obedience (Gal. 5:1–14; Acts 13:39; Rom. 6:23), freedom from guilt (Gal. 3:13; Rev. 1:5b), and freedom from the ruling power of sin (Rom. 6:6–7, 14, 17–18; 20–23; Jn. 8:31–36).

None the less, Christians do not have freedom to do wrong! Though free in a greater way than anyone apart from Christ can ever be, Christians are still in another sense *servants of God* or 'slaves of God', for they owe him their whole lives and their entire beings. True freedom, true ability to choose and do what one really *wants* to do, comes paradoxically in entire submission to God as his obedient *servants* (*cf.* Jas. 1:25; 1 Jn. 5:3). Therefore, as God's 'free servants', Christians should never use their freedom to cover up or hide wrongdoing (*as a pretext for evil* in RSV is less accurate than the NIV 'as a cover-up for evil'): freedom must result in the great joy of doing right.

---

[1] Hort (p. 145), followed by Selwyn (p. 173), says that *houtōs*, 'thus', in the Gk. text (which says literally, 'for thus is the will of God') refers back to vv. 13–14, since *houtōs* must always refer to what precedes. But BAGD, p. 598, 2, gives many examples of *houtōs* referring to what follows. Hort has simply concluded too much from the examples remaining after excluding twenty-four 'exceptions'.

[2] Hort, p. 145, understands 'as free men' to modify 'be subject' in v. 13, with v. 15 as a parentheses. This is possible grammatically, and is not inconsistent with the interpretation given here, although it would emphasize the voluntary nature of a Christian's submission.

17. Those who would live 'as servants of God' (v. 16) have differing obligations to all men generally, other Christians, God, and the emperor. The first phrase, *Honour all men*, may be taken as one command among four (RSV, NASB) or as a summary statement to be explained by the other three statements (NIV: 'Show proper respect to everyone: Love the brotherhood of believers, fear God, honour the king'; similarly NEB).

For several reasons the NIV's understanding of it as a summary statement is unpersuasive. (1) The categories 'believers', 'God', and 'the king' do not include 'all people' (Gk. *pantas*), for unbelievers are omitted, and in the very context where relationships to unbelievers are prominent (vv. 12, 15). Thus, on this reading the following three statements do not fully explain the first, as they ought to do. (2) On the other hand, it would seem somewhat unnatural to include God in the same category as men in the Greek *pantas* ('all persons') – no example like this is found in the 1,244 instances of 'all' in the New Testament. (3) The verb *honour* (*timaō*) does not seem to be so wide in range as to mean 'proper respect of various sorts' and include both 'love' and 'fear': one might well 'honour' or 'show proper respect' to a weak and evil king, for example, without either loving or fearing him. Moreover, this interpretation must give *timaō* a different sense at the end of the sentence than it has at the beginning, something unlikely if the first instance is meant as a summary of the second.

It is better therefore to take this verse as four separate commands. *Honour all men* means 'honour all people'; 'men' is not in the Greek text. 'All' (*pantas*) is common in reference to all people generally (*cf.* Mt. 10:22; Lk. 2:3; Jn. 1:7; Rom. 3:23; Jas. 1:5). Consistent with their good conduct among unbelievers (vv. 12–16), Christians should be courteous and respectful to all people. 'This principle condemns much of man's treatment of his fellows both in the political and in the industrial world' (Stibbs/Walls, p. 112).

Love the brotherhood indicates a higher obligation to fellow Christians (note 'brotherhood' also in 5:9), not only to respect them but also to show strong, deep love to them (see note on *agapaō*, 'love', at 1:22).

Fear God indicates a still higher obligation. Christians are not only to honour and love God (1:3, 8; 2:5, 9); they are also to fear him, something they should not do toward unbelievers (3:14) or toward other believers (see note at 1:17 on fear of God).

Peter now returns to 'honour', the same word with which the verse began: *Honour the emperor.*[1] In what is apparently mild irony Peter has put the emperor on the same level as 'all people'. The progression seems to be as follows:

Fear God.

Love the brotherhood.

Honour all people.   Honour the emperor.

While positively affirming the obligation to honour the emperor (consistent with vv. 13–15), he also subtly implies that, contrary to the claims of Roman emperors to be divine, the emperor was by no means equal to God or worthy of the fear due to God alone. Christians have obligations to the state, but their obligations to God and to the brotherhood of believers are higher.

C. LIVING AS SERVANTS: BE SUBJECT TO YOUR MASTERS (2:18–15)

1. *Even to evil ones* (2:18–20)

18. Peter addresses *servants*, using a less common word, *oiketēs*. The term is nearly synonymous to *doulos*, the common New Testament word for 'servant' (*TDNT* 2, p. 261), but *oiketēs* suggests a nuance of service within a household (LSJ, p. 1202). Both terms have also been translated 'slave' (NIV), but the horrible degradation of slaves in 19th-century America gives the word 'slave' a far worse connotation than is accurate for most of the society to which Peter was writing.[2] Although mistreatment

---

[1]The tense is different, however. The first 'honour' is an aorist imperative, not here specifying the beginning of an action and certainly not an action to be done only once, but rather using the aorist as the 'unmarked' tense, the one to use when an author wanted simply to command the action without specifying anything more about it. In the second case, 'honour the emperor' uses a present imperative and therefore emphasizes the continuing nature of the obligation: 'honour and keep on honouring the emperor'. *Cf.* C. F. D. Moule, *An Idiom-Book of New Testament Greek* (Cambridge: University Press, ²1959), pp. 135–136; but BDF, sec. 337 (2), unnecessarily uses a catch-all category 'complexive' for some aorist imperatives which are simply 'unmarked' with regard to the nature of the action (1 Pet. 1:17a; Jas. 5:7, *etc.*).

[2]'Most persons in slavery were treated well; they had been born in the house of their

of slaves could occur then too, it must be remembered that 1st-century slaves were generally well treated and were not only unskilled labourers but often managers, overseers, and trained members of the various professions (doctors, nurses, teachers, musicians, skilled artisans). There was extensive Roman legislation regulating the treatment of slaves. They were normally paid for their services and could expect eventually to purchase their freedom (OCD, p. 995; also p. 793, art. 'peculium').

Nevertheless, their service was involuntary (in earlier Roman history slaves had been acquired through war or kidnapping from foreign lands, but by the 1st century most slaves had simply been born into slave households). Their legal status, social standing, and opportunity for economic independence were clearly lower than others in Roman society. So a word stronger than 'servant' but weaker than 'slave' is needed – something meaning 'semi-permanent employee without legal or economic freedom'. Although 'servant' comes the closest, no single English word is adequate – perhaps because no comparable institution exists in modern Western society.

Therefore, even though there is no exact parallel to such 'servant' status in modern society, the fact that this was by far the most common kind of employee-employer relationship in the ancient world, and that it encompassed a broad range of degrees of functional and economic freedom, means that the application of Peter's directives to 'employees' today is a very appropriate one. (Free men who worked for others as day labourers were closer to 'independent contractors' today, since they seemed to resist any suggestion that their employers could tell them what to do.)[1] In fact, the word 'employee', though not conveying the idea of absence of freedom, does reflect the economic status and skill level of these ancient 'slaves' better than do either of the words 'servant' or 'slave' today.

---

owner and they had been trained to perform important domestic, industrial, business, or public tasks' (S. Scott Bartchy, *MALLON CHRĒSAI: First-century Slavery and the Interpretation of 1 Corinthians 7:21*, SBL Dissertation Series 11 [Missoula, MT: SBL, 1971], p. 174). Bartchy's description of 1st-century slavery (pp. 38–87 especially) is an excellent recent summary of the evidence. *Cf.* also *IDB* supplementary vol., pp. 830–832; and A. H. M. Jones, 'Slavery in the Ancient World', in *Slavery in Classical Antiquity*, ed. M. I. Finley (Cambridge: Heffer, 1960), pp. 1–15.

[1]See Jones, *art. cit.*, p. 2.

Servants, be submissive to your masters with all respect encourages servants to have a continuing mental attitude of acceptance of the legal and economic authority over them, and a willing obedience to the directives given by their owners or 'masters'. The same verb used in verse 13 to command submission to human authorities generally (*hypotassō*) is used here to urge submission to authorities specifically in the economic realm (see discussion at 3:1 on the meaning of this verb). The verb is participial in form but it is used as an imperative (as in 2:1; 3:1, 7).

The word translated *respect* (*phobos*) commonly means 'fear' in the New Testament (so 1:17; 3:14), but when used of relationships to human authorities does not seem quite as strong as 'fear of punishment or harm' (which would seem unnecessary for Peter to command) but rather 'a healthy desire to avoid their displeasure' (so also *phobos* in Rom. 13:7; 1 Pet. 3:2, 16; and the related verb in Eph. 5:33). Usually *respect* is taken to be the nearest English equivalent, but this will hardly do for its use in a very similar context in Ephesians 6:5, 'with fear (*phobos*) and trembling (*tromos*, 'quivering')'. ('Fear of God' might be suggested as the meaning in all these contexts, except that 'the husband' is specified as the one to fear in Eph. 5:33.) The probable sense is 'with healthy apprehension of their displeasure'. Peter affirms that such an emotion is appropriate, and thereby warns against careless disregard of, or disdain for, such authority (*cf.* 1 Tim. 6:1–2).[1]

It is easier (but by no means automatic) to give such submission to masters who are *kind* (Gk. *agathos*, 'good',) *and gentle*, but much more difficult to do so with the *overbearing* (the word *skolios* literally means 'crooked', see Lk. 3:5, but metaphorically means 'dishonest, morally evil', as in Acts 2:40; Phil. 2:15; Dt. 32:5, LXX; Ps. 78(LXX 77):8; Pr. 4:24; 8:8; 16:28; 28:18). Both 'overbearing' (RSV) and 'harsh' (NIV) are based on a supposed necessity to make the meaning opposite to 'good and gentle' in the previous phrase, but (1) no other instances of the term in this sense have been found (none are cited in BAGD, p. 756, 2); (2) the idea of moral perversity, essential to the metaphorical use

---

[1]However, my student Jonathan Lunde notes that some weighty arguments favour the sense 'fear of God' here: (1) 'All fear' seems too strong toward one's master; (2) the previous verse says to 'fear God'; (3) Peter elsewhere says not to fear men (3:6, 14).

of the term, is thereby lost; and (3) the contrast in the verse is not merely between two terms but between two kinds of masters, the best and the worst, the 'good and gentle' on the one hand and the 'crooked' or 'perverse' on the other. The 'crookedness' of such masters suggests not only physical mistreatment but also dishonesty regarding pay, working conditions, expectations, *etc*. Even to these, submission and the obedience it implies are required 'for the Lord's sake' (v. 13; note Jacob's example in Gn. 31:6–9). Yet the servant must not obey if commanded to sin (see discussion at v. 13). Though the persons exercising authority in a fallen world are necessarily sinful, such lines of authority have been established by God and must be respected.

19. *For* introduces a reason for such submission, which Peter will explain in verses 19 to 25: God is pleased when his people trust him in the midst of unjust suffering, imitating the example of Christ. (This is an additional reason to the opportunity for witness mentioned in v. 12.)

One is approved means 'approved by God' as the recipient of his favour (*charis*; for the word as meaning 'God's favour' see Lk. 2:52; 6:32–34). The person who pleases God is one who *endures pain while suffering unjustly*, although the word translated 'pain' (*lupē*) is better rendered 'sorrow' or 'grief' (see note on the related verb 'suffer' at 1:6, and *cf*. BAGD, p. 482: the term is used of mental pain or 'grief, sorrow', but never in the New Testament is the noun [sixteen occurrences] or the verb [twenty-six occurrences] used of physical pain itself). Peter's emphasis is on enduring the various kinds of mental anguish (the word is actually plural, 'sorrows') which accompany unjust suffering.

Yet he does not say that it is pleasing to God merely to endure unjust suffering and the accompanying sorrow. Rather, it is only such action endured while one is *mindful of God*, or, more accurately, 'because he is conscious of God' (NIV).[1] It is not a

---

[1] The Greek text has *dia* with accusative, which specifically means 'because'. The NASB rendering, 'for the sake of conscience toward God', does interpret the word *syneidēsis* in a common sense (it can mean either 'conscience' or 'consciousness'), but the translation is improbable because (1) it must understand the genitive *theou* 'of God', in an unnatural and perhaps unprecedented sense (an author would commonly use *pros* or *eis* with accusative to

stoic self-motivated tenacity which holds out against all opposition but rather the opposite, the trusting awareness of God's presence and never-failing care, which is the key to righteous suffering. It is the confidence that God will ultimately right all wrongs which enables a Christian to submit to an unjust master without resentment, rebelliousness, self-pity, or despair.

20. Peter here makes explicit what he implied in verse 19, namely, that it is not just any kind of endurance through suffering that God approves, but endurance through unjust suffering (note the same theme in 3:14, 17; 4:14–16). *For what credit is it* (*i.e.* there is no special approval or honour due to you) *if when you do wrong and are beaten for it you take it patiently?* Patient endurance of justly deserved punishment is not remarkable or especially commendable – many wrongdoers know that they are getting what they deserve, and bear the punishment without complaint.

Far different are the times *when you do right and suffer for it.* Although Peter may have in mind suffering specifically for the 'right' one does, the words *for it* are not in the Greek text, and it is better to understand a reference to the general situation of doing right and suffering (whether specifically for the right one has done or for some other reason). It is at such times that the natural man's sense of justice and self-protection would seek revenge, or would turn to insubordination and perhaps hatred against his master. The surprising response of a Christian is to *take it patiently* (more literally, 'you keep enduring', but the kind of endurance Peter intends, patient endurance while trusting in God, may be inferred from 'mindful of God' in v.19). This kind of endurance is something only made possible by being 'conscious of God' (v. 19 NIV) and continually trusting him to care for those rights which have been trampled underfoot by others. At such times trusting God is not easy, for it goes against our natural inclinations. But it is then that faith

say 'toward God'), and (2) it changes the emphasis of the context from trusting in God to striving to obey God, an idea not foreign to Peter but foreign to the mental attitude Peter encourages in this passage (note the model of Christ's mental attitude in v. 23, 'he trusted to him who judges justly').

shows itself to be genuine, something that in God's eyes is 'far more precious than gold' (1:7; *cf.* 3:4). Then *you have God's approval* (*i.e.* you have 'favour' (*charis*, see v. 19) in God's sight.

2. *For Christ suffered for you, trusting God* (2:21–25)

21. *For to this you have been called* indicates the situation into which Christians have been summoned by God at conversion. Although the specific focus of Peter's concern is 'servants', the general principles regarding suffering in verses 19 to 25 apply readily to all others under higher authority, whether in business, in marriage or family, in education, or in respect to government. Especially here in verses 21 to 25, the teachings are put in terms that apply to Christians generally.

Elsewhere Peter says that Christians have been called by God 'out of darkness into his marvellous light' (2:9); or called to return blessing for cursing (3:9); or called 'to his eternal glory in Christ' (5:10). But here – in a great change from his view of suffering in Matthew 16:22 – Peter says they have been called to suffer unjustly: in the phrase *to this you have been called*, 'this' must refer back to trusting in God while suffering for doing right, the theme of verses 19 to 20. The New Testament elsewhere affirms that Christians can expect to be treated unjustly (1 Pet. 5:9; Jn. 15:18–20; 16:33; Acts 14:22; 1 Thes. 3:3; 2 Tim. 3:12; *cf.* Ps. 34:19). But why are we called to suffer? Because such suffering was part of the life of Christ, which we have been called to imitate: *because Christ also suffered for you, leaving you an example, that you should follow in his steps.*

Peter uses *suffered* (*paschō*) rather than 'died' in order to focus on Christ's life of sufferings, and especially the sufferings leading up to his death, as a pattern for Christians. Later, Peter will speak of Christ's bearing the punishment that was due to us for our sins (v. 24). But here Peter has a slightly different focus. The way in which Christ suffered *for you* is explained by the phrase *leaving you an example*; that is, it is not so much Christ's bearing of the penalty for sin (what theologians call Christ's 'passive' obedience) to which Peter refers here, but his perfect obedience to God in the face of the most difficult opposition and hardship (what has been called Christ's 'active' obedience).

Moreover, while Christ's perfect obedience is elsewhere said to earn for us God's approval which Adam failed to earn and which we could not earn for ourselves (*cf.* Rom. 5:18–19), Peter here emphasizes that Christ's obedience through unjust suffering has left us *an example* to imitate, an example of the kind of life that is perfectly pleasing in God's sight. When one is suffering unjustly, trust in God and obedience to him are not easy, but they are deepened through undeserved affliction, and God is thereby more fully glorified (*cf.* 1:6–7 and notes there; also 4:13, 16, 19; Jas. 1:2–4; Lk. 24:26; Phil. 3:10; Heb. 2:10; 12:2–4).

The knowledge that we have been *called* to a life which will include some unfair suffering, while it may at first dismay us, should not ultimately unsettle our minds. We should not of course seek suffering (Mt. 6:13), but when it comes we may even 'rejoice' (1 Pet. 4:13; Jas. 1:2), knowing that in it God will draw us near to himself, and we shall know the fellowship of Christ who understands our suffering, and 'the spirit of glory and of God' (4:14) will rest upon us.

22. Peter explains in more detail the pattern of life left by Christ: *He committed no sin; no guile was found on his lips* (a quotation from Is. 53:9). The New Testament affirms Christ's total sinlessness in several places (Mt. 27:4; Jn. 8:29, 46; 18:38; 2 Cor. 5:21; Heb 4:15; 1 Jn. 3:5); here especially the absence of *guile* or deceitfulness is mentioned (see note on 'guile' in 2:1). 'This verse provides noteworthy testimony to the complete sinlessness of Jesus by one who had been on the closest terms of intimacy with Him' (Stibbs/Walls, p. 118). God's requirement of all people is perfect sinlessness even when under the most intense pressure to sin, a requirement which was fulfilled by Christ as an example and encouragement to us (*cf.* Heb. 12:3–4).

All four verses in this section are dependent on Isaiah 53. Verse 22 quotes Isaiah 53:9, and verse 23 apparently alludes to Isaiah 53:7. Verse 25 echoes Isaiah 53:6 ('All we like sheep have gone astray'). Similarly, verse 24 includes not exact quotations but words and phrases drawn unmistakably from Isaiah 53:12 ('he bore the sin [LXX: "sins"] of many'; *cf.* Is. 53:4, 11) and 53:5 ('with his stripes we are healed').

23. Christ's response to unjust treatment was that *When he was reviled, he did not revile in return; when he suffered, he did not threaten. Reviled* refers to insulting and abusive speech (note the same term in Nu. 20:3 in the LXX, where the people so 'reviled' Moses that they provoked him to a harsh retort and to smiting the rock in anger, see Nu. 20:10–11; *cf.* also Jn. 9:28; 1 Cor. 4:12). The 'reviling' of Christ was especially intense during his trial and crucifixion (Mt. 26:67–68; 27:12–14, 28–31, 39–44; Lk. 22:63–65; 23:9–11). The instinctive response of human beings when so abused is to try to get even, to hurt in return for being hurt. Or if that is impossible people will *threaten* to get even later, trying to give their enemies at least the anxiety that revenge may be taken sometime in the future.

But these responses are natural only to people who depend on themselves and believe that God does not have control of the situation. To the suffering person who trusts deeply in God and believes that God is indeed in control of every situation, there is another response, one perfectly exhibited by Jesus: *he trusted to him who judges justly.* The word *trusted* (*paradidomi*) means 'handed over, delivered, committed', an idea better conveyed by the English word 'entrusted'. The Greek text does not specify what Jesus entrusted to God, but since the options of threatening and reviling in return both have effects on the wrongdoers as well as the one suffering, we are incorrect to limit the thought just to 'entrusting himself' to God (as NIV, NASB). He entrusted not only himself but also the wrongdoers, and his followers, and indeed the entire situation 'to the one who judges justly'. The imperfect tense here implies repeated action in the past, well rendered by the NASB: 'kept entrusting'. Once again faith is seen as the attitude necessary in righteous suffering. Rather than depending on his own abilities to retaliate (which were far greater than the powers of his opponents), when Jesus was suffering he kept entrusting the situation to God the Father, knowing that God would be just and fair, for he is the one *who judges justly.*

It is important to note that Peter here commends neither the supposed therapeutic value of expressing one's anger when wronged, nor merely holding the anger in and trying to suppress it (both are self-dependent solutions), but rather repeatedly and continually committing the situation into God's hands.

When Peter calls God the one *who judges justly* it suggests that Jesus was conscious that God, as Judge, would either repay the wrongdoer justly (*cf.* 4:5), or would forgive because the punishment would be taken by Jesus himself on the cross (v. 24). This knowledge that God will ultimately right all wrongs is essential to a Christian response to suffering, for God has put within us all a sense of justice which will not allow us simply to forget wrongs suffered for which we think there will be no punishment for those who have done them. But committing the situation to God, knowing that ultimately 'the wrongdoer will be paid back for the wrong he has done, and there is no partiality' (Col. 3:25; *cf.* 2 Thes. 1:5–6; Jas. 5:7–8), means that our sense of wrong suffered can be put at rest, and enables us then to imitate Jesus in praying, 'Father, forgive them; for they know not what they do' (Lk. 23:34). We thus seek for the wrongdoers not forgiveness without cost (which is impossible in God's just universe) but forgiveness paid for by the great cost of the blood of Christ (1 Pet. 1:19).

24. Here is an explicit statement of the heart of the gospel: *He himself bore our sins in his body on the tree.* The fact that Christ bore our sins means that God the Father counted our sins against Christ and, in a way not fully understood by us, 'laid on him the iniquity of us all' (Is. 53:6). The Father thought of our sins as belonging to Christ; he 'made him to be sin who knew no sin' (2 Cor. 5:21), and then punished him with that anger against sin, separation from God, and consequent death which we deserved. In this way Christ was a substitute for his people, one who stood in their place.

Tree could also be translated 'cross', since the word is not *dendron*, 'tree', but *xylon*, 'wood, object made of wood', and is translated various ways according to the context ('clubs' in Mt. 26:47, 55; 'stocks' in Acts 16:24; 'tree' in Rev. 22:2). Peter's use of the word *xylon* rather than *stauros*, 'cross', here seems to be an intentional attempt to recall to the readers' minds the curse imagery associated with judicial punishments for sin in Deuteronomy 21:23 (*cf.* Gal. 3:13; also Acts 5:30; 10:39; 13:29).

The reason for translating it 'tree' here is that it makes the allusion to Deuteronomy 21:23 more obvious.

Bore translates a word (*anapherō*) which can mean 'carried up', and if that is the sense here it would mean Christ 'carried up' our sins in his body 'onto' (*epi*) the cross (*cf.* NASB mg., RSV mg., NEB). But *anapherō* can also mean 'bear, carry, endure' (sufferings, dangers, hardships), and since that is the sense in Isaiah 53:11–12 (and in Heb. 9:28, citing Is. 53:12), it is best to understand it to mean 'he bore our sins' here as well. (See additional note below.)

The purpose of Christ's bearing our sin, Peter says, was *that we might die to sin and live to righteousness*. The verb *die* is in a form (aorist participle before the main verb) which frequently indicates action prior to the main verb of the clause (here, 'live'). This would give the sense, 'that we, having died to sin, might live to righteousness'. Such a remarkable statement is similar to Paul's teaching in Romans 6:1–23 that at conversion Christians *have died* to (the dominating power of) sin (Rom. 6:2–11, 14), and are able to make progress in sanctification of life.

By his wounds you have been healed is drawn from Isaiah 53:5. Peter here applies the words morally: by Christ's wounds we have been 'healed' from sin. Here again is the idea of the punishment of a substitute: the punishment deserved by us Christ took on himself and thus made us (spiritually and morally) well.

25. *For you were straying like sheep* recalls Isaiah 53:6, 'All we like sheep have gone astray; we have turned every one to his own way.' This lies in the past, for *now* they have *returned* (at conversion) to Christ *the Shepherd* and they should therefore follow him in lives of 'righteousness' (v. 24). He is also *the Guardian* who watches over all their actions, protects them and expects lives of righteousness.

Returned does not suggest that they had been with Christ prior to their straying, for the verb (*epistrephō*) is used elsewhere of 'turning' or 'being converted' from sin (Acts 3:19; 9:35; 11:21; 14:15; 1 Thes. 1:9). By specifying the one to whom they turned, Peter suggests that genuine turning *away from* sin also includes turning *to* Christ and submitting to his leadership as 'Shepherd and Guardian'.

Additional Note: Did Christ 'carry our sins up to the cross'? (2:24)

BAGD, p. 63, 3 surprisingly denies that *anapherō* can mean 'bear'. Yet it occurs in this sense in Polybius (2nd century BC) 1.36.3 (to bear slander and false accusation for a time); 4.45.9 (to bear, endure the burden of war); Thucydides (5th century BC) 3.38.3 (the city itself bears, endures dangers); *cf.* LSJ, p. 125, 3: 'uphold, take upon one' (with specific reference to Is. 53:12, Heb. 9:28, and other passages from classical authors).[1] The *ana-* prefix in this case apparently conveys the nuance 'bear up under' (a burden). This is the sense in the LXX of Isaiah 53:11 and 12, where the Servant of the Lord is said to *bear* the sins of transgressors (*cf.* v. 4, where *pherō*, 'bear', is used in the same sense). Hebrews 9:28, citing Isaiah 53:12, also uses the word in this sense: 'having been offered once to bear the sins of many'.

Deissmann, pp. 88–91 argues that *anapherō* followed by *epi* with accusative (as in 1 Pet. 2:24) cannot mean 'bore (sins) *on* the tree', for that would have required *epi* with dative. He suggests that the phrase meant that Christ carried our sins '*up to* the cross'. He concludes, 'The expression thus signifies quite generally that Christ took away our sins by His death: there is no suggestion whatever of the special ideas of substitution or sacrifice' (p. 90). Indeed, he then argues that instead of saying that Christ 'bore' men's sins himself, 1 Peter 2:24 uses *anapherō* in the sense 'carried and put upon someone else', and means that Christ took our sins up to the cross and laid them 'upon the cross', thus transferring them from men not to himself but to the cross (p. 91).

Yet (1) Deissman was incorrect to say that 'on the tree' would require *epi* with dative, for *epi* with accusative can certainly mean 'on' with no necessary suggestion of 'motion to a position upon' (see 1 Pet. 4:14, 'the spirit of glory and of God rests *on* you'; *cf.* 3:12; Mk. 4:38, 'asleep *on* the cushion'; also examples in BAGD, p. 288, III.1.a. (*zēta*), and the note in Beare, pp. 149–150). The use of the accusative (instead of the genitive which is found in the LXX of Dt. 21:23) may be just a stylistic change or the result

---

[1]My student T. Matthew Arnold has called my attention to two other clear examples of *anapherō* meaning 'bear' (reproach or sin) in the LXX of Nu. 14:33; Ezk. 36:15.

of quoting from memory – it is not surprising in the light of Peter's free citation of the LXX at several points. (2) The Isaiah 53 background to 1 Peter 2:22–25 is so clear that there must be a compelling reason to take *anapherō* in a sense quite different from the sense it has in Isaiah. (3) Isaiah 53 explicitly indicates the 'bearing' of our sin when it says, 'The LORD has laid on him the iniquity of us all' (v. 6; *cf.* vv. 4, 5, 8, 10). (4) While Colossians 2:14 does say the 'bond' against us was nailed to the cross, in that passage God the Father does this action, and certainly not *instead of* putting punishment on Christ (for Paul's image of 'nailing' could only recall Christ's crucifixion and imply that the bond against us was cancelled *when* Christ bore our punishment by being *himself* nailed to the cross). (5) The teaching of the rest of the New Testament would view Christ's bearing our sins *up to* the cross (and putting them on the cross instead of bearing them himself) as something just as ineffectual as the placing of sins on a 'scapegoat' under the Old Covenant: only a man, one 'like his brothers in every respect', could be the sacrifice which would truly 'make propitiation for the sins of the people' (Heb. 2:17, NASB mg. and AV mg., *cf.* 7:27; 9:14, 22, 26, 28; 10:4, 10; Rom. 4:25; 2 Cor. 5:21).

It is best then to reject the suggestion that 1 Peter 2:24 means that Christ 'carried up' our sins to the cross. The verse affirms rather that 'he bore our sins in his body on the tree', suffering the penalty due to us for our sins.

D. LIVING AS MARRIED PERSONS (3:1–7)

1. *Wives: Be subject to your husbands* (3:1–6)

1. Just as all Christians were to be subject to government authorities (2:13–17), and servants were to be subject to their masters (2:18–25), Peter now exhorts wives to be subject to their husbands (3:1–6). Unlike the previous two sections, this one also contains instructions to those who have authority over the group addressed, namely, the husbands (v. 7). The fact that Peter writes six verses to wives and only one to husbands should not be used to argue that there were more women than men among Peter's readers (as does Kelly, p. 127) – the length of a discussion is determined by the number of words an author thinks necessary to make his message clear, not by how many readers or listeners there may be!

The word *likewise* (*homoiōs*) usually means 'in a similar way', but the degree of similarity intended can vary greatly (*cf.* Lk. 10:32, 37; 16:25; 1 Cor. 7:22; Jas. 2:25). Here the word might mean: (1) similar to the example of Christ in 2:21–25; or (2) similar to the way in which servants are to be submissive in 2:18; or (3) another possibility is that *homoios* simply means 'also', introducing a new subject in the same general area of discussion (relationships to authority), without implying similarity of conduct (see BAGD, p. 568, and 3:7; 5:5).

The second option is best here. *Likewise* modifies *be submissive*, and the reader would naturally make the connection with 2:18, the last time Peter used the verb 'be submissive' (*hypotassō*): 'Servants, be submissive' (2:18) . . . similarly, 'wives, be submissive' (3:1). (The form of expression is exactly the same in the Gk. text, with the comparatively unusual use of a participle to express a command in both cases.)

Nevertheless, Peter does not use the stronger term *kathos*, 'even as, in the same way as', nor does he say 'in every way (*kata panta*, Heb. 4:15) be similar to servants in your submission' (for wives clearly do *not* relate to husbands in every way that servants relate to masters!). The similarity intended is apparently in motive ('for the Lord's sake', 2:13), in extent of application (to good or harsh masters, 2:18, or husbands, 3:1), and in attitude (with healthy apprehension of their displeasure [or fear of God], 2:18 and 3:2), as well as in the main concept of submission to an authority (2:18 and 3:1). (See note at 2:13 about obedience to authorities in general in Scripture.)

Be submissive to your husbands means willingly to submit to your husband's authority or leadership in the marriage. The idea of willing obedience is involved in this submission, as is clear from verses 5 to 6. There Peter illustrates 'being subject to their own husbands' with the example, 'as Sarah obeyed Abraham', thus showing that obeying (*hypakouō*) is the means by which Sarah was being submissive (*hypotassō*, the same word as is used in v. 1).

Sometimes the word *hypotassō* ('be submissive') has been understood to mean 'be thoughtful and considerate; act in love' (toward another).[1] But this is not a legitimate meaning for the term, which always implies a relationship of submission to an authority. It is used elsewhere in the New Testament of the submission of Jesus to the authority of his parents (Lk. 2:51); of demons being subject to the disciples (Lk. 10:17 – clearly the meaning 'act in love, be considerate' cannot fit here); of citizens being subject to government authorities (Rom. 13:1, 5; Tit. 3:1, 1 Pet. 2:13; of the universe being subject to Christ (1 Cor. 15:27; Eph. 1:22); of unseen spiritual powers being subject to Christ (1 Pet. 3:22); of Christ being subject to God the Father (1 Cor. 15:28); of church members being subject to church leaders (1 Cor. 16:15–16 [with 1 Clement 42:4]; 1 Pet. 5:5); of wives being subject to their husbands (Col. 3:18; Tit. 2:5; 1 Pet. 3:5; *cf.* Eph. 5:22, 24); of the church being subject to Christ (Eph. 5:24); of servants being subject to their masters (Tit. 2:9; 1 Pet. 2:18); and of Christians being subject to God (Heb. 12:9; Jas. 4:7). None of these relationships is ever reversed; that is, husbands are never told to be subject (*hypotassō*) to wives, nor the government to citizens, nor masters to servants, nor the disciples to demons, *etc.* (In fact, the term is used outside the NT

---

[1]The use of the verb in Eph. 5:21 ('be subject to one another') has been usually cited to support this view, and the phrase 'mutual submission' has been used to describe the relationship thought to be advocated by this verse. However, the following context defines what Paul means by 'be subject to one another' in Eph. 5:21: He means 'be subject to others in the church who are in positions of authority over you'. This is explained by what follows: wives are to be subject to husbands (5:22–24) – but husbands are never told to be subject to wives. Children are to be subject to their parents (to 'obey' them, 6:1–3), but parents are never told to be subject to or to obey their children. Servants are to be subject to ('obey') their masters, but not masters to servants.

The misunderstanding of this verse has come about through an assumption that 'one another' (*allelous*) must be completely reciprocal (that it must mean 'everyone to everyone'). Yet there are many cases where it does not take that sense, but rather means 'some to others': for example, in Rev. 6:4, 'so that men should slay one another' means 'so that some would kill others'; in Gal. 6:2, 'Bear one another's burdens' means not 'everyone should exchange burdens with everyone else', but 'some who are more able should help bear the burdens of others who are less able'; 1 Cor. 11:33, 'when you come together to eat, wait for one another' means 'those who are ready early should wait for others who are late'; *etc.* (*cf.* Lk. 2:15; 12:1; 24:32). Similarly, both the following context and the meaning of *hypotassō* require it to mean 'those who are under authority should be subject to others among you who have authority over them' in Eph. 5:21.

to describe the submission and obedience of soldiers in an army to those of superior rank, see Josephus, *War* 2.566, 578; 5.309; *cf.* the adverb in 1 Clement 37:2; also LSJ, p. 1897, which defines *hypotassō* [passive] to mean 'be obedient').

Yet it must be remembered that submission to authority is often consistent with equality in importance, dignity, and honour – Jesus was subject both to his parents and to God the Father, and Christians who are highly honoured in God's sight are still commanded to be subject to unbelieving government authorities and masters. Thus the command to wives to be subject to their husbands should never be taken to imply inferior personhood or spirituality, or lesser importance. Indeed, Peter affirms just the opposite: wives are 'joint heirs of the grace of life' (v. 7). Moreover, the general scriptural principle of obedience to authorities 'except when commanded to sin' (see note at 2:13) also applies here.

Of course, submission to a husband's authority within a healthy marriage might not often involve obeying commands (though it will sometimes include this), for a husband may rather give requests and seek advice and discussion about the course of action to be followed (*cf.* Phm. 8–9). Nevertheless, an attitude of submission to a husband's authority will be reflected in numerous words and actions each day which reflect deference to his leadership and an acknowledgement of his final responsibility – after discussion has occurred, where possible – to make decisions affecting the whole family.

The purpose Peter mentions for this submission is *so that some, though they do not obey the word, may be won without a word by the behaviour of their wives.* Some commentators affirm that many or most of the wives to whom Peter was writing had unbelieving husbands, but the Greek text implies just the opposite. It says, 'so that *even if* some do not obey the word', and the phrase 'even if' (*kai ei*) suggests that this would be an unexpected or uncommon occurrence. It implies that Peter expected that most Christian wives among his readers had Christian husbands.

Those who *do not obey the word* are husbands who are unbelievers; the present tense verb (*apeithousin*) suggests a pattern of life characterized by disobedience not only to the gospel but also to God's standards in other areas of life. The word means not just that they 'do not believe the word' (NIV), but has a much stronger sense of active disobedience to the standards of Scripture and even rebellion against them (see note at 2:8 on *apeitheō*, 'disobey'). Some of them (not all) would have been harsh and unkind to their Christian wives, but Peter says that even such husbands can *be won* or 'gained' for God's kingdom (note the use of the same word five times in 1 Cor. 9:19–22; also Mt. 18:15, and in a commercial sense in Mt. 16:26; 25:20, 22; Jas. 4:13).

Unbelieving husbands can be won *without a word* – that is, not by continually preaching or talking about the gospel, but rather simply *by the behaviour of their wives*,[1] their Christian pattern of life (see note at 1:15 on *anastrophē*, 'conduct, behaviour'). This emphasis on conduct rather than words is also applicable to other situations in which Christians find themselves in regular daily contact with unbelievers (at work, within a family or college residence, *etc.*). Though Peter does not exactly say that Christians should never talk about the gospel message to their unbelieving husbands or friends, he does indicate that the means God will use to 'win' such persons will generally not be the Christian's words but his or her *behaviour*. To know this should increase prayer both for grace to live rightly and for God's working in the husband's heart.

2. *When they see your reverent and chaste behaviour* could also be rendered 'because they see . . .' or 'by seeing . . .'.[2] The verse gives additional emphasis to observable behaviour as the key to winning the unbeliever. *Reverent* translates *en phobō*, 'in (or with) fear'. See the note on 'fear' at 2:18 – the same sense, 'with healthy apprehension of their displeasure', would also fit here, although 'fear of God' (as in 1:17 and 2:17) is not inappropriate to the context, so it is difficult to draw a definite conclusion. Yet

---

[1]The Gk. text includes no word for 'their' (Peter could have made it clear with *autōn*), leaving open the possibility that Peter intends to say that unbelieving husbands will be won not simply by seeing the submissive behaviour of their own wives but by observing the pattern of Christian marriage exemplified by wives generally within the Christian community.

[2]The UBS Greek text has an aorist participle but the textual variant *epopteuontes* (present participle) is found in some of the best manuscripts (p72, Sinaiticus, *etc.*). It would place more emphasis on observation of the Christian wife's conduct over a period of time.

since Peter cautions wives not to fear with terror or dread (of harm) in verse 6, any such nuance should be excluded here.

The word *chaste* (*hagnos*) means 'pure, free from moral defilement', and serves as another reminder that the submission Peter commands must never go so far as to include obedience to demands to do something that is morally wrong.

The attractiveness of a wife's submissive behaviour even to an unbelieving husband suggests that God has inscribed the rightness and beauty of role distinctions in marriage on the hearts of all mankind. Such role distinctions include male leadership or headship in the family and female acceptance of and responsiveness to that leadership. Someone might object that female submissiveness is attractive to the unbelieving husband only because he is selfishly interested in gaining power for himself, or because it fits his culture's current perception of appropriate male-female relationships, but in either case (so this position would argue) such role distinctions are still wrong or still incongruent with God's ideal plan for marriage. However, this objection is unpersuasive because Peter would not encourage a sinful behaviour pattern (whether from the culture or the husband himself) to continue in order to bring someone to faith: it is 'pure' behaviour, not sinfulness, that attracts unbelievers to Christ. And this 'pure' behaviour, Peter says, especially involves wives being subject to their own husbands. The unbelieving husband sees this behaviour and deep within perceives the beauty of it. Within his heart there is a witness that this is right, this is how God intended men and women to relate as husband and wife. He concludes, therefore, that the gospel which his wife believes must be true as well.

3. The focus is now on the wife's beauty, which consists not in external, visible things which perish but in unseen spiritual realities which are eternal. *Let not yours be the outward adorning* gives the sense of the phrase quite well and prepares the reader for the contrast with 'inward adorning' in verse 4. *Adorning* refers to the focus of attention for one's attractiveness, the thing one uses to make oneself beautiful to others. Christian wives should depend for their own attractiveness not on outward things such as *braiding of hair, decoration of gold, and wearing of fine* *clothing*, but on inward qualities of life, especially 'a gentle and quiet spirit' (v. 4).

Although the RSV speaks of *fine clothing* (similarly NIV), the Greek text does not include an adjective modifying *clothing* (*himation*) and the text literally says, 'Let not your adorning be the outward adorning of braiding of hair and wearing of gold or putting on of clothing.' It is incorrect, therefore, to use this text to prohibit women from braiding their hair or wearing gold jewelry, for by the same reasoning one would have to prohibit 'putting on of clothing'. Peter's point is not that any of these are forbidden, but that they should not be a woman's 'adorning', her source of beauty.

4. *The hidden person of the heart* is the wife's inward nature, her true personality. It is not visible in itself, but it is revealed through words and actions which reflect inner attitudes. *Imperishable* is an adjective which the New Testament uses consistently to speak of heavenly realities, things which will not fade away with the passing of this present world (see note on this word at 1:4). Since Peter uses this adjective without a noun following it, some noun must be supplied by the reader from the context. Various suggestions have been made (RSV: 'imperishable jewel'; NIV: 'unfading beauty'; NASB: 'imperishable quality'; NEB: 'imperishable ornament'), but the sense is roughly the same in all of them: the beauty of a *gentle and quiet spirit* will last for eternity, in contrast to the fleeting beauty of jewelry or clothing.

The adjective *gentle* (*praüs*) only occurs three other times in the New Testament (Mt. 5:5; 11:29; 21:5), twice referring to Christ, but its related noun, translated 'gentleness' or 'meekness', is more frequent (Gal. 5:23; 6:1; Jas. 3:13; *etc.*). It means 'not insistent on one's own rights', or 'not pushy, not selfishly assertive', 'not demanding one's own way'. Such a *gentle and quiet spirit* will be beautiful to other human beings, even unbelieving husbands (vv. 1–2), but even more importantly it is something which *in God's sight is very precious*. Why? No doubt because such a spirit is the result of quiet and continual trust in God to supply one's needs, and God delights in being trusted (*cf.* 1:5, 7, 8–9, 21; 2:6–7, 23; 3:12, 5:7).

5. To underline the preciousness of inward trust in God, Peter appeals to the lives of *holy women who hoped in God*. Although he specifically mentions Sarah in verse 6, the plural 'women' refers generally to godly women in the Old Testament. 'Hoping in God' (the present participle suggests continuing in hope over a period of time), they *used to adorn themselves* 'in this way' or 'so' (*houtōs*, 'thus', referring to adorning with a gentle and quiet spirit). The verb *adorn* is related to the noun 'adorning' in verse 3, and its imperfect tense indicates continuing or repeated action over time in the past, *i.e.* 'they were repeatedly or continually adorning themselves' in this way.

And were submissive to their husbands brings us back to the theme of verses 1 to 2 and indicates that there is a relationship between a submissive attitude and the inward beauty of verses 3 to 4. Quiet confidence in God produces in a woman the imperishable beauty of a gentle and quiet spirit, but it also enables her to submit to her husband's authority without fear that it will ultimately be harmful to her well-being or her personhood.

6. Sarah is a specific example of godly submissiveness. Wives are to be submissive to their husbands (v. 5) *as Sarah obeyed Abraham, calling him lord*. Peter does not seem to be referring to any one specific incident here, for the main verb and both participles in verse 5 all indicate a continuing pattern of conduct during one's life (see above).[1]

The example of Sarah's obedience would be an appropriate encouragement to the wives to whom Peter was writing, for Sarah became the mother of all God's people in the Old Covenant (Is. 51:2; *cf.* Gal. 4:22–26), even though there had been many times in which following Abraham had meant trusting God in uncertain, unpleasant, and even dangerous situations (Gn. 12:1,

---

[1]The aorist tense here for 'obeyed' need not refer only to one incident, for the aorist indicative is frequently used in a 'constative' sense simply to say that something 'happened', with no implication of whether it happened at one point in time or over a very long period of time (*cf.* the aorist indicatives in Eph. 5:25, 'Christ loved the church'; Rom. 5:14, 'death reigned from Adam to Moses'; Rev. 20:4, 'they . . . reigned with Christ a thousand years'; also BDF, sec. 332).

Selwyn (p. 185) and Kelly (p. 131) say that Peter is referring to Gn. 18:12, but this is hardly likely since no obedience to Abraham is mentioned in the passage, and Sarah is there speaking to herself, not to Abraham.

5, 10–15; 13:1; 20:2–6 [*cf*. v. 12)]; 22:3). Yet Peter says *you are now her children* (or 'daughters'), the true members of her spiritual family, indicating (as in 1:1 and 2:4–10) that Peter sees the church, not those descended physically from Abraham and Sarah, as the true descendants of Abraham and thus the true people of God. To be Sarah's daughter is to be a joint heir of the promises and the honour given to her and to Abraham. The condition for being Sarah's daughters is *if you do right and let nothing terrify you*. Both verbs are again present participles indicating a pattern of life continued over a period of time: 'if you are doing right and not being frightened by any terror', then you are (more accurately, 'you have become') Sarah's daughter. Peter's insistence on 'doing right' is a reminder that no acts of disobedience in Sarah's life are to be imitated by Christian wives (*cf*. Gn. 16:2, 6; 18:15; perhaps 20:5); it is her submission to her husband and her trust in God that Peter commends. The condition 'if you . . . let nothing terrify you' is another way in which faith finds expression. A woman with 'a gentle and quiet spirit' who 'continues hoping in God' will not be terrified by circumstances or by an unbelieving or disobedient husband (*cf*. Gn. 20:6).

2. *Husbands: Live considerately with your wives* (3:7)

7. Now Peter speaks briefly but just as forcefully to husbands. The word *likewise* here has the sense 'also' or 'continuing on the same area of discussion' (BAGD, p. 568; *cf*. 1 Pet. 5:5), for the idea of similarity in submission is excluded by the fact that here (unlike 2:18 and 3:1) Peter does not command submission to, but rather considerate use of, authority.

The verb *live . . . with* does not carry any special nuance beyond its sense in English, except that it is used several times in the LXX to refer to a husband and wife who 'live together'.[1]

Live considerately with your wives is literally, 'living together according to knowledge' (for the use of the participle as imper-

---

[1]Kelly, p. 132, says the verb *synoikeō* has special reference to sexual intercourse, but neither BAGD (p. 791) nor LSJ (p. 1721) indicate such a sense, and it is impossible in Dt. 25:5 ('if brothers dwell together'); Wisdom 7:28 ('God loves . . . the man who lives with wisdom'); Ecclus. 25:16.

ative see the note at 1:14). Peter does not specify what kind of knowledge he means by 'according to knowledge', so some general phrase like 'in an understanding way' (NASB) is a good translation. The RSV's 'considerately' (similarly, NIV) gives too much emphasis to a considerate attitude alone while neglecting the focus on actual 'knowledge' or information which is also implied by Peter's word. The 'knowledge' Peter intends here may include any knowledge that would be beneficial to the husband-wife relationship: knowledge of God's purposes and principles for marriage; knowledge of the wife's desires, goals, and frustrations; knowledge of her strengths and weaknesses in the physical, emotional and spiritual realms; *etc.* A husband who lives according to such knowledge will greatly enrich his marriage relationship – yet such knowledge can only be gained through regular study of God's Word and regular, unhurried times of private fellowship together as husband and wife.[1]

Bestowing honour on the woman as the weaker sex affirms a theme found frequently in the New Testament, namely, that God is often pleased to give honour to those who are weaker or less honoured in the eyes of the world (*cf.* Mt. 5:3–12; 1 Cor. 1:26–30; 12:22–25; Jas. 2:5; 4:6; 1 Pet. 5:5). In this case such honour ought to include kind and affirming words both privately and in public, and high priority in choices regarding the use of one's time and money. (The NIV's 'treat them with respect' is too weak – one can treat someone with detached, formal 'respect' and yet give no special honour to the person at all.) None the less, just as wives are not to obey their husbands when commanded to disobey God (see notes on 2:13 and 3:1), so husbands must never allow love for their wives to become an excuse for sin – a principle tragically ignored by Solomon (1 Ki. 11:3–8), Ahab (1 Ki. 21:25), and perhaps even Adam (Gn. 3:6).

The woman translates a rare word (meaning, more literally 'the feminine one'). It suggests that Peter looks to the characteristic nature of womanhood or femininity and suggests that a wife's 'femaleness' should itself elicit honour from her husband.

Peter does not specify the way in which he understands the

[1]One book that deserves mention here (simply because it contains so much practical wisdom on this subject) is James Dobson, *Man to Man about Women* (Eastbourne: Kingsway, 1976; = *What Wives Wish Their Husbands Knew about Women* [Wheaton: Tyndale, 1977]).

woman to be *the weaker sex*, but the context would make it appropriate for him to have in mind any kind of weakness of which husbands would need to be cautioned not to take advantage. This would certainly include the idea that, by and large, women are physically weaker than men (*i.e.* if men tried they usually could overpower their wives physically). But the context also shows that women are 'weaker' in terms of authority in the marriage (vv. 1, 5–6), and Peter therefore directs husbands that instead of misusing their authority for selfish ends they should use it to 'bestow honour' on their wives. Yet there may also be a third sense of 'weakness' which would fit the context (because it is something husbands should not take advantage of), namely, a greater emotional sensitivity. While this is something which is also a great strength, it none the less means that wives are often more likely to be hurt deeply by conflict within a marriage, or by inconsiderate behaviour on the part of the husband. Knowing this, Christian husbands should not be 'harsh' (Col. 3:19) or fill their marriage relationship with criticism and conflict, but should rather be positive and affirming, 'living together in an understanding way', and 'bestowing honour on the feminine one, as the weaker sex'.

The word translated *sex* in 'the weaker sex' is *skeuos*, which often means 'vessel, jar, container', but is also used in the New Testament to speak of human beings as 'vessels' created by God and intended for his use (Acts 9:15; Rom. 9:21; 2 Cor. 4:7; 2 Tim. 2:21). There is no derogatory nuance here, since the fact that the woman is called the 'weaker vessel' implies that the man is also viewed as a 'vessel'. The term recalls God's creation of all people, both men and women, and is a reminder both of human frailty and of obligation to God our Creator.

It should be noted that it is also possible to understand the two phrases 'the woman' and 'the weaker sex' as relating to the command 'live together' rather than to 'bestowing honour'. This would give the sense, 'live together with your wife according to knowledge, as with the weaker sex, the feminine one' (*cf.* NASB, TEV). It is not possible to decide between this reading and that of the RSV (and NIV, AV) on grammatical grounds alone, nor do the arguments from context seem to be conclusive on either side. But there is not much difference in the end since the commands to live together and to bestow honour are both part of one large command, and the husband's knowledge of the fact that Peter calls the wife 'the feminine one' and 'the weaker vessel' should in any case modify the whole complex of actions included in 'living together in an understanding way' and 'bestowing honour'.

Since you are joint heirs of the grace of life reminds husbands that even though they have been given greater authority within marriage, their wives are still equal to them in spiritual privilege and eternal importance: they are 'joint heirs'. Here as elsewhere the New Testament authors couple their treatment of differences in roles of husband and wife with an implicit or explicit affirmation of their equality in status and importance (*cf.* 1 Cor. 11:2–3, 7–12; Eph. 5:22–33; Col. 3:18–19). Although some have argued that Paul abolished differences in role or authority when he affirmed that men and women are 'one in Christ Jesus' and both 'heirs according to promise' (Gal. 3:28–29), it is significant that here Peter sees no difficulty in affirming that wives are 'joint heirs' in a sense that includes subjection to their husbands' authority.

The RSV's *since* expresses a possible relationship between this statement and the rest of the verse, but it could also be translated, 'bestowing honour . . . *as* to those who are joint heirs . . .'. This would give slightly more emphasis to the way in which honour is bestowed instead of the reason for bestowing it, but the difference in meaning is not great.

Finally Peter adds a note of warning: *in order that your prayers may not be hindered*. Some think that *your prayers* refers only to times when the husband and wife pray together, but this view is unpersuasive because Peter is addressing this sentence to husbands only, not to both husbands and wives. 'Your' must refer to the 'you' to whom Peter is writing, namely, the husbands, and the reference therefore is to the husbands' prayers generally. This 'hindering' of prayers is a form of God's fatherly discipline, which Hebrews 12:3–11 reminds us is 'for our good' and is given to those whom God 'loves'. (The NIV unfortunately obscures the evident reference to God's discipline in the passive verb ['be hindered' in the Greek] and imports another idea, 'so that nothing will hinder your prayers' – suggesting to the reader, perhaps, that human interference is in view, from inter-personal conflict or emotional turmoil, *etc.*)

So concerned is God that Christian husbands live in an under-standing and loving way with their wives, that he 'interrupts' his relationship with them when they are not doing so. No Christian husband should presume to think that any spiritual good will be accomplished by his life without an effective minis-try of prayer. And no husband may expect an effective prayer life unless he lives with his wife 'in an understanding way, bestowing honour' on her. To take the time to develop and maintain a good marriage is God's will; it is serving God; it is a spiritual activity pleasing in his sight.

E. LIVING AS CHRISTIANS GENERALLY (3:8–22)

1. *Be humble and united in spirit* (3:8)

8. This section concludes with some general instructions on relating to others, especially those who may be hostile. *Finally, all of you, have unity of spirit, sympathy, love of the brethren, a tender heart and a humble mind.* The term translated *unity of spirit* means 'sharing the same thoughts and attitudes, thinking har-moniously' – a goal too infrequently attained in Christian churches. *Love of the brethren* refers to love for others within the church (the primary emphasis on love for fellow Christians is missed by the NIV's 'love as brothers'). *A tender heart* is a helpful translation of a word which means 'caring, compassionate', not only in actions but even more in one's feelings or emotions (note the same word in Eph. 4:32). *A humble mind* refers not only to ideas but also to attitudes and to general mental outlook – it is contrasted to pride in Proverbs 29:23.

2. *Return blessing when evil is done to you* (3:9–12)

9. Continuing with more actions which issue from a heart that is trusting in God to care for one's needs, and which imitate the supreme example of Christ's life, Peter tells his readers, many of whom are already suffering opposition, *Do not return* *evil for evil or reviling for reviling: but on the contrary bless.* (See the note at 2:23 on the related verb 'revile'; the term refers to abusive or insulting talk, 'speaking evil' against someone.) Christians are not to repay evil words with more of the same, but with the opposite, following both the teaching and example of Christ (Mt. 5:44; Lk. 6:27–29, 35; 23:34; *cf.* Rom. 12:14, 17–21; 1 Cor. 4:12). The reason given in the gospels is that they ought to imitate the goodness of God even to undeserving sinners (Mt. 5:45, 48; Lk. 6:35–36), goodness which is meant to lead them to repentance (Rom. 2:4 *cf.* Acts 14:17). Here is ample warrant to do good to all people, even those who do us harm. (It should be noted here, however, that the responsibility of government to punish evildoers in 2:14 means that there will be times when not for personal revenge but as a representative of the civil government a Christian will forcefully retaliate against evil; note the same distinction between the prohibition of personal revenge and the endorsement of forceful retribution by government in Rom. 12:14, 17–21 with Rom. 13:1–5.)

Here Peter gives another reason for the kind of actions and attitudes he commands: it is part of the Christian life, and a means of obtaining blessing from God: *For to this you have been called, that you may obtain a blessing.* Grammatically, *this* may refer either backward (to the idea of returning blessing for cursing, or to all of the righteous behaviour in vv. 8–9a) or forward (to the clause 'that you may obtain a blessing'). (The TEV, NASB, and NEB all translate the verse in such a way that the backward reference is ruled out; other versions [such as RSV, NIV] rightly leave the Eng. translation ambiguous, reflecting the two possibilities found in the Gk. text.)

However, the sense of the passage requires that *this* refers backward, to the righteous conduct Peter commands them to manifest in vv. 8–9a. This is because (1) the parallel with 2:21 ('for to this you have been called') is very close in vocabulary, in content, and in purpose. There 'this' clearly points backward to righteous behaviour (and therefore a similar construction in such a similar context would be natural for Peter); and (2) Psalm 34:12–16, quoted in verses 10 to 12, clearly promises God's blessing (God's care and his willingness to answer prayer, v. 12) in response to righteous behaviour (not speaking evil and doing right, vv. 10–11, and being 'righteous', v. 12). Therefore, verses 10 to 12 make a good ground for verse 9 if it advocates righteous behaviour in order to obtain a blessing from God. But if verse 9 simply says that Christians have been called to obtain a blessing (with no explicit connection to righteous behaviour), then verses 10 to 12 do not form a good ground for it.[1]

We may therefore represent the overall argument of verses 8 to 12 as follows: 'Finally, all of you, be like-minded, loving toward one another, compassionate, and humble (v. 8), not returning evil for evil or reviling for reviling; but on the contrary blessing, for you have been called to such a righteous life, in order that by this righteous living you may obtain God's blessing on your life' (v. 9). 'For in the Psalms God promises blessings to those who live righteously' (vv. 10–12).

Finally, does *blessing* refer to the final blessing of eternal salvation or to God's blessing in this present life? In favour of the former is the fact that the word *obtain* is *klēronomeō* ('inherit, acquire, obtain'), a verb which often speaks of heavenly inheritance, and which is related to the noun 'inheritance' in 1:4 (which is clearly future, 'kept in heaven for you'). Yet *klēronomeō* can be used simply to mean 'obtain' something in this life (*cf.* Heb. 12:17; and for the noun, Mt. 21:38; Lk. 12:13; Heb. 11:8). Peter's use of the term here may have been influenced by its use in the Old Testament (*e.g.* Ps. 37:9, 11, 22, 29) to speak of the blessings of the righteous who 'trust in the Lord, and do good' (Ps. 37:3) in the presence of the wicked (a theme exactly appropriate to Peter's concern in this context).

Moreover, the blessings specified in verse 12 clearly relate to this life: 'For the eyes of the Lord are upon the righteous, and his ears are open to their prayer.' This is even clearer in the context of the quotation from Psalm 34, which speaks throughout of God's care in this life for those who trust in him and are faithful to him (Ps. 34:4, 6, 7, 10, 17, 19).

Although Peter mentions future heavenly reward (1:4–7, 13;

---

[1]These two arguments are adopted from the thorough treatment by John Piper, 'Hope as the Motivation of Love: 1 Peter 3:9–12', *NTS* 26 (1980), pp. 212–231. Piper's discussion of the flow of the argument is excellent, even though he surprisingly fails to give much consideration to the very likely possibility that the 'blessing' of v. 9 is God's blessing in this present life, rather than final salvation.

4:13; 5:4), it would not be foreign to his thought to emphasize present blessings resulting from right actions. In fact, 1 Peter contains several examples of blessings in this life which are promised as a result of righteous conduct:

Verse	Right conduct	Resulting blessing in this life
1:8	loving Christ	unutterable joy
1:9	continuing faith	more benefits of salvation
1:17	holy life with fear	avoiding God's fatherly discipline
2:2	partaking of spiritual milk	growing up toward salvation
2:19–20	trusting God and doing right while suffering	God's approval
3:1–2	submitting to husbands	husbands won for Christ
3:7	living considerately with wives	prayers not hindered
4:14	enduring reproach for Christ	spirit of glory and of God rests upon you
5:7	casting cares on God	(implied) he will care for your needs
5:9–10	resist the devil	God will restore, establish, strengthen you

Verses 8 to 12 therefore teach that one proper motive for righteous living is the knowledge that such conduct will bring blessings from God in this life. These may take different forms but in view of the quotation from Psalm 34 they may be expected to include loving life, seeing 'good days', having God's 'eyes upon us' to care for our needs, and having his 'ears open' to hear and answer our prayers (*cf.* Jas. 5:16; 1 Jn. 3:21–22). Nevertheless, in the larger context of the whole of 1 Peter, such blessings do not include freedom from opposition or suffering – the blessings of the New Testament age generally are more spiritual, psychological, and interpersonal, and less material or physical, than in the Old Testament (see additional note on 'New Covenant Rewards' at 1:4, pp. 59f.).

10–12. The function of verses 10 to 12 has been discussed above in connection with verse 9: they provide a 'ground' or reason supporting verses 8 to 9 with a quotation from Psalm 34:12–16. It remains here only to comment on some specific terms.

To *love life* does not mean that one has a trouble-free life, either in the context of 1 Peter (for the previous verse expects 'evil' and 'reviling') or of Psalm 34 (for Ps. 34:19 concludes, 'Many are the afflictions of the righteous' before adding, 'but the LORD delivers him out of them all'). It rather suggests an enjoyment of life and contentment in the life God has given, no matter what the outward circumstances (*cf.* Eph. 5:20; Phil. 4:4, 7, 11; 1 Thes. 5:16–18). On *guile*, see the note at 2:1.

To *seek peace and pursue it* recalls Jesus' statement, 'Blessed are the peacemakers' (Mt. 5:9). To work for reconciliation and harmony among people (rather than returning evil for evil) is pleasing to God.

The phrase *the eyes of the Lord are upon the righteous* implies not merely that God sees what the righteous are doing (for that would be no greater privilege than that experienced by all people), but that he is looking after them for good, recognizing and meeting their needs (note the affirmations of God's timely care in Ps. 34:7, 8, 10, 17, 18, 19–20, 22). By contrast, the statement *But the face of the Lord is against those that do evil* is, in the context of Psalm 34, clearly a verdict of judgment, for the verse continues, 'to cut off the remembrance of them from the earth' (Ps. 34:16).

Verses 8 to 12 as a whole should not be taken as evidence for final salvation by good works, for they are addressed to those who are already Christians and already have an imperishable 'inheritance' kept for them in heaven (1:4). Yet this passage does present a bold affirmation of the relation between righteous living and God's present blessing in this life. As such it provides a needed corrective to careless, half-hearted Christians living in any age, and a powerful motivation to the kind of holy living to which Peter says all Christians have been 'called' (v. 9).

3. How to act when you suffer for righteousness (3:13 – 4:19)

a. Know that you are blessed (3:13–14a)

13. Here Peter begins a new section dealing specifically with the problem of persecution by unbelievers. Although this theme has been hinted at in 1:6; 2:12, 15, 19; 3:1 and 9, this is the first time Peter confronts persecution as his primary subject and deals with it at length.

In the first sentence, the phrase *to harm you* may also be translated 'who will harm you' or 'who is going to harm you' (NIV). The sentence is a rhetorical question with the force, 'Is there really anyone who will harm those who are eager to do good?' It implies that harm is not the normal expectation, for usually those who do what is right are rewarded, not punished. (This is a witness to the restraining influence of God's 'common grace' given to all people, as it finds expression in conscience and human government.)

14a. None the less, this is not always so. Though persecution of the righteous is abnormal, it does happen, so Peter recognizes the possibility that Christians may *suffer for righteousness' sake.* The verb form (optative) is the one a writer would use to speak of an event he considered unlikely, and the phrase *even if* contributes further to the sense of unlikelihood implied. (Though suffering of all kinds may be widespread, suffering *for righteousness' sake* may still be unlikely.) Yet Peter must realize that this 'unlikely' possibility is happening to some of his readers, and he must tell them how to respond.

You will be blessed (or, 'you are blessed'; the Gk. text does not contain a verb but a plural adjective which applies to the readers, 'if you suffer . . . (you) blessed ones', and it most naturally indicates blessing which comes at the same time as the suffering, not after it). This blessing includes the favour of God in general, but more specifically the readers would think of the blessing promised to the 'righteous' in verse 12. The word *makarios* ('blessed') has the sense 'blessed, happy', with emphasis on blessing which comes from God (*cf.* Mt. 5:11–12).

b. Trust Christ (3:14b-15a)

14b. Peter makes specific reference to the persecutors when he says, *Have no fear of them.* The passage is an inexact but fairly close quotation from Isaiah 8:12–13 (LXX), which (at least in the Heb. text) is a warning not to fear what the faithless people fear (see NIV). But this context does not concern avoiding the groundless fears which unbelievers experience: it rather counsels Christians not to be afraid when facing hostile opposition. So the sense, 'Do not fear a fear of them' or 'Do not fear them' is preferable, and it is certainly an acceptable way of translating Peter's words.[1]

Though it is generally better to understand New Testament citations of the Old Testament as carrying the same sense in both places, where the New Testament context strongly favours a slight change of sense or referent we must adopt an interpretation which is faithful to its new context (especially when, as in this case, there is no formal citation but simply a duplication of several expressions). Peter is apparently borrowing a familiar phrase from the Old Testament but using it in a different context and with different application.

Nor be troubled uses a term (*tarassō*) which means 'be shaken up, disturbed, frightened', and often implies emotional turmoil (note its use in Mt. 2:3; 14:26; Jn. 13:21; 14:1; *etc.*).

15a. The alternative to fear is to focus attention on someone else: *But in your hearts reverence Christ as Lord. Reverence* translates *hagiazō*, which normally means 'sanctify, make holy', but here seems to have the sense, 'treat as holy, regard reverently' (it has a similar sense in Mt. 6:9, 'hallowed be thy name', or 'may your name be reverenced'). The phrase is also an adaptation of part of Isaiah 8:13, 'But the LORD of hosts, him you shall regard as holy; let him be your fear, and let him be your dread.' Thus the sense of fear or reverence for the Lord rather than fear of men is reinforced – yet Peter stops short of applying to Christ the admonitions to 'fear' the Lord in Isaiah 8:13. To *reverence Christ*

---

[1]Note a very similar construction in 3:6, 'not fearing any fear'; *cf.* also Mk. 4:41, 'they feared a great fear' (*i.e.* 'they were greatly afraid'); Mt. 2:10. This is a common Heb. idiom ('cognate accusative') found frequently also in the LXX; *cf.* BDF, sec. 153 and Robertson, *Grammar*, pp. 477–479.

as Lord means really to believe that Christ, not one's human opponents, is truly in control of events. To have such reverence *in your hearts* is to maintain continually a deep-seated inward confidence in Christ as reigning Lord and King, who even now has 'angels, authorities, and powers subject to him' (3:22).

c. Use this opportunity to witness while doing right (3:15b–17)

15b. Yet the stance of Christians toward unbelievers must never be merely passive or neutral, and Peter does not stop with an admonition not to fear. He goes on to encourage preparation for active witness which will win the unbeliever to Christ. Peter envisages the need to respond to allegations of wrongdoing which Christians face from their opponents, so he says: *Always be prepared to make a defence to any one who calls you to account for the hope that is in you.* The word *defence* (*apologia*) almost always has a sense of 'reply to an accusation' (*cf.* Acts 22:1; 25:16; 1 Cor. 9:3; Phil. 1:7, 16). Although some maintain that formal legal charges are in view here (so Beare, p. 164), Kelly's point that *always* and *any one* are extremely general (p. 143) is well taken: whether to formal charges or informal accusations, Christians should be prepared to give an answer (Kelly notes the non-technical uses of *apologia* in 1 Cor. 9:3; 2 Cor. 7:11; Plato, *Politicus* 285e).

However, since the questioning is concerning *the hope that is in you*, Peter must be assuming that the inward hope of Christians results in lives so noticeably different that unbelievers are prompted to ask why they are so distinctive (*cf.* 4:4). Christians therefore should always be ready (prepared) to give an answer. Paul provides a good example of seizing the offensive and bearing testimony to Christ even when on trial himself (Acts 22:1–21; 24:10–24; 26:1–23, 25b–29). In hostile situations the opportunity for witness to Christ often comes unexpectedly; the Christian who is not always ready to answer will miss it.

Yet such witness must be given *with gentleness and reverence*, not attempting to overpower the unbeliever with the force of human personality or aggressiveness, but trusting the Holy Spirit himself quietly to persuade the listener. (The word *gentleness* and its related adjective 'gentle' are discussed in the note at 3:4.)

16. *Keep your conscience clear* (or 'good, morally right': *agathos*) demands far more than mere outward morality. This does not imply that sinless perfection is possible, but it does imply that a Christian should aim to have a 'good conscience' before God. This can be maintained by (1) avoiding conscious or wilful disobedience to God throughout each day; and (2) continuing to practise immediate repentance and prayer for forgiveness (and therefore for a cleansing of the conscience) whenever one becomes aware of any sin in one's life.

While other parts of the New Testament mention effectiveness in prayer (1 Jn. 3:21–22) and confidence of access to God in worship (Heb. 10:22) as benefits of a clear conscience, here witness to others is the motive: Christians should keep their consciences clear *so that, when you are abused, those who revile your good behaviour in Christ may be put to shame.* (A similar motive for righteous conduct is given in 2:12, 15; *cf.* 3:1–2.) *Abused* refers to verbal, not physical abuse, since it translates *katalaleō*, 'speak evil of' (the same term is used in 2:12, and three times in Jas. 4:11). *Revile* implies insulting or threatening speech, while *behaviour* represents *anastrophē*, the word Peter frequently uses to speak of conduct or pattern of life (see note at 1:15). The hope that opponents will *be put to shame* does not suggest that their shame is something good in itself, but that it will issue in the silencing of their slander and subsequently in their considering and believing the gospel (*cf.* 2:12, 15; Mt. 5:16; Rom. 12:20–21).

17. Developing a theme he had touched on earlier when addressing servants (2:19–20), Peter again emphasizes the value of suffering unjustly. Although the RSV translates *it is better to suffer for doing right . . . than for doing wrong*, the Greek text does not make it explicit that the suffering is specifically *for* the right that one does; this sense has to be derived from the larger context (see v. 14, where Peter speaks of suffering 'for righteousness' sake'). The phrase *if that should be God's will* again (as in v. 14) uses the unusual optative mood, indicating something which Peter thought possible but unusual, not ordinarily to be expected.

But why is it *better* to suffer for doing right than for doing wrong? In this context, it is because such wrongful suffering patiently endured is so remarkable that it becomes a powerful form of witness, leading unbelievers to salvation (*cf.* 2:12; 3:1–2). This understanding is confirmed by the following verse, which shows that Christ himself also suffered unjustly 'that he might bring us to God'. (Verse 18 begins with a *hoti*, 'for, because', indicating that the verse gives a reason to support v. 17.) Just as Christ endured unjust suffering for our salvation, Peter reasons, so we are blessed by God if we endure unjust suffering for the salvation of others.

Of course, the parallel is not complete at every point, for Jesus' suffering not only bore witness, but also actually earned our salvation because he died as our substitute (see notes at 1:19; 2:24). By contrast we can in no sense bear the wrath of God against the sins of others. None the less the example of Christ's willingness to suffer for our sake provides a powerful encouragement for us to be willing even to suffer while witnessing, in order that others might be saved (*cf.* Col. 1:24). This kind of suffering is much 'better', for deserved suffering because of wrong one has done is hardly a witness to others.

(i) For Christ suffered in order to bring you to God (3:18)

18. For the purpose of this verse, see the discussion of verse 17 above. Instead of *died* (*apothnēskō*) many manuscripts have 'suffered' (*paschō*), which makes the connection with 'suffer' in verse 17 more explicit. But since Christ's suffering for sins resulted in his death, this would make little difference to the sense (the textual evidence clearly favours 'died', but some think it abrupt for the context). The difference between *bring us to God* (RSV, NASB) and 'bring you to God' (NIV) is also based on a difference among ancient Greek manuscripts, and again carries no great significance for the overall force of the passage.

Peter says that Christ died *once* (Gk. *hapax*, meaning 'one time, once') and this, together with the verb tense of *died*, indicates that Christ's suffering and dying for sins has been completed. The words *for all* are not intended by the RSV translators to mean 'for all people', but simply 'for all time' (the words do not represent an additional phrase in the Greek text but are simply part of the translation of *hapax*, 'once').

Christ's death was *for sins*, a compressed way of saying that he paid the penalty for our sins. This is made more explicit when Peter adds *the righteous for the unrighteous* – more literally, 'the righteous one (singular) for unrighteous people (plural)'. Precisely because Christ had no guilt of his own to pay for (he was 'righteous'), he could be the substitute who died in our place, bearing the punishment we deserved.

Being put to death in the flesh indicates the fact that Jesus' 'flesh' or physical body was put to death (so NIV: 'He was put to death in the body'). Although 'flesh' (*sarx*) has a range of meanings in the New Testament, whenever, as here, 'flesh' is contrasted with 'spirit' (*pneuma*), the contrast is between physical, visible things which belong to this present world and invisible things which can exist in the unseen 'spiritual' world of heaven and the age to come. (See 4:6; *cf.* Mt. 26:41; Mk. 14:38; Jn. 3:6; Rom. 8:4–6; 1 Tim. 3:16; *etc.*)

But made alive in the spirit, in view of the contrast noted above, must mean 'made alive in the spiritual realm, in the realm of the Spirit's activity'. Here it refers specifically to Christ's resurrection, because 'made alive' must be the opposite of 'put to death' in the previous phrase. 'In the spiritual realm, the realm of the Holy Spirit's activity, Christ was raised from the dead.' This is important because in the New Testament generally this 'spiritual' realm is the realm of all that is lasting, permanent, eternal.

The NIV translation 'but made alive by the Spirit' (similarly, AV), is also possible since there is no distinction in Greek between 'spirit' and 'Spirit'. But it would be somewhat unusual to expect readers to see exactly the same grammatical structure (in Greek) in parallel parts of the same sentence, and yet to know that Peter wanted the two parts understood differently (put to death *in* the body but made alive *by* the Spirit).

The contrast *put to death in the flesh but made alive in the spirit* fits in with the whole letter's emphasis on the relative unimportance of temporary suffering in this world compared to the enjoying of an eternal inheritance in the next (*cf.* 1:6–7, 8, 11, 13, 23; 2:11; 3:3–4, 14; 4:1–2, 6, 13, 14, 16, 19; 5:1, 4, 10). Our Lord willingly suffered physical harm, even death, for the sake of eternal, spiritual gain – *that he might bring us to God*. Peter's readers should not therefore be surprised to find themselves 'following in his steps'.

(ii) Another example: Noah witnessed when persecuted (3:19–20)

19. *In which* refers back to 'in the spirit' in verse 18.[1] It means 'in which realm, namely, the spiritual realm'. It does not necessarily mean 'in the resurrection body'[2] (which Peter could easily have said, had he wanted to), but rather 'in the realm of the Spirit's activity' (the realm in which Christ was raised from the dead, v. 18).

Peter frequently makes a transition from one section to another by the use of a relative pronoun like this ('which' or 'whom'), and it should indicate to us that the following statements, while related to the overall argument of the section, may introduce a different subject. The pattern of introducing related but clearly distinct subjects in this way (sometimes with, sometimes without, a preposition) is seen in 1:6, 8, 10; 2:4, 22; and 3:21; and, with transitions to less different but none the less distinct material, in 1:12; 3:3, 6b; 4:4; and 5:9.[3]

The Greek text has the word *kai*, 'and, also', following *in which*, giving the sense, 'in which *also* he went . . .'. This simply adds emphasis to the impression that a distinct subject is being introduced: Christ was made alive in the spiritual realm (v. 18), and he also did something else in the spiritual realm (vv. 19–20).

That other action is this: *He went and preached to the spirits in prison.* The meaning of this phrase is much disputed. The issues are:

1. Who are the spirits in prison?
   – unbelievers who have died?
   – Old Testament believers who have died?
   – fallen angels?

---

[1]Selwyn, pp.197, 315, 317 says 'in which' (*en hō*) cannot refer to 'in the spirit' in v. 18, because there are no other instances in the NT where a relative pronoun (here , *hō*, 'which') has as its antecedent an 'adverbial dative'. This objection is unpersuasive, however, and factually incorrect (see discussion in Appendix, pp. 227f.).

[2]As argued by France, pp.268–269. France rightly sees the contrast in v. 18 as between the 'natural human sphere of existence' and the 'eternal spiritual state of existence' (p. 267), but then (p. 268) overly restricts the 'eternal, spiritual sphere' to mean only the resurrected state of Christ. The 'flesh-spirit' contrast in v. 18 is rather between two spheres of activity than between the pre- and post-resurrection states of Christ.

[3]Reicke, pp. 110–111, understands *en hō* to mean not 'in which' but 'on which occasion' (as in 2:12; 3:16). But the words and the phrase itself are so common that there is no reason to think that Peter only used it in one specialized way: relative pronouns should be understood to refer to whichever (grammatically correct) antecedent makes the most sense in each

2. What did Christ preach?
   – second chance for repentance?
   – completion of redemptive work?
   – final condemnation?
3. When did he preach?
   – in the days of Noah?
   – between his death and resurrection?
   – after his resurrection?

Various answers have been given to these questions; the five most common views are set out in the Appendix on p. 204. The following discussion will argue for View 1, *i.e.* that Christ was preaching through Noah when the ark was being built. (For a fuller discussion of these two verses, see the Appendix, pp. 203ff.)[1]

Taken by itself, the phrase *spirits in prison* could refer either to human spirits in hell or to fallen angelic spirits in hell. 2 Peter 2:4 and Jude 6 speak of sinful angels being imprisoned and punished, while Luke 16:23–24 and 2 Peter 2:9 refer to unbelievers who have died and are in a place of punishment. The word *spirits* could refer either to angelic spirits, good and evil (Mt. 8:16; Heb. 1:14) or to human spirits of people who have died (Mt. 27:50; Lk. 23:46; Jn. 19:30; Acts 7:59; 1 Cor. 5:5; Heb. 12:23; Eccl. 12:7). This is also the case in extra-biblical literature. (For example, in 1 Enoch, which Selwyn and Dalton claim as their primary evidence for View 5 [see appendix, p. 207], *pneuma* refers twenty times to angelic spirits and seventeen times to human spirits, and in both cases the spirits are imprisoned and awaiting final judgment.) Some contend that when 'spirit' is found without a defining phrase attached to it (like 'of men', *etc.*), it means angelic or demonic spirits, never human spirits. But this argument is invalid, for *pneuma* by itself is simply ambiguous, and in every case where it means 'angelic spirit' as well as every case where it means 'human spirit' the context makes it clear what kind of spirit is meant.

particular context. Here, 'spirit' is near at hand and makes good sense; it is the antecedent Peter's readers would have naturally understood.

[1]In the Appendix, I examine the arguments of Selwyn and Dalton in detail and compare them with an extensive survey of extra-biblical literature.

20. The spirits in prison are those *who formerly did not obey* (better: 'disobeyed', since the word has a sense of active rebellion), *when God's patience waited in the days of Noah, during the building of the ark.* These phrases indicate that only human spirits can be intended, for nowhere in the Bible or in Jewish literature outside of the Bible are angels ever said to have disobeyed 'during the building of the ark'. Genesis 6:5–13 clearly emphasizes the *human* sin which provoked God to flood the earth in judgment. Furthermore, extra-biblical literature, some of which was probably familiar to many of Peter's readers, frequently describes the mockery which Noah had to endure from his contemporaries, *e.g.* 'They derided him and said, "Old man, what is this ark for?"' (*b.Sanh.* 108b). *When God's patience waited in the days of Noah* also suggests human, rather than angelic, disobedience. God's patience waited for human beings to repent before bringing the judgment of the flood (this is also a frequent theme in extra-biblical literature), but never is there any hint that fallen angels have a chance to repent – it is only given to sinful human beings (*cf.* 2 Pet. 2:4; Jude 6).

But why does Peter refer to 'spirits' if he has in view disobedience by human beings who were not just 'spirits' but bodies as well? This is best explained by understanding the text to mean 'spirits who are now in prison' (*i.e.* at the time Peter was writing), but who were people on earth at the time of Noah, when Christ was preaching to them. (The NASB translates, 'the spirits *now* in prison'.) A similar expression is found a few verses later at 4:6, 'For this is why the gospel was preached even to the dead', which is best understood to mean 'the gospel was preached to those who are now dead' (but who were alive when the gospel was preached to them; see discussion below). One can speak the same way in English: 'Queen Elizabeth was born in 1926' is an appropriate statement, even though she was not Queen when she was born – we mean 'She who is now Queen Elizabeth was born in 1926.'

The phrase *who formerly did not obey* is better translated 'when they formerly disobeyed',[1] thus specifying that this was the time when Christ 'in spirit' preached to these people: *i.e. 'when they*

---

[1] See below, pp. 233–236, for discussion of grammatical point.

formerly disobeyed when God's patience was waiting in the days of Noah, during the building of the ark.' Peter elsewhere mentions ideas similar to the thought that Christ 'in spirit' preached through Noah, for in 1:11 the Spirit of Christ is said to have been active in the prophets of the Old Testament era (*cf.* 1 Cor. 10:4).

Although Peter does not specifically call Noah a prophet in 2 Peter 2:5, he terms him a 'herald of righteousness', and uses the noun (*kēryx*) which is related to the verb 'preached' (*kēryssō*) in 3:20.

By saying that Christ *went and preached* rather than just saying that he 'preached', Peter suggests that Christ did not stay in heaven but 'went' to where people were disobeying, and there preached to them through the lips of Noah. The content of this preaching was not a message of final condemnation (see Views 3 and 5 on p. 204) or the completion of redemption (see View 4 on p. 204), but concerned the need to repent and come to God for salvation. This is what Noah would have preached to those around him (even without extra-biblical literature we would draw this conclusion from 2 Pet. 2:4). It is the right message to preach when people are disobeying 'while God's patience is waiting' (*cf.* 2 Pet. 3:9).

This interpretation is very appropriate to the larger context of 3:13–22. The parallel between the situation of Noah and the situation of Peter's readers is clear at several points:

(1) Noah and his family were a minority surrounded by hostile unbelievers; so are Peter's readers (vv. 13–14; 4:4, 12–13).

(2) Noah was righteous in the midst of a wicked world. Peter exhorts his readers to be righteous in the midst of wicked unbelievers (vv. 13–14, 16–17; 4:3–4).

(3) Noah witnessed boldly to those around him. Peter encourages his readers to be good witnesses to unbelievers around them (vv. 14, 16–17), being willing to suffer, if need be, to bring others to God (just as Christ was willing to suffer and die 'that he might bring us to God', v. 18).

(4) Noah realized that judgment was soon to come upon the world. Peter reminds his readers that God's judgment is certainly coming, perhaps soon (4:5, 7; 2 Pet. 3:10).

(5) In the unseen 'spiritual' realm Christ preached through Noah to unbelievers around him. By saying this Peter can

remind his readers of the reality of Christ's work in the unseen spiritual realm and the fact that Christ is also in them, empowering their witness and making it spiritually effective (*cf.* 1:8, 11, 12, 25; 2:4). Therefore, they should not fear (v. 14) but in their hearts should 'reverence Christ as Lord' and should 'always be prepared' to tell of the hope that is in them (v. 15).

(6) At the time of Noah, God was patiently awaiting repentance from unbelievers, before he brought judgment. So it is in the situation of Peter's readers: God is patiently awaiting repentance from unbelievers (*cf.* 2 Pet. 3:9) before bringing judgment on the world (*cf.* 2 Pet. 3:10).

(7) Noah was finally saved, with 'a few' others. Peter thus encourages his readers that, though perhaps few, they too will finally be saved, for Christ has triumphed and has all things subject to him (3:22; 4:13, 19; 5:10; 2 Pet. 2:9).

This passage, once cleared of misunderstanding, should also function today as an encouragement to us to be bold in our witness (as Noah was), to be confident that, though we may be few, God will certainly save us (as he did Noah), and to remind us that just as certainly as the flood eventually came, so final judgment will certainly come to our world as well, and Christ will ultimately triumph over all the evil in the universe.

At the end of verse 20, Peter mentions that in the ark *a few, that is, eight persons, were saved through water*. Although this is the usual translation, it is more likely that the sense is '*into* which (*i.e.* the ark) a few, that is, eight persons, *escaped through* water'.[1] This is a common sense of the verb *diasōzō* in this form (aorist passive/deponent: so Gn. 19:19; Jos. 10:20; Jdg. 3:26; 2 Ki. (LXX 4 Ki.) 19:37, A text; Is. 37:38 [all with *diasōzō* plus *eis* in the sense 'escaped to . . .']; Acts 27:44; 28:1, 4), and the idea that Noah and his family 'escaped through water' is consistent with Genesis 7:13, which specifies that Noah and his family entered the ark 'on this same day' as the flood came (v. 11). The advantage of this translation is that it gives the preposition *dia* its very common sense 'through', as well as allowing *eis* to mean 'into' (its most common sense) rather than just 'in' (for which we

[1] I am following here the perceptive analysis of David Cook, *JTS* 31 (1980), pp. 72–78. Cook lists several other parallel examples from secular Greek writers where this construction means 'escaped into . . .'.

might have expected *en*), and it follows the sense of the construction as it is used elsewhere.

The mention of 'eight persons' is one of many New Testament examples where seemingly minor details in the Old Testament are quoted as historically reliable. Peter picks up the detail about Noah entering the ark with his wife, his three sons, and their wives (Gn. 6:10; 7:7) and affirms its truth. God shows his mercy to the family of a righteous man (including even children by marriage), enabling each of them to give heed to Noah's preaching and be saved, despite the extreme wickedness (Gn. 6:5) around them.[1]

(iii) God will save you (as he did Noah and Christ) (3:21-22)

21. 'Through water' (v. 20) leads Peter to make a transition to baptism: *Baptism, which corresponds to this, now saves you. . . .* The grammar of the Greek text is puzzling, but the RSV translation given here represents a good understanding of the force of the words. If our understanding of 'escaped through water' in verse 20 is correct, then the word *which* (*ho*) at the beginning of the verse refers back to 'escaping through water'. Baptism *corresponds to* escaping through water in that the water of baptism is in some ways a counterpart to the waters of the flood. For if, as is nearly certain, baptism when Peter wrote was by immersion (going completely under the water – note how incongruous the mention of 'removal of dirt from the body' would be if Peter thought that only a few drops of water were sprinkled on the head), then going down into the waters of baptism was a vivid symbol of going down into the grave in death. (*Cf.* 'we were buried therefore with him by baptism into death', Rom. 6:4.)

The water of baptism is like waters of judgment – similar to the waters of the flood, and showing clearly what we deserve

[1]Verses 18 to 19 have sometimes been used to support the idea that between his death and resurrection Christ 'descended into hell'. The phrase itself comes from the Apostles' Creed ('suffered under Pontius Pilate, was crucified, dead, and buried, he descended into hell; the third day he rose again from the dead . . .'), while scriptural support for this concept has been found primarily in 1 Pet. 3:18–19, along with Acts 2:27, 31; Rom. 10:7; Eph. 4:8–9; and 1 Pet. 4:6. However, many question whether any of these texts clearly support this idea, and the phrase itself is a late addition – it does not appear in any versions of the Apostles' Creed until AD 390 and then not again until AD 650 (see Phillip Schaff, *Creeds of Christendom* [New York: Harper, 1882], vol. 2, p. 54). Against the view that Christ descended into hell may be mentioned Lk. 23:43, 46; Jn. 19:30.

for our sins. Coming up out of the waters of baptism corresponds to being kept safe through the waters of the flood, the waters of God's judgment on sin, and emerging to live in 'newness of life' (*cf.* Rom. 6:4). Baptism thus shows us clearly that in one sense we have 'died' and 'been raised' again, but in another sense we emerge from the waters knowing that we are still alive and have passed through the waters of God's judgment unharmed. As Noah fled into the ark, so we flee to Christ, and in him we escape judgment.

But what does Peter mean by saying that *baptism . . . now saves you*? It saves you *not as a removal of dirt from the body*[1] (*i.e.* not as an outward, physical act which washes dirt from the body – that is not the part which saves you), *but as an appeal to God for a clear conscience* (*i.e.* as an inward, spiritual transaction between God and the individual, a transaction symbolized by the outward ceremony of baptism). We could paraphrase, 'Baptism now saves you – not the outward physical ceremony of baptism but the inward spiritual reality which baptism represents.' Thus Peter guards against any 'magical' view of baptism which would attribute saving power to the physical ceremony itself.

An appeal to God for a clear conscience is another way of saying 'a request for forgiveness of sins and a new heart'. When God gives a sinner a *clear conscience*, that person has the assurance that every sin has been forgiven and that he or she stands in a right relationship with God (Heb. 9:14 and 10:22 speak this way about the cleansing of one's conscience through Christ). To be baptized rightly is to make such an appeal to God: 'Please, God, as I enter this baptism which will cleanse my body outwardly I am asking you to cleanse my heart inwardly, forgive my sins, make me right before you.' In this way baptism is an appropriate symbol for the beginning of the Christian life. Once we understand baptism in this way, we can appreciate why 'Repent, and be baptized . . . for the forgiveness of your sins' (Acts 2:38) was an evangelistic command in the early church.

Some have argued that 'pledge' is a better word than *appeal*

---

[1]Kelly (pp. 161–162) follows Dalton (pp. 215–224) in seeing 'removal of dirt from the body' as a reference to circumcision. But they adduce no direct linguistic parallels, only some expressions which are conceptually similar at certain points, but dissimilar at others, and the argument is unpersuasive.

(NIV: 'the pledge of a good conscience towards God'). This is because *eperōtēma*, which usually means 'question', has not elsewhere been found with the meaning 'appeal'. It has the sense 'pledge' in later Greek papyri (but none at the time of the NT – the earliest is 2nd century AD; *cf.* LSJ, p. 618), so this meaning has been advocated here (so Selwyn, pp. 205–206). However, 'pledge' is still a derived sense which may have come into use after the time of the New Testament.

Moreover, although no examples have been discovered of the noun meaning 'appeal', the related verb is used with the sense to 'make a request, ask for something' (Mt. 16:1, 'they asked him to show them a sign from heaven'). So this word may well have been easily understandable to Peter's readers in the sense 'request'.

More importantly, 'pledge' introduces a theological problem. If baptism is a 'pledge to God' to maintain a good conscience (or a pledge – to live an obedient life – which flows from a good conscience), then the emphasis is no longer on dependence on God to give salvation but on dependence on one's own effort or strength of resolve. And since this phrase is so clearly connected with the beginning of the Christian life as the thing about baptism which 'saves you', the translation 'pledge' seems to be inconsistent with the New Testament teaching on salvation by faith alone: it would be the only place where a promise to be righteous is said to be the thing which 'saves you'. And since the lexical data are inconclusive for both senses (while suggesting that both senses are apparently possible), it is better to adopt the translation 'appeal' as a sense much more in accord with the rest of the New Testament.

Those who support the view that only people who are old enough to profess faith in Christ should be baptized might well see in this verse some support for their position: baptism, it might be argued, is appropriately administered to anyone who is old enough personally to make 'an appeal to God for a clear conscience'.

Yet it is not even a request to God for a clean conscience which actually provides the basis for our salvation. That salvation has ultimately been earned for us by Christ, and all that baptism represents comes to us not on the merits of any response from us, but *through the resurrection of Jesus Christ.* His resurrection marked his once-and-for-all exit from the realm of death and judgment on sin, and our union with him in his resurrection is the means by which God gives us new life (see note at 1:3, above). Our rising out of the waters of baptism is a picture of our being raised with Christ; by being brought safely through these 'waters of judgment' through Christ's resurrection we are indeed given a clear conscience by God. (The sense 'pledge' would not fit this idea of a clear conscience as a gift from God nearly as well.)

22. Peter completes this discussion with a mention of Christ's ascension into heaven. Jesus Christ *has gone into heaven* and now *is at the right hand of God.* Though modern thinkers largely reject such a notion, the New Testament writers do not hesitate to talk about heaven in spatial terms.

Jesus' ascension to heaven also was the occasion when he received new authority and power which he had not had before as God-man. (Though, as God the Son, he had possessed infinite power for all eternity, he had not previously exercised this power in the role of the person who was both God and man.) Peter emphasizes this by saying that Jesus *is at the right hand of God.* In the ancient world, to sit at the right hand of a king signified that one acted with the king's authority and power (*cf.* Ps. 110:1 and Eph. 1:20–21, with similar emphasis on authority). This theme of Christ's 'session' (*i.e.* his sitting at God's right hand) is often mentioned in the New Testament (Mt. 22:44, 26:64; Acts 2:33–34; 5:31; 7:56; Rom. 8:34; Col. 3:1; Heb. 1:3, 13; 10:12; 12:2; *cf.* Ps. 110:1). It is used by the New Testament authors as an indication of Christ's present universal authority, the finality of his completed work of redemption, and his immeasurable worthiness to receive our praise (note Phil. 2:9; 1 Tim. 3:16; Rev. 5:12). Moreover, Christ's ascension foreshadows our future ascension and rule with him (1 Thes. 4:17; Rev. 2:26–27; 3:21).

Peter focuses here on Christ's authority in the unseen spiritual world: he has *angels, authorities, and powers subject to him.* The three terms can be applied to both good and evil spiritual beings elsewhere in Scripture, and without specific restrictions in the context it is best to understand them as a reference to all spiritual beings in the universe, both good and evil. When Paul says not only that we have been raised with Christ but also that God has 'made us sit with him in the heavenly places' (Eph. 2:6), it indicates that even now Christians have a share in the spiritual authority which belongs to Christ, an authority which finds expression in our lives especially in terms of power in spiritual warfare (2 Cor. 10:3–4; Eph. 6:10–18), freedom from fearing demonic powers (Eph. 6:13; Jas.4:7; 1 Pet. 5:9; 1 Jn. 4:4), and authority to rebuke, if need be, the demonic forces which oppose us (Lk. 10:17–20; Acts 16:18).

d. Decide that you are willing to sufer for righteousness (4:1–6)

(i) For a Christian who has suffered for doing right has made a clear break with sin (4:1–2)

1. *Since therefore Christ suffered in the flesh* resumes the theme Peter had begun in 3:18, the value of imitating Christ's example of willingness to suffer, if necessary, in order to do God's will. But whereas there his concern was to encourage his readers to give a good Christian witness, here his emphasis shifts to the related theme of willingness to suffer in order to avoid sinning.

Arm yourselves with the same thought means to think as Christ did about obedience and suffering: to be convinced that it is better to do right and suffer for it than to do wrong (*cf.* 3:17–18). The word *thought* means here not so much an attitude of mind but the insight which one has gained into the nature of God's dealings with people.

There is a motive for this: they should be willing, like Christ, to suffer for doing right *for whoever has suffered in the flesh has ceased from sin*. As a general statement, without qualification, this would not be true, for there are many people who have suffered physically and yet still sin very much. Nor is Peter simply saying that physical suffering somehow purifies and strengthens people – it strengthens some, but others become rebellious toward God and embittered. Rather, we must read the sentence in the light of the theme of suffering for doing right which is found in the preceding context (3:14, 16–18). The kind of suffering in the flesh which Peter means is defined by 3:17:

'For it is better to suffer for doing right, if that should be God's will, than for doing wrong.'

Therefore *whoever has suffered in the flesh has ceased from sin* means 'whoever has suffered for doing right, and has still gone on obeying God in spite of the suffering it involved, has made a clear break with sin'. The phrase *has ceased from sin* cannot mean 'no longer sins at all', for certainly that is not true of everyone who has been willing to suffer for doing right, and several passages in Scripture rule out the idea that anyone can be absolutely free from sin in this life (1 Ki. 8:46; Pr. 20:9; Ec. 7:20; Jas. 3:2; 1 Jn. 1:8). It rather means 'has made a clear break with sin', 'has most definitely acted in a way which shows that obeying God, not avoiding hardship, is the most important motivation for his or her action'. Thus, following through with a decision to obey God even when it will mean physical suffering has a morally strengthening effect on our lives: it commits us more firmly than ever before to a pattern of action where obedience is even more important than our desire to avoid pain.

2. Peter now explains 'ceasing from sin' in more detail. It is for the purpose of living a life governed not by human feelings but by God's will: one breaks clearly with sin *so as to live for the rest of the time in the flesh* (*i.e.* the rest of one's life on earth) *no longer by human passions but by the will of God*. (See note on the word for *passions* at 1:14.)

Of course the initial repentance from sin which is part of any genuine conversion to Christ is also in some sense a 'clear break with sin' and a resolve to live 'not by human passions but by the will of God'. But Peter here seems to be saying that obeying God, even though the price is physical suffering, involves an even stronger moral commitment than that first decision of the will. Yet we must be careful not to make this into some kind of uniform 'second experience' which all mature believers must experience in the same way. Rather, Peter is speaking of something which may happen many or few times in a Christian's life, and with many different degrees of intensity. For Christians living under hostile governments the suffering endured may be great indeed; for those living elsewhere something related to such suffering 'in the flesh' may be seen in less intense form in physical weariness or other discomfort which one endures in order to be obedient to God's will.

(ii) Give no more time to sin (4:3)

3. *Let the time that is past suffice* is not the best translation because it omits the conjunction 'for' with which Peter begins the sentence. This verse supplies a reason for living not 'by human passions' but 'by the will of God' (v. 2). Why should Peter's readers not live by following (sinful) human passions? Because they have done enough living like that in 'the time that is past'. Peter does not just encourage them to 'let the time that is past' be sufficient experience of sin; he tells them bluntly that their past experience of sin *is* sufficient! They should not want to live any longer the kind of life which was given to following sinful human desires. To the Christian who wonders whether ever in the future he or she might indulge in one more unrestrained time of sin, one more time of *doing what the Gentiles like to do*, Peter's answer is clear: The 'time that is past' is 'sufficient', is 'enough' of living that way. Indeed, those who live that way will someday have to give an account to God (v. 5).

He then explains what he means by *doing what the Gentiles like to do*. (Since Peter has frequently viewed Christians as the new people of God, the true Israel, earlier in this letter [see the summary at 2:10] it is quite natural for him to carry through this terminology by using the term '*Gentiles*' to refer not to people who are not Jews, but to people who are not Christians.)

To 'do what the Gentiles like to do' is to spend one's time *living in* various kinds of sin which Peter names. *Licentiousness* (*aselgeia*) is living without any regard for moral restraint, especially in giving oneself over to acts of sexual immorality or acts of physical violence (the same word is used in Rom. 13:13; Gal. 5:19; Eph. 4:19; 2 Pet. 2:7 [of Sodom]; 2:18; Philo, *Moses* 1.305). *Passions* (*epithymia*) are sinful human desires which can be allowed to exert strong influence on one's behaviour (see note at 1:14). *Drunkenness* (*oinophlygia*) is also characteristic of a life bent on following physical desires, as are *revels* (*kōmos*; banquets and feasts given to wild immorality) and *carousing* (*potos*; drinking parties or drinking bouts). The expression *law-*

less idolatry is actually plural (*athemitoi eidōlolatriai*), meaning 'lawless acts of idol worship'. The word *lawless* cannot mean 'against God's law', for all idol worship is that. *Lawless* here must rather mean 'against the civil laws' – implying particularly evil kinds of idol worship which involved or incited people to kinds of immorality even forbidden by the laws of human governments. This suggests that sensual living is often connected with idol worship and the demonic forces behind those idols which incite people to yet greater sin (*cf.* 1 Cor. 10:20, where, in a discussion of idol worship which uses this same word, *eidōlolatreia*, Paul says 'what pagans sacrifice they offer to demons and not to God').

(iii) There is a judgment coming for Gentiles who abuse you (4:4–5)

4. Such behaviour was part of the normal life of these Christians before their conversion, for their neighbours *are surprised that you do not now join them in the same wild profligacy.* The phrase *join them* is literally 'running with them', an expression which vividly reflects the frenetic pace of their continually disappointing search for true pleasure. *The same wild profligacy* is literally 'the same rapid pouring out of unrestrained indulgence' or 'the same torrent of debauchery' (NIV: 'that you do not plunge with them into the same flood of dissipation'). The word translated *profligacy* (*asōtia*) refers to uncontrolled indulgence in the seeking of pleasure (the same word is used in Eph. 5:18, and the related adverb is used of the 'loose living' of the prodigal son in Lk. 15:13 – it suggests wastefulness, perhaps both of money and of life). The whole picture is one of people rushing headlong toward destruction.

The fact that unbelievers are 'surprised' that Christians do not join in their profligacy suggests that Peter's readers included not only many who had been converted from Judaism, but also many won from a Gentile background, for there would be no surprise involved if former Jews, who had previously led a morally upright life, did not participate in pagan life.

But when Christians did not join in sins of unbelievers, the result was not just surprise. The unbelievers became hostile, for Peter says *they abuse you.* It is primarily verbal abuse and slander that are intended, for the term means 'speak evil of, defame, injure the reputation of someone' (so in Mt. 27:39; Lk. 22:65; 23:39; Rom. 3:8; 14:16; 1 Cor. 10:30; Tit. 3:2; 2 Pet. 2:2). Why did this happen? No doubt because silent non-participation in sin often implies condemnation of that sin, and rather than change their ways unbelievers will slander those who have pained their consciences, or justify their own immorality by spreading rumours that the 'righteous' Christians are immoral as well.

5. Yet unbelievers cannot escape responsibility for their actions as easily as that, for God will one day hold them accountable: *They will give account to him who is ready to judge the living and the dead.* The phrase *give account* is used of human accountability to an employer (Lk. 16:2) or to government authorities (Acts 19:40), and also of men's accountability to God at the final judgment (Mt. 12:36; Heb. 13:17). The fact that God is *ready* to judge suggests the possibility that judgment could come suddenly, without warning (*cf.* v. 7; Jas. 5:9; 2 Pet. 3:10). It is not only *the living* who will be judged, but also *the dead* – a statement which clearly implies that death will not enable anyone to escape judgment, but that all people will consciously stand before God on that day.

(iv) For the gospel was preached to Christians who have died to save them from eternal judgment (4:6)

6. In fact, it is the fate of believers who have now died to which Peter now turns. His readers may have wondered about the benefits of being a Christian for those believers who had already died. This may have included some who died as a direct result of persecution, but the text does not allow us to limit its application to such; it simply speaks of 'the dead'.

He says, *For this is why the gospel was preached even to the dead.* The word *this* refers back to the subject of the previous sentence, the final judgment. In other words, 'It was because of the coming final judgment that the gospel was preached, even to those who believed in Christ and then later died.' In this way *the dead* means 'those who are now dead' (when Peter was writing), though when the gospel was preached to them they were still living on the earth. (See discussion above on the similar expression 'the spirits in prison' at 3:19.) The NIV has 'those who are now dead'. The fact that they died should not trouble the minds of those left alive, for, short of the second coming of Christ, the gospel was never intended to save people from physical death. All people, both Christians and non-Christians, still have to die physically (and this is the apparent meaning of *judged in the flesh like men*). But even *though* they are *judged in the flesh like men* (the judgment of death which came with the sin of Adam still affects them as it does all men), the gospel of Christ *was preached* to them so that *they might live in the spirit like God*. It was with respect to the final judgment ('for this reason', referring to v. 5) that the gospel was preached, and it will save them from final condemnation.

The expressions *like men* and *like God* are legitimate translations (BAGD, p. 407, II.5.b; *cf.* 1 Pet. 1:15), but it is also possible to translate them 'according to men' and 'according to God' (NIV), *i.e.* 'according to the way men are judged generally' and 'according to the way God lives, in the spiritual realm'. There is not much difference between the views, for in both cases the expressions refer to physical death and to continuing spiritual life. (However, this translation may not be used to justify the sense 'in the opinion of men' and 'in the opinion or evaluation of God', for the Greek *kata* with accusative cannot take that specific sense of the English 'according to'; *cf.* BAGD, p. 407, II.5.)

Since *spirit* is without the definite article in the Greek text, it could be translated 'in the spiritual realm' (see the discussion at 3:18). We are assured here that believers who have died are none the less living and enjoying blessings in the unseen 'spiritual' and eternal realm, which is characterized by the Holy Spirit's activity.

On this interpretation, the word *dead* means 'believers who have died' here in verse 6, but 'all people who have died' in verse 5. Alford objects strongly to this, saying that if the same word can mean two different things so close together, then 'exegesis has no longer any fixed rule, and Scripture may be made to prove anything' (p. 374). But he himself takes 'judge' (*krinō*) in verse 5 to refer to final judgment, yet in verse 6 he says that *krinō* means something different, namely, physical death. There is no fixed rule in any language that when a word is used twice in close succession it *must* be used in the same sense both times. It is best simply to choose from the possible senses the one that best fits the context in each case. Moreover, in this case the senses 'all who have died (physically)' and 'believers who have died (physically)' are not far apart, and the transition in thought in the readers' minds would not be difficult.

Some have argued that *the gospel was preached even to the dead* in this verse means 'to those who are spiritually dead, or unbelievers'. But this is unconvincing because it allows no meaning to the word 'even', and does not fit the past tense of 'was preached' (preaching to the 'spiritually dead' was still happening when Peter was writing; it was not something confined to the past).

One other common view has been that this verse means that the gospel was preached to people after they died, giving them a 'second chance' to repent and believe the gospel. But such a meaning does not fit the context: what kind of warning would it be to say that God is ready to judge people for wickedness (v. 5) and then add that it really does not matter much what they do in this life for there will be a second chance for them to be saved after they die? Moreover, it could hardly encourage Peter's persecuted readers to persevere as Christians in the hard path of obedience if the easy road of debauchery could all be renounced and forgiven after they died. Finally, the entire missionary activity of the early church, as well as some specific texts of the New Testament (Lk. 16:26; Heb. 9:26–28; Mt. 25:10–13), argues against such a view.

e. This final judgment is near, so act this way within the church . . . (4:7–11)

(i) Pray more and love each other more (4:7–9)

7. *The end of all things is at hand* means that all the major events in God's plan of redemption have occurred, and now all things are ready for Christ to return and rule. Rather than thinking of world history in terms of earthly kings and kingdoms, Peter thinks in terms of 'redemptive history'. From that perspective all the previous acts in the drama of redemption have been completed – creation, fall, the calling of Abraham, the exodus from

Egypt, the kingdom of Israel, the exile in Babylon and the return, the birth of Christ, his life, death and resurrection, his ascension into heaven, and the pouring out of the Holy Spirit to establish the church. The great 'last act', the church age, had been continuing for about thirty years by the time Peter wrote. Thus the curtain could fall at any time, ushering in the return of Christ and the end of the age. All things are ready: *the end of all things* (the 'goal' to which 'all' these events have been leading) *is at hand*.

Christians who realize that the end of the age could happen at any time should act in a certain way: *therefore keep sane and sober for your prayers*. The word translated *sane* means 'having a sound mind, thinking about and evaluating situations maturely and correctly' (the same word and its related terms are used in Lk. 8:35; Rom. 12:3; 2 Tim. 1:7; Tit. 1:8). For *sober*, see comments at 1:13. Such attitudes of mind are in many ways opposite to the sins mentioned in verses 3 to 5.

The reason given for being *sane and sober* is *for your prayers*; the plural suggests specific, individual prayers throughout each day. The idea is not simply 'so that you can pray' (NIV), but 'in order to pray more effectively, more appropriately', Christians should be alert to events and evaluate them correctly in order to be able to pray more intelligently. Peter's words also imply that prayer based on knowledge and mature evaluation of a situation is more effective prayer (otherwise there would be no relationship between being 'sane and sober' and one's prayers). What this verse teaches could well be put into practice when reading the newspaper, listening to the news, travelling to work, and so on.

8. *Above all hold unfailing your love for one another* (*cf.* notes on the related verb for *love* [*agapaō*] at 1:22). *Unfailing* inadequately translates *ektenēs*, which here has the adverbial sense of 'earnestly'. A better translation is therefore 'keep loving one another earnestly' (see note on the cognate word *ektenōs* at 1:22). The reason for doing so is *since* (or 'because') *love covers a multitude of sins*. Where love abounds in a fellowship of Christians, many small offences, and even some large ones, are readily overlooked and forgotten. But where love is lacking, every word is viewed with suspicion, every action is liable to misunderstanding, and conflicts abound – to Satan's perverse delight (*cf.* Heb. 12:15; by contrast, 1 Cor. 13:4–7). A similar idea is expressed in Proverbs 10:12: 'Hatred stirs up strife, but love covers all offences.'

9. Earnest love, which seeks the good of others before one's own, finds practical expression in *hospitality* (v. 9) and in using every gift 'for one another' (v. 10). *Hospitality*, though a Christian duty, is to be offered *ungrudgingly to one another* without resenting the time and expense which may be involved. The words translated *ungrudgingly* are more literally 'without grumbling' or 'without murmuring' (the term is used to refer to repeated words of complaint, often spoken to others with the result of stirring up rebellion: Ex. 16:7–9; Acts 6:1; Phil. 2:14; *cf.* the verb in 1 Cor. 10:10). Such grumbling is ultimately a complaint against God and his ordering of our circumstances, and its result is to drive out faith, thanksgiving, and joy. Though hospitality to all people is certainly pleasing to God, Peter's emphasis on hospitality *to one another* – that is, to other Christians within the household of faith – is consistent with the rest of the New Testament (*cf.* Gal. 6:10).

(ii) Glorify God in using your gifts (4:10–11)
10. Within the fellowship of the church, earnest love for one another (v. 8) will find expression in the use of spiritual gifts, not for self-advancement or to draw attention to ourselves, but for the benefit of others: *As each has received a gift, employ it for one another, as good stewards of God's varied grace.*

Each implies that every person in the fellowship of believers – in every church to which Peter was writing – had received a 'spiritual gift' (*charisma*) for use in the life of the church (Paul teaches this explicitly: 1 Cor. 12:7–11). The word *as* might mean 'to the extent to which', 'to the degree that' (BAGD, p. 391, 2), but the idea of 'receiving' a gift does not fit well with the idea of different degrees (either one has received a gift or one has not). It is better to take it to mean 'in the same way in which' each person has received a gift (*i.e.* freely, out of grace, not merit), 'employ it for one another'. This sense certainly fits the context of love for one another (v. 8) and stewardship of God's gracious gifts.

The expression *a gift* is indefinite and implies 'at least one gift', but it should not be taken to mean that each person receives one and only one gift (*cf.* 1 Cor. 12:31; 14:1, 13, 39). A spiritual *gift* (*charisma*, the same word used in 1 Cor. 12 – 14 for 'spiritual gifts') is any talent or ability which is empowered by the Holy Spirit and able to be used in the ministry of the church. There are five different lists of spiritual gifts in the New Testament (Rom. 12:6–8; 1 Cor. 12:7–11; 12:28–30; Eph. 4:11; 1 Pet. 4:10). Since the lists are all different (no one gift is on every list, and no list includes all the gifts), and since 1 Corinthians 7:7 indicates two gifts not on any list (marriage and celibacy, which Paul calls *charismata*), it is legitimate to conclude that they are not exhaustive. In fact, since there are various types within any one gift (people with the gift of evangelism may differ in the kinds of evangelism they do best; similarly with teaching, helping, *etc.*), one could say there is an almost limitless variety of different spiritual gifts, all manifestations of the richly varied and abundant grace of God.

Varied (*poikilos*) means 'many faceted, having many different aspects or differing kinds' (note its use in Mt. 4:24, 'various diseases'; 1 Pet. 1:6, 'various trials'). As God's grace is richly varied, so are the gifts flowing from his grace. Yet if all these various gifts are to be used 'for one another', then churches should be willing to welcome a great variety of ministries and ways of using gifts.

Good stewards of God's gift will not hide it, but *employ it* for the benefit of others (*cf.* the parable of the talents, Mt. 25:14–30; similarly, Lk. 19:11–27). God's rule for our gifts is that we use them, with the confidence that resources expended in faithful stewardship will be replenished by a faithful Master.

11. *Whoever speaks* includes not just teaching or preaching, but many kinds of gifts involving speech-activity: evangelism, teaching, prophesying, and perhaps singing or sharing words of praise and testimony in the assembled congregation. In all these cases the Christian must do it *as one who utters oracles of God*. *Oracles* (*logia*) means 'sayings', but especially sayings spoken from God to man (used in Acts 7:38; Rom. 3:2 of Old Testament Scripture). Yet this cannot mean 'as claiming that the words he speaks are God's own words', because that would only be true of Scripture, not of every word spoken during a church meeting. It means rather 'with the seriousness of purpose which one would use if one were speaking God's words'.

Whoever renders service is again a very broad category, which includes any kind of helping or encouraging ministry for the benefit of others in the church (or, by extension of the idea, any Christian service or ministry to others outside the church). The source of such service is (literally, 'out of') *the strength which God supplies*; service performed by merely human energy and for one's own status in the eyes of others can soon become a wearying activity (see Gal. 6:9; 2 Thes. 3:13) and increase one's pride rather than one's faith. While service is directed to helping fellow believers (and others) and to building up the church, its ultimate purpose is that *in everything God may be glorified through Jesus Christ* (*cf.* 1 Cor. 10:31). The translation 'God may be praised' (NIV) gives a connotation that is too exclusively verbal: *glorified* applies not only to words but also to attitudes and actions which honour God.

Finally, Peter closes this section with his own doxology. To Jesus Christ whom he knew in the flesh as a man, Peter writes words of praise appropriate only to one who is also fully God: *To him belong glory and dominion for ever and ever. Amen.* The word translated *dominion* can also mean 'power'; if that is the sense here it cannot mean that Peter wants Christ (who is all powerful) to have in himself more power, but rather that he wants the powers of the creation, and especially the powers of man, to be given more fully into Christ's service (*cf.* Rev. 4:11; 5:12; 7:12). But that sense is in any case very similar to *dominion*.

f. Do not be surprised at your trials, but rejoice (4:12–16)

Some have seen verse 12 as beginning a separate section of the letter, or even a separate letter which has been added on later, but the doxology and 'Amen' at the end of verse 11 do not require this (*cf.* Rom. 1:25; 9:5; 11:36; Gal. 1:5; Eph. 3:21; 1 Tim. 1:17). However, is the subject matter so distinct that we need to think of this section as written to a different situation, one where persecution was not just a possibility but actually happening?

To answer this question we must bear in mind that 1 Peter is addressed to Christians in ten or more major churches (with no doubt other readers in many other local churches that had grown out of them) scattered through four provinces in Asia Minor (see 1:1 and 'Destination and readers' in the Introduction). From the first spread of the gospel there had been hostility and even violent opposition in many places – sometimes opposition stirred up by unbelieving Jews (Acts 4:1–3; 5:17–18, 40–41; 7:57–60; and 8:1–3, in Jerusalem; 13:50–52 at Pisidian Antioch; 14:4–6 at Iconium; 4:19 at Lystra; 17:5–9 at Thessalonica; 17:13 at Beroea; 18:12–17 at Corinth; 20:3 probably again at Corinth; 21:27–36 at Jerusalem); and sometimes persecution by local officials, whether for political purposes (Acts 12:1–3) or because of false accusation from Gentiles whose profits from sin were threatened (Acts 16:19–25 at Philippi, *cf.* Acts 19:23 – 20:1 at Ephesus).

Thus, we have specific evidence of violent opposition to the gospel from the time it first reached some of the cities to which Peter was writing (at least Pisidian Antioch, Iconium and nearby Lystra, and Ephesus – if Ephesus be counted as a likely recipient of the letter), and it is not unreasonable to think that similar opposition would have broken out from time to time in the other cities to which Peter was writing.

Given this historical background, we must then ask whether Peter would have written to so many different churches (1) as if none of them were experiencing persecution; (2) as if some of them were experiencing persecution; or (3) as if all of them were experiencing persecution. Even if he had not had recent news of actual persecution currently being endured, it would not be surprising if, in a general letter to spread-out groups of churches, the apostle would write as though varying degrees of formal and informal persecution were a live possibility for some readers and a present experience for others.

In fact, that is what we find in 1 Peter as a whole. Some passages regard persecution as just a possibility (1:6–7; 2:12, 21; 3:14; 4:1–2, 14, 16. Others suggest that for some readers persecution, or at least some kind of unjust treatment, is actually happening (2:15, 18–20; 3:9, 14, 16; 4:4, 17, 19; 5:9–10). And it is significant that two very clear statements about present persecution do not localize the phenomenon but rather universalize it, saying that it is the characteristic experience of the church generally: 4:17 and 5:9.

Thus, although persecution is specifically in view in verses 12 to 19, it is not necessary to see them as addressed to a different situation than the earlier parts of the letter. This section continues the long discussion, begun at 2:11, on living as a Christian in a hostile world. The theme of suffering as a Christian has been prominent since 3:13, with only verses 7 to 11 forming a minor parenthesis about life within the church in the end times.

12. Suffering as a Christian is not to be thought of as unusual or strange: *Beloved, do not be surprised at the fiery ordeal which comes upon you to prove you, as though something strange were happening to you.* The word translated *fiery ordeal* means 'fire, burning' (as in Rev. 18:9, 18), but Peter probably has in mind the use of the word in Proverbs 27:21 (LXX), 'Fire is the means of testing silver and gold.' Because of this sense, the word could also be translated 'refining fire'. The imagery is similar to that used in 1:7.

The image of a refiner's fire suggests that such suffering purifies and strengthens Christians. This idea is reinforced by the fact that it *comes upon you* (or: 'among you') *to prove you.* Here he uses the same word (*peirasmos*) which he used in 1:6 ('trials') in its positive sense of a trial expected to have a positive outcome. The readers are encouraged to see God's good purpose behind their difficulties, enabling them to grow stronger in faith and give more glory to God. This he explains in the following verses, showing that such trials are not to be thought unusual or *strange*, for they are a normal part of the Christian life.

13. Instead of being thrown off balance by trials, Christians are to *rejoice in so far as* (*i.e.* to the degree that) they *share Christ's sufferings.* Both verbs have a suggestion of continuation over time: 'In so far as you are sharing Christ's suffering, keep on rejoicing.' It is amazing to think that increased sufferings seem only to increase the believer's joy in the Lord, but Scripture testifies that this is so (Acts 5:41; *cf.* 16:25; Rom. 5:3; Col. 1:24; Heb. 10:34). Moreover, suffering as a Christian confirms to us the fact that we are indeed Christ's: 'To share, therefore, in Christ's sufferings here, is to be on the sure road to a share in His consequent glory hereafter' (Stibbs/Walls, p. 159). This is because union with Christ involves not only union with him in his death and resurrection (Rom. 6:5), but also union with him in the whole pattern of his life, which includes his suffering for righteousness (1 Pet. 2:20–21; 3:17–18; Rom. 8:17; Phil. 3:10; Col. 1:24; 2 Tim. 3:12; 1 Jn. 2:6).

Thus, rejoicing in suffering for Christ now will certainly lead to great rejoicing in his presence when he returns: 'Rejoice in so far as you share Christ's sufferings, *that you may also rejoice and be glad when his glory is revealed*' (*cf.* Rom. 8:17). The phrase *rejoice and be glad* is more expressively rendered, 'rejoice with great spiritual rejoicing', for Peter adds to this clause the verb *agalliaō*, 'to exult with spiritual joy, joy in the Lord' (see note on this term at 1:6).

14. A specific example of suffering as a Christian is now given: *If you are reproached* (reviled, abused, slandered) *for the name of Christ*. Again the verbs suggest continuation over time: 'If you are being reproached . . . you are blessed . . . the spirit . . . is resting on you.'[1]

The blessing named in verse 13 was future; the blessing named here is present. *The spirit* ('Spirit', as in NIV, NASB, TEV would be better, since it is certainly the Holy Spirit who is the Spirit of God) *of glory and of God rests upon you* indicates an unusual fullness of the presence of the Holy Spirit to bless, to strengthen,[2] and to give a foretaste of heavenly glory. The words echo the Messianic prophecy of Isaiah 11:2, speaking of the branch out of Jesse: 'And the Spirit of the LORD shall rest upon him' (the same word for 'rest', *anapauō*, is used both in the

[1] The grammatical construction here ('first class condition') does not imply that Peter thinks the readers actually are being reproached, but only that Peter assumes it momentarily for the sake of the argument (see note on 'you may have to suffer' at 1:6).

[2] The idea of the Holy Spirit's strengthening would be assumed if not stated, for strength is what one needs in time of trial. The rather strongly attested textual variant 'and of power' would make it explicit.

LXX and here. Peter sees this Messianic blessing extending also to those who bear the name of the Messiah (or 'Christ') – see some examples in Acts 5:41; 6:15; 7:55, 59–60; 16:25. Yet the word *glory* in the verse suggests another theme as well: the New Testament fulfilment of the Old Testament cloud of God's glory (the 'shekinah glory') is to be seen in the powerful dwelling of the Holy Spirit within Christian believers (see 'Additional Note: The dwelling place of God' at 2:5, p. 102 above).

15–16. Such a blessing is not bestowed upon every kind of suffering, however: *But let none of you suffer as a murderer, or a thief, or a wrongdoer* (a general term, referring to anyone who 'works evil'), *or a mischief-maker.* The last term is extremely rare (only one other example of its use is known; *cf.* BAGD, p. 40) and various meanings have been proposed. The sense 'meddler' (NIV; *cf.* 'troublesome meddler', NASB) seems best, since the separate parts mean 'one who looks carefully on others' affairs' (or: on the possessions of others), and the general idea would then be that of wrongdoing by meddling in affairs which are not properly one's concern.

On the other hand, *if one suffers as a Christian, let him not be ashamed.* The world may think suffering for conscientious adherence to Christianity is disgraceful, but actually it is an honour in God's sight, and should be so in the eyes of Christians as well. The word *Christian* is found in the New Testament only here and at Acts 11:26 and 26:28; it means 'follower of Christ' – not 'little Christ', as some popular explanations claim (for it is formed like the word 'Herodian', see Mk. 3:6; 12:13, which means 'follower or supporter of Herod').

Instead of being ashamed Peter suggests another alternative: *but under that name let him glorify God.* The sense is that the one being reviled as a Christian should so act and speak that God is continually honoured in his or her life. The idea of living so that in everything God is glorified is stated explicitly in verse 11, but is frequently implied in previous verses as well (see notes on 1:7, 16; 2:5, 9; 3:4).

Under that name (or, more literally, 'in that name') seems to have the sense 'acting in Christ's name, as the one who represents Christ to others'. The NIV's 'But praise God that you bear that name' is difficult to derive from the Greek, unless it is based on an uncommon use of the word 'name' (*onoma*) to mean 'category' (BAGD, p. 573, II), which is then extended to mean 'praise God in that matter' (the matter of bearing Christ's name). Yet this is unlikely, for (1) the presence of the name 'Christian' in the sentence makes it likely that *onomati* is being used in its common sense, 'name', rather than to mean 'matter'; (2) the nuance of the present imperative (*doxazetō*, 'let him glorify or praise') makes better sense as 'let him continually glorify' (in life) than as 'let him continually praise God' (that he bears that name); and (3) the disciplining process of God's judgment (v. 17, which begins with 'for') is a good reason to live generally in a way that glorifies God, but not nearly as clear a reason to praise God that one bears the name 'Christian'.

(i) For God's judgment is beginning from God's own house (4:17–18)

17. *For the time has come for judgment to begin with the household of God* puts verses 12 to 16 in a broader theological context. 'What is going on in the world?' the readers might wonder. 'Why are God's people suffering and evildoers going unpunished?' Peter explains that the 'fiery ordeal', or 'refining fire', of verse 12 is really a fire of God's *judgment*. Yet this word for *judgment* (*krima*) does not necessarily mean 'condemnation' (which would be *katakrima*) but is a broader term which can refer to a judgment which results in good and bad evaluations, a judgment which may issue in approval or discipline as well as condemnation. The picture is that God has begun judging within the church, and will later move outward to judge those outside the church. The refining fire of judgment is leaving no one untouched, but Christians are being purified and strengthened by it – sins are being eliminated and trust in God and holiness of life are growing.

The translation *household of God* emphasizes the family-like nature of the church. But this translation seems hardly justifiable in terms of the Greek phrase *oikos tou theou* ('house of God'). Dennis Johnson[1] has argued persuasively that this phrase in the

[1]Dennis E. Johnson, 'Fire in God's House: Imagery from Malachi 3 in Peter's Theology of Suffering (1 Peter 4:12–19)', *JETS* 29:3 (Sept, 1986), pp. 291–292. O. Michel says, '*oikos theou* is a fixed term for the sanctuary in the LXX' (*TDNT* 5, p. 120).

LXX never refers to the 'household' of God's people, but always to the Temple, the 'house of God' in terms of the building in which God dwells. Thus, it is likely that it should be translated 'house of God' here as well.

This argument gains support when we recall Peter's only other use of the word *oikos*, 'house', in 2:5: 'Coming to him, you are being built into a spiritual house' (see note at 2:5 regarding the reference to the temple here). Moreover, the text literally reads not *with* but 'from' (*apo*): 'The time has come for judgment to begin *from* the house of God.'

Such a translation allows Johnson correctly to see this verse in the light of two other Old Testament passages, Ezekiel 9 and Malachi 3. Ezekiel 9 pictures the Lord calling to 'the executioners' of judgment to 'draw near' (9:1) to bring judgment on Jerusalem for its horrible sins. One messenger of God puts a mark on the forehead of all who were found to 'sigh and groan' over the 'abominations' committed in Jerusalem (9:4–5). Then the 'executioners' of judgment are told to kill all who do not have the mark on their foreheads (9:5–6). Significantly, God tells the executioners, 'Begin from[1] my sanctuary,' and Ezekiel adds, 'So they began from the elders who were inside the house' (9:6). The words 'begin from', used twice here, are the same words Peter uses to say that it is time for judgment to 'begin from (*archomai apo*) the house of God'. 'House' (*oikos*) is also the same word in both places. Both 1 Peter 4:17 and Ezekiel 9:6 have mention of God's glory before and after them (1 Pet. 4:14 and 5:1; Ezk. 9:3 and 10:4). Finally, whereas Ezekiel's judgment begins with 'the elders' who are in God's house, Peter begins his next section of admonition, '*Therefore*, I exhort the elders among you . . .' (5:1; the word for 'elders' is *presbyteroi* in both cases). It seems very likely that the judgment scene of Ezekiel 9 is in Peter's mind when he writes, indicating that God's judgment will begin with God's house (now the church; *cf.* note at 2:5) and then spread outward to destroy all unbelievers.

But the mention of the 'fiery ordeal' or 'refining fire' (v. 12) which does not destroy but purifies God's people calls to mind a

---

[1] I have given my own translation of the LXX here, to bring out the verbal parallels with 1 Pet. 4:17.

second Old Testament passage, whose vivid imagery may have been joined with that of Ezekiel 9 as Peter wrote. Malachi 3 predicts that the Lord himself 'will suddenly come to his temple' as 'the messenger of the covenant' who 'is like a refiner's fire' (3:1–2; 'fire' is *pur* in the LXX, not the same word but a related word to *pyrōsis*, 'refining fire', in 1 Pet. 4:12). Malachi adds, 'He will sit as a refiner and purifier of silver, and he will purify the sons of Levi and refine them like gold and silver, till they present right offerings to the LORD' (Mal. 3:3). 'Then I will draw near to you for judgment . . .' (on unbelievers: Mal. 3:5).

Johnson rightly points out that though Peter's *language* may have been more influenced by Ezekiel 9, the *concepts* in 1 Peter 4:12–19 are closer to the picture of Malachi 3: the Lord himself is acting as a refining fire, purifying the priests ('the sons of Levi'; *cf.* 1 Pet. 2:5, 9) so that they may offer sacrifices pleasing to the Lord (*cf.* 1 Pet. 2:5). Then the judgment which began at God's house (the temple, Mal. 3:1) will move from there to unbelievers, no longer as a purifying fire but as a judgment of condemnation – which brings us directly back to 1 Peter 4:17: 'For the time has come for judgment to begin with the house of God; *and if it begins with* (Greek 'from', *apo*) *us, what will be the end of those who do not obey the gospel of God*?' 'The thought is simply: "If the purifying fire of God's eschatological visitation . . . entails, for those united to Christ, such anguish as Peter's readers are undergoing, what shall the consummation of that purifying divine presence mean for those who have rejected God's good news – if not a conflagration of utter destruction?"'[1]

The application of this passage to Peter's readers should be clear: if the Lord is already in the midst of his new temple (*i.e.* his people), they should 'not be surprised at the refining fire which comes among you (Greek *en humin*, 'in the midst of you') to prove you . . . the Spirit of glory and of God is resting upon you' (vv. 12, 14). He is the 'messenger of the covenant in whom you delight' (Mal. 3:1), so they can 'rejoice' (v. 13) in his presence. But with him also comes a refining fire, and they

[1]Johnson, *art. cit.*, p. 292.

must purify themselves of all iniquities in order to avoid the pain of his disciplining judgment, even while they continue trusting him who alone can enable them to stand before himself (v. 19).[1]

18. This verse has the same theme, but expressed this time in words taken exactly from Proverbs 11:31 (LXX): '*If the righteous man is scarcely saved, where will the impious and sinner appear?*' The fire of God's holiness is so intense that even *the righteous* feel pain in its discipline. The *impious* (a godless person, a person without true reverence for God) *and sinner* will, by implication, find it to be a fire of eternal destruction.

(ii) Therefore do right and trust God continually (4:19)

19. What should Christians do in such circumstances? They should *do right*, maintaining moral purity in their lives (*cf.* 1:15, *etc.*), and should continue not to trust themselves but to *entrust their souls to a faithful Creator*. In this one verse is summarized the teaching of the entire letter. Christians do not suffer accidentally or because of the irresistible forces of blind fate; rather, they suffer *according to God's will*.

While this may at first seem harsh (for it implies that at times it is God's will that we suffer), upon reflection no better comfort in suffering can be found than this: it is God's good and perfect will. For therein lies the knowledge that there is a limit to the suffering, both in its intensity and in its duration, a limit set and maintained by the God who is our creator, our saviour, our sustainer, our Father. And therein also lies the knowledge that this suffering is only for our good: it is purifying us, drawing us closer to our Lord, and making us more like him in our lives. In all of it we are not alone, but we can depend on the care of a *faithful Creator*; we can rejoice in the fellowship of a Saviour who has also suffered (v. 13); we can exult in the constant presence of

[1] Readers of less literal modern translations, in particular the NIV and TEV, have no chance of discovering these OT parallels which make the passage understandable, for the two key terms have been lost in translations which only contain generally related ideas: 'purifying fire' has become 'painful trial' in the NIV in v. 12, with the idea of 'fire' totally lost; and 'house of God' has become 'family of God' in v. 17. (The TEV is similar, with 'painful test' and 'God's own people'; RSV and NASB are better, but still have 'household of God' instead of 'house of God'; only the AV has 'house of God'.)

a Spirit of glory who delights to rest upon us (v. 14).

Some have thought that the phrase *according to God's will* refers to the way Christians act while they are suffering, not to the reason for suffering. However, such an understanding is not possible because it would make the phrase *do right* redundant: the verse would in essence then say, 'Let those who suffer while doing right, do right.' But this is meaningless repetition. It is necessary, therefore, to understand the sentence to mean, 'Let those who suffer because God has willed that they suffer do right . . .'.

The phrase *entrust their souls* does not use the usual word for 'trusting' God, but a verb (*paratithēmi*) which means 'to give to someone for safekeeping, to turn over to someone to care for' (*cf.* Lk. 23:46, 'Father, into thy hands I *commit* my spirit', quoting Ps. 31:5; see also Acts 14:23). *Souls* may also be translated 'selves' (NIV: 'commit themselves to their faithful Creator' – however, see note on 'soul' at 1:22). The mention of 'souls' here, together with the possible echo of Jesus' words on the cross (Lk. 23:46), suggests the idea of the believer's soul living on even after his body is destroyed, and puts the question of temporary suffering in the proper perspective.

F. LIVING AS CHURCH MEMBERS AND OFFICERS (5:1–7)

1. *Elders: Shepherd God's flock rightly* (5:1–4)

1. *So I exhort the elders among you* seems at first unrelated to the previous section, but the word *so* or 'therefore' (*oun*) suggests that this section follows logically on from the previous one. It is likely that the thought of judgment beginning from the house of God (4:17) prompted Peter to focus on the need for purity of heart before God in relationships among those in the church, beginning with the leaders of the church. This pattern may even have been suggested by Ezekiel 9:6, from which Peter borrowed the language about judgment beginning 'from the house of God', for there it says, 'So they began with the elders who were before (LXX: in) the house.' The connection is: since purifying judgment is beginning with God's house, and especially with the leaders of God's house, therefore *I exhort the elders among you.*

Lest he seem to be too haughty in this prediction of judgment, Peter immediately classes himself with the elders: *as a fellow elder.* This lets the elders know that he thinks of himself as one of those with whom judgment will begin – even he, an apostle, is not exempt, nor should any among his readers think themselves too important or too sanctified to be exempt. Moreover, as he is about to encourage them to be 'examples' to the flock (v. 3), so he demonstrates in the next phrase how he himself is willing to be an example for those leaders to whom he writes.

While it is remarkable that Peter the apostle would take the less exalted title 'fellow elder' to speak to elders, it is even more remarkable that he should describe himself as *a witness of the sufferings of Christ.* Had he said 'witness of the resurrection' it would have been a claim for the truthfulness of his message (as in Acts 2:32; 3:15; *cf.* 1:22). Even 'witness of his transfiguration' would have been a claim to authenticity (*cf.* 2 Pet. 1:16–18). But 'witness of the sufferings of Christ' bluntly recalls, for Peter and for anyone familiar with the details surrounding Christ's crucifixion, the most painful episode in Peter's life – for we remember just what kind of 'witness' Peter was: one whose courage failed and who three times denied that he even knew Christ (Mt. 26:69–75).

Why does Peter recall this? Probably to demonstrate that restoration even from grievous sin is possible with Christ (*cf.* Paul's similar use of his life as an example of restoration totally by grace, 1 Tim. 1:16), and thus to encourage in the elders a humble willingness to be penitent for sin rather than a hypocritical pride and an unwillingness ever to admit to doing wrong.

The fact that Peter is also *a partaker in the glory that is to be revealed* shows that full restoration from sin is certainly available through Christ. This phrase could refer to Peter's presence on the Mount of Transfiguration, when the cloud of God's glory overshadowed those with Jesus (Mt. 17:1–8; *cf.* 2 Pet. 1:16–18), but had he meant this he would probably have said something like, 'as well as a witness of the glory that *was* revealed'. The fact that he mentions this partaking in glory after he mentions his witnessing of the sufferings of Christ, and the fact that he says the glory is still *to be revealed*, suggest that he is thinking of the future glory that will come to believers when Christ returns (note this theme in 1:7; 4:13; 5:4, 10). Peter is an 'elder' who has sinned, repented, been restored, and will share with Christ in glory. He can rightly 'exhort' any elder in whose life there is sin likewise to repent and be restored before God's disciplinary refining fire reaches him.

On another level, the reference to Christ's sufferings may also function as a reminder to the elders that just as Christ was willing to suffer for them, so they should be willing to endure hardship and suffering for the sake of those in their churches (*cf.* the note on the function of 3:18 in its context). Yet in the context of Peter's speaking about himself as fellow elder/witness/ partaker in glory, the primary emphasis of this phrase does not seem to be on Christ's example but on Peter's own experience.

2. Peter exhorts the elders, *Tend the flock of God that is your charge.* There is a play on words, since the verb *tend* (*poimainō*, 'serve as shepherd, serve as pastor') and the noun *flock* (*poimnion*) come from the same root. We could translate, 'Shepherd the sheep of God'. The verb Peter uses is the same one Jesus used when he said to Peter, 'Tend (*poimainō*) my sheep' (Jn. 21:16). The phrase *that is your charge* is more literally 'that is among you'.

At this point the RSV mg. adds *exercising the oversight*, a phrase which translates the verb *episkopeō*, 'functioning as overseer (or bishop)'. The phrase should be included in the text here (so NIV, 'serving as overseers'; the three main manuscripts omitting it are all from one geographical area, while those including it are diverse in location, and several are also quite early). The combination of the term 'elder' with the verbs related to 'pastor' and 'bishop' ('overseer') in such close connection in verses 1 to 2 is good evidence that the terms 'pastor', and 'bishop, overseer' were interchangeable during the New Testament period.

Peter now tells the elders how they are to act, listing three sins to which elders are especially prone and three antidotes to which they should give attention.

Calvin introduces this section with a perceptive summary:

187

In exhorting pastors to their duty, he points out three vices especially which are often to be found, namely sloth, desire for gain, and lust for power.[1]

Not by constraint but willingly means not doing the job simply out of obligation or because 'someone has to do it', but because the elder has freely and willingly chosen to carry out this valuable work (*cf.* 1 Tim. 3:1). The phrase in the RSV mg. *as God would have you* (literally, 'according to God', meaning 'according to God's will') is also well attested in ancient manuscripts and should be included in the text (so NIV, NASB). No-one should be pressured into accepting a church office which he does not really want to have – God wants our ungrudging service, and he will provide another solution. An elder is to serve *not for shameful gain but eagerly*. The word translated *eagerly* places somewhat more emphasis on a positive emotional desire to do the work, whereas 'willingly' in the previous phrase simply focused on the element of unconstrained or free choice, the decision of the will that one will do the work.

It may be questioned whether the prohibition against serving for *shameful gain* means one should never engage in church-related work in order to earn money, or whether it means one should not do it in order to earn money 'shamefully' (*i.e.* with greedy or selfish motives, or by dishonest or unfair practices). The second view seems preferable, both because Peter says *shameful gain*, not just *gain*, and because Scripture elsewhere indicates that it is right at least for some elders (probably those whose source of income or full-time work is their eldership activities) to earn money from this work (1 Tim. 5:17–18) – therefore, the desire for such earnings must be correct also, at least as part of their motivation. Yet the contrast is not: 'not for shameful gain but for honest gain', but a much higher one: 'not for shameful gain *but eagerly*'. Greed and selfish interest are so near at hand in all human hearts that especially in this work they must be constantly guarded against.

3. *Not as domineering over those in your charge but being examples*

---

[1]Calvin, p. 314.

to the flock shifts attention from inward motivation to outward behaviour. But even here attitude is determinative, for an elder greedy for power over others will 'domineer', delighting in the use of his authority and seeking to increase, preserve or flaunt it. By contrast the elder who seeks not his own status but the edification of others (*cf.* Phil. 2:3–4, 5–8, 20–21; Mt. 23:11) will strive continually to make his life an 'example' to others, a pattern to imitate.

The term translated *domineering* (*katakyrieuō*) means 'forcefully ruling over, subduing', and can carry the nuance of a harsh or excessive use of authority (note its use in Mt. 20:25; Mk. 10:42; Acts 19:16; also LXX Gn. 1:28; 9:1; and, in the context of military conquests, Nu. 21:24; 32:22, 29; Ps. 110:2, *etc.*). The word always seems to involve bringing something into subjection by the use of force, whether physical, military, or political. Here Peter forbids the use of arbitrary, arrogant, selfish, or excessively restrictive rule. He implies that elders should govern not by the use of threats, emotional intimidation, or flaunting of power, nor generally by the use of 'political' force within the church, but rather by power of example whenever possible. Nevertheless, verse 5, in commanding others to 'be subject' to the elders, implies that they have genuine governing authority in the church, and that at times they can give directions which the church ought to obey. (Paul's use of his own authority as an apostle, especially in 2 Corinthians and Philemon, is a profitable example for study.)

Although we may already recognize that God himself is our example to imitate (Eph. 5:1) and that Jesus is our perfect example for a human life pleasing to God (1 Pet. 2:21; 1 Jn. 2:6; *etc.*), we are probably surprised to find how often the early Christians expected all their leaders to live in a way which others could imitate as well: they did not have to be perfect in order to be *examples to the flock*. Paul frequently urged others to imitate his example (1 Cor. 4:16; 11:1; Phil. 3:17; 4:9; 2 Thes. 3:7–9), and told both Timothy (1 Tim. 4:12) and Titus (Tit. 2:7–8) that they were to live as examples of the Christian life to others (*cf.* Heb. 6:12; 13:7).

Thus all in leadership positions in the church should realize that the requirement to live a life worthy of imitation is not optional – it is a major part of the job, challenging though such responsibility may be. Moreover, those who select church leaders should realize that academic excellence and administrative or financial skills do not automatically qualify one for leadership in the church (as they would for leadership in the university or business worlds).

Recognizing that one has such responsibility should never engender pride, but rather a continual humility in the awareness that the sin remaining in one's heart is still hateful, and that any growth in holiness of life has only come about by God's grace. Indeed, to take pride in one's own spiritual progress would be to set exactly the wrong example for others. Those who like Paul cry out, 'Who is sufficient for these things?' (2 Cor. 2:16b) are most likely to set the best example, for, as Peter himself says in this context, 'God opposes the proud but gives grace to the humble' (v. 5b).

Those in your charge has been thought by some to indicate that each elder had certain individuals assigned to him to care for, but there is not enough evidence to conclude this. The expression could just mean 'your shares or portions of responsibility' before God.

4. Peter promises no earthly reward but rather directs the elders to look beyond this present world: *And when the chief Shepherd is manifested you will obtain the unfading crown of glory.* When elders are viewed as shepherds, as they are here, it is natural to call Christ the *chief Shepherd* (the term occurs only here, in the NT, but *cf.* 2:25; also Heb. 13:20; Mt. 26:31; Jn. 10:11–16). *When [he] is manifested* means 'when he is made visible, when he appears', and thus refers to the time of Christ's visible return to earth. At that time (and not even at death: see note at 1:7), Peter says, *you will obtain the unfading crown of glory.*

Crown (*stephanos*) is used of a victor's crown or 'wreath' in athletic contests (1 Cor. 9:25), or a golden crown given by a Roman general to soldiers most valiant in battle (Josephus, *War* 7.14), or a crown worn by a king (2 Sa. (LXX 2 Ki.) 12:30; *cf.* Rev. 6:2; 14:14). In every case it is a sign of special honour, given not to all but only to those worthy of particular public recognition, commonly as a reward for some kind of unusually meritorious activity. Such an idea would fit this verse, where Peter mentions this *unfading crown of glory* specifically when speaking to 'elders', and when speaking of a reward which is given in the age to come, following after a description of righteous conduct in the exercise of the office of elder during this life. Moreover, the term *glory* carries the nuance of an outwardly visible evidence of honour. Finally, the 'twenty-four elders' in Revelation have 'golden crowns' (Rev. 4:4) which they cast before God's throne (Rev. 4:10) – even though these are not identical to the elders in local churches to whom Peter is writing, the 'crowns' there are none the less marks of honour said to be possessed by particular individuals, not by all.

There are other passages of Scripture which suggest that some kind of 'crown' will be given to all believers (2 Tim. 4:8; Jas. 1:12; Rev. 2:10; 3:11). Yet in these passages the 'crown' seems to be a metaphor for the heavenly life in general. The 'crown' of righteousness' in 2 Tim. 4:8 which the Lord will give not only to Paul but also to all who have loved his appearing' (*i.e.* all believers) probably means 'righteousness, which will be like a crown'. Similarly, the 'crown of life' in Jas. 1:12; Rev. 2:10; *cf.* Rev. 3:11) is probably 'eternal life in heaven, which is a reward like a crown received at the end of a race'. 1 Corinthians 9:25 implies that all believers should strive to obtain an 'imperishable' crown, but in the context it may also be viewed as a heavenly reward not for all believers but only for those who have continued through life faithful and obedient to God in a way worthy of special reward (*cf.* 1 Cor. 9:24, and note degrees of reward in 1 Cor. 3:12–15).

1 Peter 5:4, then, seems to indicate that elders in local churches should fulfil their office in ways pleasing to God, not in order to obtain honour or wealth in this life, but to obtain a special reward, an *unfading crown of glory*, when Christ returns (*cf.* note at 1:7). In churches today this should be the reward which elders work for, but it often is not.

2. *Younger people (and all others): Be subject to the elders* (5:5a)

5a. Peter uses the word *likewise* to shift attention to a different group of people, yet still within the same general subject area, just as he did in 3:7 (see notes there and at 3:1 on *homoiōs*). The term *likewise* in both places means not 'act in the same way' but 'continuing the same subject' (at 3:7, relations within marriage; here in 5:5, relations between officers and others in the church).

You that are younger be subject to the elders commands submission to the governing authority of the elders within the church. *Be subject* indicates a general willingness to support the elders' directions (see note on *hypotassō* at 3:1), except if they should ever direct one to sin (see note at 2:13).

The word *elders* (*presbyteroi*) in the New Testament can mean either 'older people' or 'those who have the office of elder', and the precise sense can only be determined from context. Therefore some have thought that *the elders* in this verse must mean 'older people generally' in the church (so NIV: 'those who are older'), since Peter does not say, 'All of you be subject to the elders', but speaks directly to *you that are younger*. The contrast between *younger* and *elders*, it is said, indicates a contrast in age, not church office.

However, several considerations make it more likely that we should understand *elders* here, as in verse 1, to refer to those who have the office of 'elder' within the church, not to older people generally. (1) The first word of verse 5, 'likewise', indicates that Peter is continuing the discussion begun in verses 1 to 4, just as 'likewise' in 3:7 indicates the continuation of the discussion begun in 3:1–6. And since the subject in verses 1 to 4 is those who hold the office of 'elder', verse 5a is to be seen as an instruction about relating to those who hold the office. However, if this were general instruction about relations between older and younger people generally, an entirely new subject would be introduced (on relationships). (2) Unless there were clear contextual indications otherwise, those reading verse 5 would naturally give the same sense to the word 'elders' which it had as the subject of the discussion in verses 1 to 4. (3) The word *hypotassō*, 'be subject', implies submission to an authority, not just deference or respect (see note at 3:1), and older people generally did not have governing authority in churches, but those in the office of 'elders' did.

Even so, the question remains why Peter spoke only to *you that are younger*, and not to the whole church, in commanding submission to the elders. It is probably because the younger people were generally those who would most need a reminder to be submissive to authority within the church (and there is no need to restrict this to 'young men', NIV, or 'younger men', NASB, since the masculine plural noun would be used to refer to a mixed group of men and women as well). This would not imply that the others were free to rebel against the elders, but quite the opposite: if those who are likely to be most independent-minded and even at times rebellious against church leaders are commanded to *be subject to the elders*, then it follows that certainly everyone else must be subject to the elders as well. This idea finds confirmation in the fact that the *Epistle of Polycarp* 5.3 uses the same words as Peter did for the 'younger' (*neōteroi*) and for 'be subject' (*hypotassō*) in commanding the 'younger' to 'be subject to the elders and deacons as to God and Christ', and the context clearly indicates that church officers are in view (note the phrase 'elders and deacons'; also the instructions to deacons in 5:2 and elders in 6:1).

3. All of you: Be humble toward each other (5:5b)

5b. There should be a new verse and a new paragraph beginning with the sentence, *Clothe yourselves, all of you, with humility toward one another, for "God opposes the proud, but gives grace to the humble."* This is because Peter has moved from a discussion of relationships between elders and others in the church to a distinct section (vv. 5b–7) dealing more generally with all interpersonal relationships in the church. (Our verse divisions were introduced by the publisher Stephanus in 1551,[1] and were not present when Peter wrote. Modern paragraph divisions are even more recent, since they are decided by each modern translator and will vary from translation to translation.)

Peter uses a metaphor of 'clothing' or fastening on garments to speak of the atmosphere of humility toward one another which should characterize relationships among Christians. No one is exempt, for Peter includes church officers and non-officers, young and old, new Christians and mature believers in

[1]*ODCC*, p. 1308.

the address *all of you*. The term *humility* speaks of an attitude which puts others first, which thinks of the desires, needs, and ideas of others as more worthy of attention than one's own. This word (*tapeinophrosynē*) is well defined by Philippians 2:3–4: 'Do nothing from selfishness or conceit, but in *humility* count others better than (NASB: 'more important than') yourselves. Let each of you look not only to his own interests, but also to the interests of others' (Christ himself is the great example of this in Phil. 2:5–8).

The reason for putting on humility is that *God opposes the proud but gives grace to the humble*, a quotation from Proverbs 3:34 (also quoted in Jas. 4:6). Why does God act this way? Apparently because the proud (those who are haughty or arrogant, thinking of themselves as more important than everyone else) trust in themselves, while the humble trust in God, and God delights in being trusted. Moreover, the proud seek glory for themselves while the humble give glory to God – and glory rightfully belongs to God, not us (1 Cor. 4:7; also 1 Cor. 1:26–31; Rev. 4:11). *Grace* is God's undeserved favour toward us, and is needed not only to save us from eternal judgment but also to enable us to live the Christian life. The whole quotation applies well to daily Christian living, since the present tense verbs give the sense 'God is continually opposing the proud but continually giving grace to the humble'.

a. Humble yourselves before God (5:6)

6. From humility before others, Peter passes to humility before God: *Humble yourselves therefore under the mighty hand of God*. 'Therefore' connects this statement with the quotation in verse 5: if God opposes the proud it is true wisdom to humble oneself before him. Among other things this will involve bowing to God's wisdom, accepting the twists and turns of his providence, and entrusting all our concerns to him. Though this may well mean personal disadvantage in this life, it is always in the believer's interest to humble himself or herself before God so *that in due time he may exalt you*.

Neither the specific time nor the kind of 'exaltation' are specified, so it is best to understand the statement generally: 'that in the time God deems best, whether in this life or in the life to come, he may lift you up from your humble conditions and 'exalt' you in the way that seems best to him – perhaps only in terms of increased spiritual blessing and deeper fellowship with himself, perhaps also in terms of responsibility, reward, or honour which will be seen by others as well.

b. Gain humility by casting your cares on God (5:7)

7. *Cast all your anxieties on him, for he cares about you.* No new sentence begins here in Greek, and an important connection between verses 6 and 7 is missed by those English translations (such as RSV and NIV) which start a new sentence at verse 7. Peter continues the command of verse 6 ('Humble yourselves . . .') with a participial phrase telling how this is to be done. Proper humility is attained by 'casting all your anxieties on him, for he cares about you'.

Peter recognizes that a great barrier to putting others first and thinking of them as more important is the legitimate human concern 'But who then will care for me?' The answer is that God himself will care for our needs. He is able to do so far better than we are (his hand is 'mighty', v. 6), and he wants to do so, for he continually *cares* for his children. Therefore casting *all your anxieties* on him is the path to humility, freeing a person from constant concern for himself and enabling him or her truly to be concerned for the needs of others.

Cast means to throw something upon someone or something else (so in Lk. 19:35). The background for this statement is the use of this same term in the LXX of Psalm 55:22, 'Cast your burden on the LORD, and he will sustain you.' Moreover, the word translated 'anxieties' is used for 'burden' in Psalm 55:22 (LXX 54:23). It means 'cares, concerns, things one is anxious or worried about' (note its use in Lk. 21:34; 2 Cor. 11:28).

G. LIVING AS CHRISTIANS IN SPIRITUAL CONFLICT (5:8–11)

1. Beware of the devil (5:8)

8. A new section begins here with an admonition to spiritual watchfulness. Just as a person walking down a dangerous road might be advised to be alert and careful, so Peter's readers are warned, *Be sober, be watchful.* (See note on *sober* [*nēphō*] at 1:13; the same spiritual alertness of mind and soundness of judgment is urged 'for your prayers' at 4:7.) *Watchful* translates a word (*grēgoreō*) which also indicates spiritual alertness, with perhaps more of an emphasis on one's focus of attention ('watching' for sin, for attacks of evil: so of Jesus and the disciples in the Garden, Mt. 26:38, 40–41; *cf.* also Acts 20:31; Col. 4:2; and, translated 'awake', in Rev. 3:2, 3; 16:15). The opposite of this sober watchfulness is a kind of spiritual drowsiness in which one sees and responds to situations no differently than unbelievers, and God's perspective on each event is seldom if ever considered.

One great reason for alertness is the genuine danger of attacks by the Enemy: *Your adversary the devil prowls around like a roaring lion, seeking some one to devour.* The metaphor is apt, for a prowling lion attacks suddenly, viciously, and often when its unsuspecting victim is engaged in routine activities. *Devour* means 'swallow, swallow up something' (the same term is used of the great fish swallowing Jonah in Jon. 1:17).

The devil (*diabolos*) refers to a personal spiritual being who is in active rebellion against God and who has leadership of many demons like himself (Mt. 4:1–11; 13:39; 25:41; Rev. 12:9; *etc.* – the Greek term translates the Hebrew word *satan*, 'Satan', eighteen times in the LXX). But when *diabolos* is not used to refer to one individual being, the devil, the term is a noun meaning 'slanderer, false accuser' (as in 1 Tim. 3:11; 2 Tim. 3:3; Tit. 2:3; the word is applied to Haman in the LXX of Esther 8:1). Peter here views Satan as a cunning and evil personal being who has the ability and the propensity to attack (and presumably harm) Christians.

A survey of the results of demonic influence in the New Testament will indicate certain characteristics which a *sober* and *watchful* Christian may suspect to be caused, at least in part, by the devil or demons: bizarre or violently irrational evil behaviour, especially in opposition to the gospel or to Christians (Mk. 1:24; 5:2–5; 9:18; Acts 16:16–18; Rev. 2:10); malicious slander and falsehood in speech (Jn. 8:44; 1 Jn. 4:1–3); increasing bondage to self-destructive behaviour (Mk. 5:5; 9:20); stubborn advocacy of false doctrine (1 Jn. 4:1–6); the sudden and unexplained onslaughts of emotions (such as fear, hatred, depression, anxiety, violent anger, *etc.*) which are both contrary to God's will and inappropriate in one's situation (note the 'flaming darts of the evil one' in Eph. 6:16); and simply the deep spiritual uneasiness which might be called the 'discernment' (*cf.* 1 Cor. 12:10) of spiritual evil.

Yet caution is appropriate here, for there is much evil in the world which is not directly from Satan or demons but simply from sin remaining in our own hearts or in the lives of unbelievers around us. And excessive curiosity about the devil's workings is also harmful – we are to 'be babes in evil' (1 Cor. 14:20).

2. *Resist the devil with firm faith* (5:9)

9. Far from saying that Christians should fear such a formidable adversary, Peter says, *Resist him, firm in your faith.* This is an encouraging verse, for it gives hope that Christian resistance to the devil's attacks will be successful. While it is wrong to ignore the devil's existence, it is also wrong to cower before him in fear: *Resist him!* The phrase *firm in your faith* implies a confidence that God will intervene and give the Christian victory, not defeat. In a similar way, James tells Christians to *resist* the devil, and promises, 'and he will flee from you' (Jas. 4:7). In both passages the word *resist* implies active, determined opposition, often through confrontation (it is used of the Egyptian magicians who opposed Moses in 2 Tim. 3:8; *cf.* its use in Acts 13:8; Rom. 13:2; Gal. 2:11; 2 Tim. 4:15).

How should Christians resist the devil? Peter does not tell us, but Paul's discussion of the equipment for spiritual warfare in Ephesians 6:10–18 is a good commentary on this passage. In practical terms, all the positive resources of the Christian life are to be used – prayer, the word of God, praise, the help of fellow believers, verbal rebuke of the enemy (Lk. 10:17–20; Acts 16:18), renewed holiness of life (note 'righteousness' in Eph. 6:14); in short 'the whole armour of God' (Eph. 6:11).

Therefore the command, *Resist him, firm in your faith*, signifies that defeat is not inevitable. Christians must resist, expecting that the enemy will flee, God's kingdom will advance, they will grow in faith and holiness through conflict, and God will take

Satan's plans for evil and turn them to their good.

When Peter adds, *knowing that the same experience of suffering is required of* (or: 'is being accomplished, experienced by') *your brotherhood throughout the world*, he seeks to encourage them by showing that their circumstances are not unusual but in fact to be expected by Christians everywhere.

3. *God will restore you after you have suffered* (5:10–11)

10. The transition to this verse is better marked by 'But' than by the RSV's *And*, for Peter regularly (twenty-eight times in 1 Peter) uses this conjunction (*de*) to indicate a distinct contrast with a previous statement.[1] The sense is that the suffering and the attacks of the devil which accompany the suffering – and are the cause of some of it – may seem difficult *but* they will not last long. Indeed, *after you have suffered a little while* – an expression intentionally vague in the amount of time it implies, allowing for restoration either in this present life or later – *the God of all grace* will *restore* them or 'make them fully prepared and complete' with respect to any resource or ability which they have lost through this suffering. He will *establish* them firmly in any position, rightful privilege, or responsibility which this suffering has taken from them. He will *strengthen* them for any weakness they have been made to suffer, any inadequacy for overcoming evil which they may have known. And we should add (with RSV mg., similarly NIV, NASB) that he will *settle* (or: found, establish, firmly place) them in any rightful place from which the suffering has wrongfully removed them. In sum: all loss will soon be made right, and that for eternity.

This comforting thought is strengthened by the reminder that God is the God *who has called you to* (or 'into', *eis*) *his eternal glory in Christ*. That is the realm that really counts, for it lasts for ever. In that realm, the manifold excellence of God's character is given spectacular expression in *his eternal glory* – something that ordinarily would cause us to remain distant in fearful awe. Yet God has decided that we should not remain distant, but that we

[1]See 1:7, 8, 12, 20, 25 (twice); 2:4, 7, 9, 10 (twice), 14, 23; 3:8, 9, 11, 12, 14, 15, 18; 4:6, 7, 16 (twice), 17; 5:5 (twice), 10.

should be summoned into the midst of his own glory – yes, even that we should come *in Christ* (*i.e.* in union with Christ) to share in it,[1] partially now and more fully in the life to come. Here is promise of abundant grace sufficient to overcome any suffering in this life.

11. A concluding brief doxology appropriately looks to God's power and rule over a world where so much evil is present, a world so badly in need of God's just reign: *To him be the dominion for ever and ever, Amen.*

IV. CLOSING GREETINGS (5:12–14)

Peter ends the letter with a brief concluding section. In verse 12 he begins by noting the role of Silvanus, but then immediately reverts to another word of exhortation. Verses 13 and 14 contain personal greetings and a benediction of peace.

A. I AM SENDING THIS BY FAITHFUL SILVANUS (5:12a)

12a. *Silvanus* is also closely connected with Paul's ministry (he is mentioned in 2 Cor. 1:19; 1 Thes. 1:1; 2 Thes. 1:1), and is the same person whom Luke calls 'Silas' in Acts (mentioned twelve times between Acts 15:22 and 18:5). In fact, Acts 15:22 names Silas as a messenger carrying the apostolic letter from Jerusalem. (A. T. Robertson, *Grammar*, pp. 172–173, gives a long list of Gk. names which had both long and short forms in the same pattern as Silas/Silvanus.)

By Silvanus, a faithful brother as I regard him, I have written briefly to you has been thought by some commentators to indicate that Silvanus was a messenger who carried Peter's letter, by others to indicate that he was the 'amanuensis' (secretary) who recorded the letter as Peter spoke (*cf.* Rom. 16:22; the use of an amanuensis explains Paul's habit of adding a personal postscript 'with my own hand': 1 Cor. 16:21; Gal. 6:11; Col. 4:18; 2 Thes.

[1]Note the same concept in 2 Pet. 1:3 (RSV).

3:17; Phm. 19). The evidence presented in the Introduction clearly favours the 'messenger' view, not the 'amanuensis' view (see pp. 23f.). (The NIV translation, 'With the help of Silvanus [see mg.] . . . I have written to you briefly', is apparently based on the view that Silvanus is the amanuensis.)

In addition to the sense of the phrase 'by Silvanus' (see p. 23), further evidence that this sentence merely designates Silvanus as the messenger is found in the fact that Peter calls him *a faithful brother as I regard him.* This commendation of the bearer of a letter is common and appropriate (apparently found, for example, in 1 Cor. 16:10–11; Eph. 6:21–22; Col. 4:7–9; Tit. 3:12–13), but nowhere is there a clear example of such a commendation given for an amanuensis who helped to write a letter, nor would there seem to be a good reason for Peter to do so. (Although Tertius mentions himself in Rom. 16:22, no NT author himself specifically mentions or commends an amanuensis.)

Of course, one could argue that even though this verse designates Silvanus as the bearer of the letter, he could also have been the amanuensis who wrote at Peter's direction and (perhaps) polished the style of composition. But if this verse is entirely explained as a designation showing Silvanus to be the bearer of the letter (see discussion in Introduction), then there is nothing here which also designates him as the amanuensis, nor is there historical data elsewhere which would indicate this role for Silvanus. It is best, therefore, to conclude that there is no clear evidence in the letter indicating that Silvanus had a role in its composition.

B. STAND IN THE GRACE I HAVE DESCRIBED (5:12b)

12b. *I have written briefly to you* is similar to the expression of brevity found in Hebrews 13:22. Looking back over both Hebrews and 1 Peter, one cannot help being struck by how much the authors have actually said in a very short space: many present-day readers may see in that fact additional evidence of divine as well as human authorship of this letter (certainly that has been true of the present author's own experience while working closely on the letter over many months).

Peter says he has been *exhorting and declaring that this is the true grace of God*, thus summarizing his letter as a combination of moral commands (*exhorting*) and factual doctrinal teaching (*declaring that this is the true grace of God*). The word *this* is best understood to refer to the entire way of life described in the letter as a whole. The entire Christian life is one of *grace* – God's daily bestowal of blessings, strength, help, forgiveness, and fellowship with himself, all of which we need, none of which we ever deserve. All is of *grace*, every day. From continual trust in that grace and from continual obedience empowered by it Christians must not move: rather, they must *stand fast in it* – until the day of their death.

C. GREETINGS FROM THE CHURCH IN ROME AND FROM MARK (5:13)

13. *Babylon* can hardly be the ancient city of Babylon in Mesopotamia which is prominent in the Old Testament, for by the first century it was a small and obscure place (see Introduction, p. 33), for which there is no evidence of a visit by Peter (or Mark: see the end of this verse), or even of a Christian church. But there is good evidence outside the New Testament that Peter was in Rome about the time this letter was written (see Introduction, pp. 34f.), and it is best to understand *Babylon* as a reference to Rome (just as in Rev. 16:19; 17:5; 18:2). It is not that Peter was trying to disguise his location, but rather that he is carrying through the imagery of the church as the new people of God, the true Israel (see note at 2:10), which he has maintained since the word 'Dispersion' in 1:1. Just as in the Old Testament Babylon was the centre of worldly power and opposition to God's people, so in the time of the New Testament Rome is the earthly centre of a world-wide system of government and life which opposes the gospel. Yet there Peter is in the midst of it.

And Peter is not alone. *She who is at Babylon, who is likewise chosen*, must mean the church at Rome – for no one individual would be so well known to all the churches of Peter's readers as to be identifiable from such an anonymous reference. The whole church at Rome *sends you greetings. And so does my son Mark* indicates the presence of Mark with Peter and shows a close association with the author of the second Gospel. *Son* means not physical son but spiritual 'son', close associate and assistant in the service of Christ (*cf.* 1 Tim. 1:2; 2 Tim. 1:2).

D. GREET ONE ANOTHER (5:14a)

14a. *Greet one another with the kiss of love* is similar to a closing exhortation in several of Paul's letters (Rom. 16:16; 1 Cor. 16:20; 2 Cor. 13:12; 1 Thes. 5:26). Such a kiss was free from romantic overtones, since Paul always calls it a 'holy kiss'. Although we may dismiss this as simply a custom belonging to first-century culture, we would do well to recognize the benefits in interpersonal relationships which come from such close physical expressions of friendship and fellowship in Christ. It is much harder to get mad at someone you have just hugged or kissed, and it is much easier to feel accepted in a fellowship which has given such a warm welcome! 'Give each other a handshake all round' (Phillips) is far too distant and formal – probably a 'holy hug' would come much closer to fulfilling Peter's intention. And it should be a genuine expression *of love* in Christ.

E. PEACE TO ALL WHO ARE IN CHRIST (5:14b)

14b. *Peace to all of you that are in Christ* is what these believers needed – peace within for troubled minds and hearts, and peace without when God grants them rest from their sufferings (*cf.* 'peace' in 1:2b). To be *in Christ* is to be united with him for all the benefits of redemption: it is the status of all true believers as soon as they have become Christians, and they remain *in Christ* for all eternity.

APPENDIX

CHRIST PREACHING THROUGH NOAH: 1 PETER 3:19–20 IN THE LIGHT OF DOMINANT THEMES IN JEWISH LITERATURE

Near the end of chapter 3 in this first letter, Peter writes,

> [18]For Christ also died for sins once for all, the righteous for the unrighteous, that he might bring us to God, being put to death in the flesh but made alive in the spirit; [19]in which he went and preached to the spirits in prison, [20]who formerly did not obey, when God's patience waited in the days of Noah, during the building of the ark, in which a few, that is, eight persons, were saved through water.

The difficulties of this passage have given rise to a number of interpretations, especially of the meaning of verse 19, *in which he went and preached to the spirits in prison*.

The issues where commentators differ, as already stated on pp. 157f., are at least these:

1. Who are the spirits in prison?
   – unbelievers who have died?
   – Old Testament believers who have died?
   – fallen angels?
2. What did Christ preach?
   – second chance for repentance?
   – completion of redemptive work?
   – final condemnation?
3. When did he preach?
   – in the days of Noah?
   – between his death and resurrection?
   – after his resurrection?

Among all the possible answers to those questions, the following five views have been the most commonly held (the italicized words indicate the identity of 'the spirits in prison' in each view):

View 1: When Noah was building the ark, Christ 'in spirit' was in Noah preaching repentance and righteousness through him to *unbelievers who were on the earth then* but are now 'spirits in prison' (people in hell).[1]

View 2: After Christ died, he went and preached to *people in hell*, offering them a second chance of salvation.[2]

View 3: After Christ died, he went and preached to *people in hell*, proclaiming to them that he had triumphed over them and their condemnation was final.[3]

View 4: After Christ died, he proclaimed release to *people who had repented just before they died in the flood*, and led them out of their imprisonment (in Purgatory) into heaven.[4]

View 5: After Christ died (or: after he rose but before he ascended into heaven), he travelled to hell and proclaimed triumph over the *fallen angels* who had sinned by marrying human women before the flood.[5]

[1]St. Augustine, Letter 164, chs. 15–17; Thomas Aquinas, *Summa Theologica*, part 3, question 52, art. 2, reply to obj. 3; Leighton, pp. 354–366; Zahn, p. 289; W. Kelly, *Christ Preaching to the Spirits in Prison* (London: Morrish, 1872), pp. 3–89; D. G. Wohlenberg, *Der erste und zweite Petrusbriefe und der Judasbrief* (Leipzig: Deichert, 1923), pp. 106–115; Guthrie, *NTI*, p. 842; recently, P. Patterson, *A Pilgrim Priesthood* (Nashville: Nelson, 1982), pp. 134–146, 195–199, with several theological objections to other views.

[2]Reicke, esp. pp. 90–91, 118, 120–122, 130–131 (includes preaching also to disobedient angels); Cranfield, pp. 84–86 (but hesitantly); A. M. Hunter, *IB*, vol. 12, pp. 132–133 (preaching to the rebellious generation of the flood); Hart, pp. 68–69 (preaching to disobedient angels, who repented); Bigg, pp. 162–163; Beare, pp. 170–173; Best, pp. 140–147; others listed in Reicke, pp. 47–49 and in Dalton, p. 21, note 34; A. T. Hanson, *ExpT* 93 (1981–82), pp. 100–115.

[3]Reicke, pp. 44–45, lists several 17th-century supporters of this view, which he calls the 'orthodox Lutheran theory'; it is strongly supported by Lenski, pp. 160–169.

[4]This position began with Robert Bellarmine in 1586, and has been common among Roman Catholic interpreters; so H. Willmering in *A Catholic Commentary on Holy Scripture*, ed. B. Orchard (London: Nelson, 1953), p. 1179; others listed in Reicke, pp. 42–44, and Dalton, pp. 30–31.

[5]This is probably the dominant view today, primarily because of the influence of Selwyn's commentary, pp. 197–203, 314–362, and then of the detailed work by Dalton, esp. pp. 135–201. (Dalton sees the preaching as having occurred during an 'invisible ascension' of Christ on Easter Sunday morning, just after his appearance [Jn. 20:17] to Mary in the Garden: see pp. 185–186.)

Others who favour this view (but who place the preaching at various times, either before

There are other views than these but they are usually different combinations of the details listed above (offering salvation to unbelieving people and angels, or proclaiming triumph over sinners and complete redemption to believers, *etc.*).[1] For our purposes this list is sufficient.

The following discussion will argue for View 1 (Christ preaching through Noah when the ark was being built), a view which has received the support of very few commentaries, and which is frequently dismissed in discussions of this passage because Augustine, who first proposed it, took *in prison* to refer to 'the darkness of ignorance' in which unbelievers lived – obviously a metaphorical (or 'allegorical', to use Dalton's term) sense of 'prison' not intended by Peter. But this sense of 'in prison' is by no means essential to the view that Christ was preaching at the time of Noah, and a more common understanding ('spirits in hell') is certainly consistent with it (see below). The other common objection to this view is that it has no clear relationship to the context, but it will be argued that on closer inspection the context lends more support to this view than perhaps to any of the others.

Although most of the views mentioned above depend on backgrounds familiar to readers of the Bible generally, a word of explanation should perhaps be given regarding View 5. This view argues that certain extra-biblical Jewish traditions, especially the tradition in 1 Enoch about Enoch going and proclaiming a message of condemnation to disobedient angels, were well known to Peter's readers. Therefore, when Peter said that Christ went and preached to the 'spirits in prison', his readers would immediately have recognized the allusion to 1 Enoch and known that Peter was portraying Christ as a 'second Enoch' who in a far greater way 'went and proclaimed' his victory over fallen angels, and announced to them, as had Enoch long before, that they were eternally condemned for their sin. The fact that they 'formerly disobeyed' is then understood

---

Christ's resurrection, immediately after it, or at his ascension) include: Kelly, pp. 151–158; J. Fitzmyer, *JBC*, vol. 2, pp. 366–367; Stibbs/Walls, pp. 142–143; Blum, pp. 241–243; Leaney, pp. 50–52; France, pp. 264–281 (a good recent statement of this position).

[1] For the view of R. Harris (1902), E. Goodspeed (1945), and others that the text should be emended to read, 'Enoch went and preached . . .', see objections in Reicke, pp. 41–42. Most

to refer to the sin of angels who married human wives in Genesis 6:2, 4, a story well-attested in extra-biblical literature.[1]

Dalton has performed a valuable service in his careful tracing of the history of different views, and in his gracious evaluation of those views which he rejects. Because his extensive arguments have convinced many scholars from a wide spectrum of theological positions, somewhat more interaction in the subsequent discussion will be with Dalton's argument.

I shall consider the three questions mentioned above in the order given:

I. Who are the spirits in prison?
II. What did Christ preach?
III. When did he preach?

I. WHO ARE THE 'SPIRITS IN PRISON'?

A. THE MEANING OF 'SPIRIT' (PNEUMA)

1. General meaning: angels or human spirits?

If the phrase 'the spirits in prison' appeared in the text without any further specification, it could refer either to human or to angelic spirits, depending on the larger context. This is because the word *spirits* (*pneumata*, plural, or *pneuma*, singular) both in the Bible and in extra-biblical literature can be used to refer to human spirits or to angels (or demons).

Examples of the word used to refer to a human spirit are found, for example, in Ecclesiastes 12:7 ('and the spirit returns to God who gave it' is a description of death; the LXX has *pneuma* here); Mt. 27:50 (Jesus 'yielded up his spirit'); Lk. 23:46 ('Father,

---

commentators have been left unpersuaded by this view, preferring to interpret the text as it stands rather than attempting to alter it by inserting the name 'Enoch', a proposal supported by no ancient manuscript.

[1]The fullest statement of this position is in Dalton, pp. 135–201, but a briefer yet very clear statement of this view is found in France, pp. 264–281, or in Kelly, pp. 151–158.

into thy hands I commit my spirit!');[1] Jn. 19:30 (Jesus 'bowed his head and gave up his spirit'); Acts 7:59 (as Stephen was dying he prayed, 'Lord Jesus, receive my spirit'); 1 Cor. 5:5; 7:34; 14:14; Heb. 12:23; Jas. 2:26; *cf.* Nu. 16:22; Josephus, *War* 7.185; *etc.*

Examples of the meaning 'angel' (or 'evil angel, demon') are found in Matthew 8:16 ('he cast out the spirits with a word'); 10:1 ('he gave them authority over unclean spirits'); 12:43, 45; Mark 1:23; Luke 10:20; Acts 23:8; *etc.*

2. Does pneuma, 'spirit', have a special meaning when used 'absolutely'?

Those who understand the spirits in prison to be fallen angels (View 5 above) have claimed that the word 'spirit' is never used 'absolutely' (or without a 'defining genitive phrase') to refer to human spirits (the objection apparently originated with Selwyn, p. 199, and is repeated by Dalton, p. 147, and France, p. 269). Those who make this objection claim that *pneuma* is used 'absolutely' to refer to good or evil angelic spirits.

However, this is simply one example of an error in exegetical method which occurs frequently in Selwyn's commentary – that of drawing conclusions about the meaning of words or phrases from insufficient data or from artificially created distinctions in style which really have no significant influence on the meanings of the words used. In this case, the objection is invalid for three reasons:

(a) *Pneuma* is used 'without a defining genitive' to refer to a 'departed' human spirit (the spirit which had left Abel after Cain killed him) in 1 Enoch 22:6 and again in 22:7; another example is found in 1 Enoch 20:6 (Gk. text).[2] These examples are significant because Selwyn, Dalton, and France all emphasize 1 Enoch as the supposed background for this passage in 1 Peter. Other examples of *pneuma* used 'absolutely' of a human spirit are

---

[1] Some have suggested that this verse means simply, 'Into your hands I commit myself' (so Dalton, p. 146). However, in the light of the very similar expressions in Mt. 27:50, Jn. 19:30, and Acts 7:59, where such a meaning is not possible, this suggestion is not persuasive.

[2] Gk. text in M. Black, *Apocalypsis Henochi Graece* and A.-M. Denis, *Fragmenta Pseudepigraphorum Quae Supersunt Graeca* (Leiden: Brill, 1970), p. 32. A recent English translation by E. Isaac is found in *OTP*, vol. 1, pp. 13–89.

Ecclesiastes 12:7; Matthew 27:50 (Gk. text); John 19:30 (Gk. text).

(b) But the larger issue is not whether we can find examples of *pneuma* used without a 'defining genitive' ('of men', *etc.*) to refer to human spirits, for that is simply an artificial distinction. The real issue is whether the context specifies more clearly what type of spirit is meant. If by *pneuma* used 'absolutely' Selwyn and Dalton mean *pneuma* used with no further specification or definition from context, then it should be pointed out that no examples of *pneuma* meaning 'angelic spirits' have been found without further definition from context, either.

In fact, the three examples of an 'absolute' use cited by Dalton, p. 147 – Matthew 8:16; 12:45; Luke 10:20 – are all further defined by the immediate context: Matthew 8:16 mentions people who were 'demon possessed' in the previous phrase; Matthew 12:45 is in a paragraph where the subject had been defined as 'an unclean spirit' in verse 43; Luke 10:20 is in response to verse 17, 'Lord, even the demons are subject to us in your name!' These three are not instances showing that *pneuma* generally, without other indications from context, means 'evil spirits' – for all these instances have prior contextual specification.

But this is simply because of an obvious linguistic fact: *pneuma* has a range of meanings, and can refer to human spirits, to angelic spirits, to God's Holy Spirit, *etc.* Because of this, there will always be a further specification of the type of spirit intended in context if the author wishes to communicate to the reader the sense in which he is using the term.

(c) Thirdly, 1 Peter 3:19 is not itself an example of *pneuma* used without further definition from its context, for the sentence itself defines further the kind of 'spirits' intended. They are spirits 'in prison' who 'disobeyed in the days of Noah' and who did so 'while the patience of God was waiting during the building of the ark'.

3. 'Spirits' in 1 Enoch

It has been argued that for Peter's readers the phrase 'spirits in prison' would automatically call to mind the use of *pneuma* in 1 Enoch to refer to 'angels who sinned and were consigned to a place of punishment awaiting final judgment' (Dalton, pp. 166–

168). But even if one grants for the sake of argument that all of Peter's readers had just finished reading 1 Enoch the night before Peter's letter arrived, it does not follow that 'spirits in prison' would mean 'fallen angels' to Peter or to his readers.

The extant Greek sections of 1 Enoch use *pneuma* thirty-seven times.[1] Of these thirty-seven times, the word is used twenty times to refer to angelic or demonic spirits. But it is used seventeen times to refer to human spirits (1 Enoch 9:10; 20:3, 6 [twice]; 22:3, 6, 7, 9 [twice], 11 [twice], 12, 13 [twice]; 98:3, 10; 103:4). We are therefore not justified in drawing from this data any firm conclusion about what Peter's readers would have thought the phrase 'spirits in prison' meant.

Moreover, in some instances the human spirits of those who have died are seen to be bound or confined in a place of waiting until they face the final judgment (1 Enoch 22:3–13, which uses *pneuma* ten times in this sense; *cf.* 98:3), and could readily be said to be 'in prison'.

4. Are the spirits 'in prison' now, or when Christ preached to them?

Although it might appear on an initial reading that 'spirits in prison' must refer to those who were incarcerated at the time the preaching took place, this is not necessarily the case. Verse nineteen could equally well be understood to mean 'he preached to the spirits who are now in prison', *i.e.* those who are spirits in hell at the time Peter is writing but who were formerly human beings on earth at the time of the flood. (NASB translates, 'He went and made proclamation to the spirits *now* in prison, who once were disobedient, when the patience of God kept waiting in the days of Noah, during the construction of the ark.') It is quite natural to speak in terms of a person's present status even when describing a past action which occurred when the person did not have that status. For example, it would be perfectly correct to say, 'Queen Elizabeth was born in 1926,' even though she did not become Queen until long after 1926.

[1]This count is taken from the concordance in C. Wahl, *Clavis Librorum Veteris Testamenti Apocryphorum Philologica* (Graz, Austria: Akademische Druck- und Verlagsanstalt, 1972), p. 548), and excludes the variant readings.

In fact, the great majority of commentators, no matter what view they take of 3:19–20, interpret 4:6 in similar fashion, understanding it to mean that the gospel was preached to those who, at the time of writing, were now dead. It was declared to them in order that they might be saved from final judgment, even though they would not be spared dying. So 'the gospel was preached to the dead' in 4:6 means that the gospel was preached to 'those who are now dead' (at the time Peter is writing) even though they were alive on earth at the time the gospel was preached to them (see Commentary, pp. 170ff.). Therefore, in understanding 1 Peter 3:19–20, the possibility must be left open that 'he *preached to the spirits in prison*' means 'he preached to those who are now spirits in hell but who at the time of the preaching were human beings living on the earth'.

5. Conclusion regarding the phrase 'spirits in prison'

We must conclude that by itself the phrase 'the spirits in prison' could refer either to human or to angelic spirits, and the larger context must be decisive. The term 'spirit' is used frequently to refer both to human spirits and to angelic spirits. Since the evidence from 1 Enoch is ambiguous, no clear conclusion can be drawn from it. Furthermore, the brief phrase 'spirits in prison' could mean either 'spirits who were in hell when Christ preached to them' or 'those who are now spirits in hell but who at the time of Christ's preaching were people on earth'. Thus, the phrase itself is not clear apart from further definition by its larger context. It is to an examination of this context that we now turn.

B. EVIDENCE FROM FOUR OTHER DEFINING PHRASES

The phrase 'the spirits in prison' does not stand by itself but is followed by four additional defining phrases:

who formerly did not obey
(better: 'disobeyed', see pp. 106f. and 159)[1]

[1] At this point in the discussion I shall assume, for the sake of argument, the validity of the

in the days of Noah
when God's patience waited
during the building of the ark

These four phrases, upon examination, all indicate that the 'spirits in prison' must be understood to be human spirits, not angelic spirits. This can be seen by an investigation of the biblical and extra-biblical evidence pertaining to these phrases.

1. Evidence for angelic disobedience

a. The sons of God in Genesis 6:2, 4

Those who favour View 5 above (the spirits in prison as fallen angels) point to the many places in extra-biblical Jewish literature where the 'sons of God' who married 'the daughters of men' in Genesis 6:2, 4 and begot children by them, are understood to be sinful angels who married human women. This understanding of Genesis 6 is frequent in extra-biblical literature, being attested in at least the following nine texts: Josephus, *Ant.* 1:73; Philo, *On the Giants* 6; *Q.Gen.* 1.92; CD 2.18; 1 Enoch 6.2, 6; 106.13–14; Jubilees 5.1; 10.1–6; 2 Baruch 56.12–15.

However, it is often not appreciated that such an interpretation of Genesis 6 is far from uniform in Jewish tradition. The following list shows nine other texts where non-angelic interpretations are held:

While Philo himself calls these 'sons of God' angels in one place, he later calls them 'good and excellent men' *Q.Gen.* 1.92).[1]

---

common Eng. translation *'who* formerly disobeyed', even though at a later point I shall argue on grammatical and contextual grounds that it would be better to translate this phrase, *'when* they formerly disobeyed'.

[1]Although the meaning of Gn. 6:2, 4 is still widely disputed, something near to this statement of Philo seems to be the most satisfactory interpretation: note the emphasis on sonship as including likeness to one's father in Gn. 5:3, and the tracing of descendants from God through Adam to many 'sons' in all of chapter 5. The structure of the narrative is tracing the parallel development of the godly (ultimately Messianic) line of Seth and the ungodly descendants of the rest of mankind. Thus 'sons of God' are (as in Dt. 14:1) people belonging to God and like him, walking in righteousness (note Gn. 4:26 as an introduction to Gn. 5), and 'daughters of men' are the ungodly wives whom they marry. *Cf.* the argument of H. C. Leupold, *Exposition of Genesis* (Grand Rapids: Baker, 1953), vol. 1, pp. 249–254; also J. Murray, *Principles of Conduct* (Grand Rapids: Eerdmans, 1957), pp. 243–249. (But also note the view of Meredith G. Kline, *WTJ* 24 (1961–62), pp. 187–204, who sees the 'sons of God' as human kings.)

Moreover, the Targums and the Rabbinic literature are unanimous in viewing the 'sons of God' as human beings. Targum Onkelos on Genesis 6:2 and 4 reads 'sons of princes' (or great men, *rbrby'*), and Targum Pseudo-Jonathan has the same. Targum Neofiti has 'sons of the Judges' (*dyyny'*) in both verses.[1]

Tosefta, *Sotah* 3.9a[2] interprets 'sons of God' as men of the generation of the flood. In the Midrash Rabbah, they are understood as 'sons of judges' (*dyyn*) and as 'leaders' (Gen.R. 26.5 on Gn. 6:2, quoting Rabbi Simeon ben Yohai, *c.* AD 140), or as the generation of men at the time of the flood (Num.R. 9.24, on 5:27). The Babylonian Talmud at *b.Sanh* 108a understands them as men at the time of the flood. Symmachus translates Genesis 6:2 as 'the sons of the rulers' (*tōn dynasteuontōn*).

Although this material is admittedly somewhat later than 1 Enoch and Jubilees, which are both to be dated in the second century BC, the citations from Philo and the Targums are certainly not irrelevant for New Testament exegesis – indeed, the Rabbinic material generally represents a stream of Jewish tradition which is certainly relevant as a background for New Testament studies. And the citations in this second group are diverse and frequent enough to give strong indication of the existence of a 'non-angelic' view of the 'sons of God' in Judaism, especially more orthodox Judaism, before or during the time of the New Testament.

Our understanding of this point is not crucial, for one could be convinced that Peter's readers all thought that Genesis 6:2, 4 referred to fallen angels who took human wives and still hold that 1 Peter 3:19–20 spoke of human beings who disobeyed during the building of the ark. (Peter does not, of course, say 'he preached to the spirits in prison who disobeyed by marrying human women' but rather 'spirits . . . who disobeyed when the ark was being built'.) But this evidence is none the less helpful in showing that one cannot simply assume that the readers of 1 Peter had an 'angelic' interpretation of Genesis 6:2, 4 in their minds. Indeed, Peter would not have assumed an 'angelic'

---

[1]However, a marginal gloss of unknown date at Targum Neofiti on Gn. 6:4 reads 'sons of the angels'.

[2]Neusner, vol. 3, p. 156.

interpretation in his readers' minds either, for no uniform interpretation of this passage can be demonstrated for the first century AD.

b. Other references to angelic disobedience

Even if there is no uniform interpretation of Genesis 6:2, 4 as involving the sin of angels, is there none the less other evidence in Jewish literature showing a common tradition of interpretation in which angels are said to have sinned 'in the days of Noah' or 'when God's patience waited' or 'during the building of the ark'?

Something near to this idea is found in Jubilees 10:4-5, where Noah, speaking of evil spirits (who are called 'Watchers'), says to God, 'You know what your Watchers . . . did in my days, and also these spirits who are alive. Shut them up and take them to the place of judgment.'

Then with reference to the reason for the flood, the *Testament of Naphtali* says that 'the Watchers departed from nature's order; the Lord pronounced a curse on them at the flood. On their account he ordered that the earth be without dweller or produce' (*T.Naph.* 3:5). Here the flood is specifically said to have been caused by the sin of angels. In addition, 1 Enoch 67:8-13 says that the waters of the flood will first become hot – to punish sinful angels – and then become cold – to punish sinful men.

However, Jewish tradition does not uniformly link the sin of angels with the flood. This sin is more frequently put in the days of Enoch and Methuselah, two and three generations before Noah (Jubilees 4:22, *cf.* 4:20, 20:8), or in the time of Jared, four generations before Noah (1 Enoch 6:6 [Greek text]; 106:13). While a difference of two to four generations may seem insignificant to the modern reader who may have only a vague idea of the genealogy leading to the birth of Noah, it would certainly matter to the authors or readers of these writings, for they go into great detail when narrating the events of the lives of people like Enoch, his son Methuselah, his grandson Lamech, and his great grandson Noah.[1]

More significantly, even in these three texts which make a

---

[1] See the detailed chronologies in other Jewish literature, such as Josephus, *Ant.* 1.81–88 (with extended note in LCL edition, vol. 4, pp. 38–39); also Babylonian Talmud, *Abodah Zarah* 9a (with note in Soncino Eng. tr. [ed. I. Epstein; London: Soncino, 1961], *Nezkin*, vol. 4, p. 44).

connection between angelic sin and the flood, there is no mention of two elements which Peter specifically mentions – God patiently waiting (for repentance), and the disobedience which occurred 'during the building of the ark'.

One final strand of evidence for the idea of angelic sin as a background to 1 Peter 3:19 might be found within the New Testament itself: it might be argued that 2 Peter 2:4–5 (and perhaps Jude 6) connects the sin of angels and consequent judgment with Noah and the flood, or perhaps with the sin concerning 'the daughters of men' in Gen. 6:2, 4.

However, this conclusion cannot be sustained after a closer look at 2 Peter 2:4–7, for there in the same sentence Peter mentions not only angelic sin and the flood, but also 'the cities of Sodom and Gomorrah' and the rescue of Lot (vv. 6–7). Yet Peter hardly thinks the judgment on Sodom and Gomorrah happened at the same time as the flood! This means that, far from seeing events such as angelic sin and the flood as contemporaneous, he is simply picking out three separate examples of sin and judgment from the Old Testament to emphasize that judgment on sin will come and that God will save the righteous from it (vv. 9–10).

Jude 6 is even less persuasive. It mentions angelic sin and judgment on angels, but does not specify the sin except for a general statement that angels 'did not keep their own position' (a probable reference to rebellion against God's authority). And there is no connection with the time of the flood but rather the following sequence:

v. 5 exodus from Egypt; judgment on unbelievers (Ex. 14; Nu. 14)

v. 6 sin of angels; judgment

v. 7 Sodom and Gomorrah; judgment (Gn. 19).

No chronological connection is implied; Jude, like Peter, simply selects three noteworthy examples of judgment from the Old Testament. In neither text is there an implication of angelic sin at the time of the flood, or of angelic sin with human women.

Nevertheless, if there were no other references indicating a tradition of human disobedience just before the flood, these three pseudepigraphal texts which briefly mention angelic disobedience in a general way, though not precisely parallel to

Peter's statement about the spirits in prison, might still be thought to provide a helpful background against which Peter's readers would have understood 1 Peter 3:18–20. However, before such a conclusion is drawn, it is necessary to examine the evidence for a tradition of human, not angelic, disobedience 'during the building of the ark'.

2. Evidence for human disobedience

a. Who disobeyed 'during the building of the ark'?

(i) Old Testament evidence

The Old Testament narrative indicates that there were human beings who disobeyed God 'when God's patience waited in the days of Noah, during the building of the ark', but there is no indication of angelic disobedience during that time (cf. Gn. 6:5–7, 12–13).

Though there are different views on whether Genesis 6:1–4 refers to the sin of angels when it talks about the 'sons of God' (see above), there can be no dispute that the entire section immediately preceding the command to build the ark (Gn. 6:5–13) clearly emphasizes human sin, and human sin alone, as the reason God brings the flood upon the earth. God is not sorry that he has made angels, but that he made man (v. 6). He does not decide to blot out fallen angels, but man (vv. 6, 13); it is not the violence and corruption of angels which arouses his anger, but the violence and corruption of man (vv. 5, 11, 12, 13).

At this point it could be objected that human disobedience is sometimes seen as having been caused by prior angelic disobedience, and that therefore the two are closely connected. While this connection is made in some extra-biblical literature, it is certainly not a uniform interpretation, and it is clearly not a connection made in the biblical text itself. In addition, 1 Peter 3 speaks not of those who disobeyed long before the flood (as angels did), but of those who disobeyed precisely when the ark was being built.

(ii) New Testament evidence

In the New Testament, 2 Peter 2:5 mentions Noah as a 'herald of righteousness' in the midst of 'the world of the ungodly'. Similarly, in Matthew 24:37–39 and Luke 17:26–27 Jesus clearly emphasizes human disregard of impending judgment in the days of Noah. Furthermore, he says that a similar situation will occur again: 'As were the days of Noah, so will be the coming of the Son of man . . .' (Mt. 24:37). In this context, the warning about the need for human watchfulness, and the parallels with activity in the days of Noah, mean that human disobedience in the days of Noah is clearly in view. Once again, angelic disobedience is never specifically connected with the judgment of the flood itself.

(iii) Extra-biblical evidence

The *Sibylline Oracles*, 1.171–172, say that the people who heard Noah's exhortations to repentance from their wicked life mocked him: 'When they heard him they sneered at him, each one, calling him demented, a man gone mad' (this mocking occurs in the middle of Noah's sermon about their sins, after the ark has been built: note lines 190–191, 205).[1] Similarly, the Babylonian Talmud at *b.Sanh.* 108b says that those watching Noah 'derided him', saying, 'Old man, what is this ark for?' Genesis Rabbah 30.7 (on 6:9) says that Noah was mocked by those who watched him build the ark. They despised him and called him 'contemptible old man'. Moreover, when Noah cut down trees to build the ark and told them a flood was coming they responded, 'It will come only on your father's house.' In Ecclesiastes Rabbah on 9:14 (sec. 1), when Noah warns the people, 'Tomorrow a flood will come, so repent', they refuse to listen and mock him, 'If punishments begin they will begin with your house'. These specific citations quite clearly speak of *human* disobedience 'while the ark was being built', and should be seen in contrast to the total absence of references to angelic sin during the building of the ark.

Furthermore, Jewish literature frequently mentions human, not angelic sin, as the reason why God brought the flood on the earth. The texts are too numerous to cite here but it is sufficient

---

[1]This section of the *Sibylline Oracles* is dated in the late 1st century BC or very early 1st century AD by J. J. Collins, in agreement with A. Kurfess: see J. J. Collins, 'Sibylline Oracles' in *OTP*, vol. 1, p. 331.

to give the references: Targums Onkelos, Pseudo-Jonathan, Neofiti, and the Fragmentary Targum on Genesis 6:5 and 6:11–13; Gen.R. 26.5 (on 6:2); 26.7 (on 6:4); 28:8 (on 6:7); 31.1–5 (on 6:13); 31.6 (on 6:13); Eccl.R. on 2:23, sec.1; Num.R. 5.3 (on 4:18); 9.18 (on 5:21); 9.24 (on 5:27); *b.R.H.* 12a; *b.Sanh.* 108a; Philo, *Q.Gen.* 1.99, 100; 2.13; *Abr.* 40–41; Josephus, *Ant.* 1.74, 75, 98; CD 2.20–21; 1 Enoch 65.6, 10–11; 67.8–10; 2 Enoch 70.4–8; 3 Enoch 4.3; Jubliees 5.2–4, 7–9; Apocalypse of Adam 3.3; Pseudo-Philo, *Biblical Antiquities*, 3.2, 6; *Sib. Or.* 1.130–131, 150–179; 3 Maccabees 2.4. And the phrase 'the generation of the flood' is used frequently in Rabbinic writings as a paradigm of extreme human wickedness: Mishnah, *Sanhedrin* 10:3; Eccl.R. on 2:23, sec.1; SongR. on 1:4, sec.3; Num.R. 9.18 (on 5:21); 14.6 (on 7:54); 20.2 (on 22.2), *etc.*

All of these texts (forty-five listed here, from every strand of Jewish tradition) must be seen in contrast to the slight evidence of a tradition of angelic sin at this time: one text (Jubilee 10:4–5) which mentions angelic sin in Noah's day and two (*T.Naph.* 3:5; 1 Enoch 67:8–13) which say angels were punished at the flood (one of which, *T.Naph.* 3:5, also says the earth was made 'without dweller or produce' because of angels' sin). Not one text from any strand of Jewish tradition mentions angels disobeying 'during the building of the ark'. The overwhelming weight of extra-biblical tradition – as well as the biblical evidence itself – emphasizes human sinners, not angels, as the most likely to be meant by Peter's phrases, *who formerly [disobeyed]*[1] . . . *in the days of Noah, during the building of the ark.*

b. For whom was the patience of God waiting?
That the 'spirits in prison' are further stated to be those *who . . . [disobeyed]*[1] *when God's patience waited,* strongly suggests that God was waiting for them to repent, otherwise there would be no point in Peter's mentioning God's patience. Furthermore, the word *apekdechomai,* 'waiting', has the nuance of hopeful or expectant waiting for something to happen.[2]

The 'angelic' interpretation of this passage does not seem appropriate here, because neither the Old nor New Testaments

---

[1]For 'disobeyed', see pp. 106f. and 159.   [2]BAGD, p. 83: 'await eagerly'.

teach that fallen angels ever have a chance to repent (*cf.* 2 Pet. 2:4; Jude 6). But if Peter is referring to human beings who disobeyed, the statement is entirely consistent with repeated instances, throughout the Bible, of God's patient waiting for repentance before bringing judgment (Gn. 6:3; Pss. 103:7–12; 106:43–46; Ho. 11:8–9).

In extra-biblical Jewish literature also, God's patience is specifically connected with the years leading up to the flood. Targum Neofiti on Genesis 6:3 reports God saying to Noah, 'Behold I have given you 120 years, hoping that they might do repentance.' The same idea is repeated in Targum Onkelos, Targum Pseudo-Jonathan, and the Fragmentary Targum on Genesis 6:3. Mekilta, *Shirata* 5:38–39 (on Ex. 15:5–6)[1] says that God gave an extension of time 'to the generation of the flood that they might repent'. The Mishnah (*Aboth* 5.2) says that all the generations from Adam to Noah continued to provoke God, thus making known how 'long-suffering' God is, until he finally brought upon them the water of the flood. Similar statements about God's waiting for men to repent are found in Gen.R. 32.7 (on 7:10); Num.R. 14.6 (on 7:54). And Philo (*Q.Gen.* 2.13 on Gn. 7:4, 10), in discussing the delay of the flood, says that God 'grants repentance of sins . . . in order that when they see the ark . . . they may believe the announcing (*to kērygmati*) of the flood . . . and that they may turn back from impiety'.[2]

Thus, with respect to the background for Peter's phrase *when God's patience waited*, the extra-biblical literature gives frequent and diverse witness to God's waiting for human repentance, but it is entirely silent regarding any waiting for angelic repentance – something the New Testament even seems to deny as a possibility (2 Pet. 2:4; Jude 6).

c. Noah as a preacher to his generation

There remains one further strand of extra-biblical Jewish tradition relevant to the background of biblical interpretation against which Peter was writing his letter. This concerns a widespread testimony to Noah's efforts as a 'preacher of righteousness'. Of

[1]Lauterbach, vol. 2, pp. 39–40.
[2]Here Philo uses the noun *kērygma*, 'announcement, proclamation', which is cognate with Peter's verb *kēryssō*, 'preach, proclaim', in 1 Pet. 3:19.

course, this evidence is of primary value merely to confirm the conclusions of the two previous sections that (a) it was humans who were thought to be sinning at that time, for they are the ones Noah tells to repent, and that (b) God's patience is waiting for the repentance of the human beings to whom Noah preaches. But the fact that Noah is frequently said to be a 'preacher' of repentance and righteousness to those around him during the building of the ark should at least prompt us to consider the possibility that when Peter speaks of preaching 'to the spirits in prison, who formerly disobeyed . . . during the building of the ark', he is in some way alluding to the preaching activity of Noah, familiar to his readers from Jewish tradition.

What is interesting is the frequency with which Noah is called a 'preacher' or 'herald' using the word *kēryx* and related words, all of which are cognate to *kēryssō* in 1 Peter 3:19 (Christ 'preached' to the spirits in prison). For example, in the early material from the *Sibylline Oracles*, Book 1,[1] we find that lines 150–198 contain two long speeches by Noah calling for repentance from those around him and warning that the flood was coming. In fact, *Sib. Or.* 1.128–129 records God as commanding Noah, 'Proclaim repentance to all the peoples . . . so that all might be saved.' The verb for 'proclaim' is *kēryssō*, the same verb used in 1 Peter 3:19.

Philo's use of the cognate noun *kērygma* to refer to warnings about the flood has just been cited (see above). Josephus does not use this term of Noah, but he says that Noah 'urged them to come to a better frame of mind and amend their ways' (*Ant.* 1.74, referring to human sinners).

In connection with Noah's preaching, Gen.R. 30.7 (on 6:9) quotes Rabbi Abba (3rd century AD?) as saying, 'The Holy One, blessed be He, said, "One herald arose for me in the generation of the flood, and this was Noah."' (The word for 'herald' used here is *kārôz*, an Aramaic loanword from Gk. *kēryx*, cognate to *kēryssō* in 1 Pet. 3:19; *cf.* BDB, p. 1097.) Other examples of Noah's preaching are found in Eccl.R. on 9:14, sec. 1; *b.Sanh.* 108a, 108b.

---

[1]This section was written perhaps fifty years before the time of the NT: see above, p. 216, n. 1.

Moreover, in early Christian literature we read, 'Noah preached repentance and those who obeyed were saved' (1 Clement 7.6), and that Noah proclaimed a 'new beginning to the world' (1 Clement 9.4). In both cases Clement (writing in AD 95) uses *kēryssō* to speak of Noah's preaching activity.

It is also relevant here to notice that Noah is called a preacher, 'herald [or, *kēryx*] of righteousness' in 2 Peter 2:5.

Thus, there is a widespread Jewish and early Christian tradition about Noah's activity as a preacher to those around him before the flood. And Peter's verb *kēryssō* and its cognates are used with surprising frequency in these traditions, even once by Peter himself.

3. Conclusion from a survey of background material

When Peter defined the 'spirits in prison' as those 'who disobeyed in the days of Noah when God's patience waited during the building of the ark', it is very unlikely that he would have expected his readers to identify them as disobedient angels. There is no evidence in biblical or extra-biblical literature which suggests that disobedient angels fit these characteristics.

Our conclusion is that the 'spirits in prison' are the human beings who disobeyed at the time Noah was building the ark and who were destroyed in the flood. This conclusion can be avoided only by disregarding the crucial defining phrases in 1 Peter 3:20.

C. ADDITIONAL NOTE:
CAN WE ASSUME THAT PETER'S READERS KNEW 1 ENOCH?

There is one further consideration which may appropriately be mentioned here. Those who take the 'spirits in prison' to be fallen angels must argue that 1 Enoch, the primary location of a detailed story about angelic sin and subsequent imprisonment, was widely known in the ancient world, so widely known that Peter could allude to a section of 1 Enoch without mentioning the work by name and still assume (if he wished to communicate effectively) that all his readers scattered throughout four provinces in Asia Minor would understand the allusion and interpret his sentence correctly in light of that allusion. (I have argued above that even if 1 Enoch were that widely known, readers would not automatically think of angels when they read the phrase 'spirits in prison'. As we saw, even in 1 Enoch there are human as well as angelic spirits imprisoned and waiting judgment, and there is human as well as angelic disobedience, with the human sin coming nearer the time when God's patience was waiting during the building of the ark. Nevertheless, this question is still relevant, since it speaks to a major part of Dalton's argument.)

It seems that we must entertain serious doubts about whether 1 Enoch was that widely known, and whether Peter would have been justified in making such an allusion. It is one thing to agree that Jude 14–15 quotes 1 Enoch by name and does so in a way in which even readers who have never heard of 1 Enoch can still understand the force of what Jude is saying. It is quite another thing to say that Peter would allude to 1 Enoch without mentioning it by name, and would do so in such a way that readers who were not familiar with 1 Enoch would be completely unable to understand Peter's meaning. Yet this is what advocates of the 'preaching to fallen angels' view must claim.

Against this claim must be put the fact that even though 1 Enoch is quoted in Jude 14–15, no one has ever demonstrated that 1 Enoch was that widely known or even familiar to the great majority of churches to which Peter was writing. In a recent introduction to 1 Enoch, E. Isaac writes:

> Information regarding the usage and importance of the work in the Jewish and Christian communities, other than the Ethiopian Church, is sparse. . . . It seems clear, nonetheless, that 1 Enoch was well known to many Jews, particularly the Essenes, and early Christians, notably the author of Jude.[1]

Yet this statement says nothing about whether it was known at all among Gentiles in Asia Minor – indeed, it implies that we have no positive evidence which would indicate such know-

[1]E. Isaac, '1 Enoch', *OTP*, vol. 1, p. 8.

ledge. 1 Enoch is cited or alluded to by several early Christian writers from the second century AD onward, but once again that gives no reason to think that it was known by Peter's readers in the first century who were far removed both geographically and culturally from the Palestinian Jewish origins of this book. Yet if this crucial fact must simply be assumed rather than demonstrated by those advocating the view that Christ preached to fallen angels, then it must be seen as an additional fundamental weakness in the position.

Furthermore, a hermeneutical and to some extent theological question arises for the modern interpreter: is the usual nature of the New Testament writings such that knowledge of a specific piece of extra-biblical literature would have been required for the original readers to understand the meaning (not the historical origin, but the meaning) of a specific passage? Is there any other text in the New Testament where readers simply would not have understood the meaning of the passage unless they were familiar with some extra-biblical text? I, at least, am unaware of one.

The reason this is seldom if ever the case is not far to seek: the New Testament writers were writing in order to communicate clearly with wide audiences of diverse backgrounds. In such a situation, they could of course assume knowledge of the Old Testament, for that was the 'Bible' for all Christians. But other than that, there was no one piece of literature which they could assume to be familiar to all their readers. And if they could not assume that, then it would seem to be irresponsible if they had ever written something which *required* knowledge of another piece of literature in order to be understood.

Of course, for the modern interpreter extra-biblical literature frequently provides information which gives more precise understanding of specific details about the force of a passage, and in many passages (as in this one) it can provide additional certainty about the correctness of an interpretation. But advocates of the 'fallen angels' view are claiming more than either of those things: they are claiming that a knowledge of the content of specific parts of 1 Enoch is necessary today (and, by implication, was necessary for the original readers) if one is to come anywhere near a correct understanding of the force of the passage.

On the other hand, and again in favour of the 'human disobedience' view, we must consider the fact that the New Testament authors regularly assume a knowledge of the Old Testament on the part of their readers. In the case of 1 Peter 3:19–20 that means that the Old Testament background must be given greater weight in evaluation of the reader's understanding than any background derived from extra-biblical literature. And for readers with only the background of the Old Testament, a reference to disobedience *when God's patience waited, during the building of the ark* would not be ambiguous, needing to be explained by acquaintance with extra-biblical literature. The phrases would be understandable and they would point unmistakably toward human beings who sinned during the time of Noah.

Who then are the 'spirits in prison'? A vast preponderance of biblical and extra-biblical literature seems to require the conclusion that they were not sinful angels but human beings who sinned while Noah was building the ark.

II. WHAT DID CHRIST PROCLAIM?

The citations regarding Noah's preaching which were quoted in the previous section indicated a frequent use of Peter's verb *kēryssō* in connection with Noah's preaching which called people to repentance and faith. This is not a necessary meaning of *kēryssō*, for the word simply means 'to proclaim', and the specific message proclaimed must be understood from other elements in the context. However, it must be noted that the verb is very commonly used in the New Testament and the LXX to refer to evangelistic preaching – preaching the gospel of Christ, or calling people to repentance and faith. Moreover, Peter's use of the related noun (*kēryx*) in 2 Peter 2:5 must be taken as very significant. Whether one understands this verse to mean that Noah preached righteousness, or that Noah was a righteous preacher (a less likely but grammatically possible view), in either case it is Noah's preaching of repentance to those around him which is in view. Furthermore, it was noted earlier that the phrase 'when God's patience waited', in connection with 'who formerly disobeyed', strongly suggests that this preaching calls for repentance on the part of those who are disobeying – otherwise the mention of the patience of God 'expectantly or eagerly waiting' would be without point.

If only a proclamation of condemnation were in view (as Dalton argues), Peter would have had to make that clear by further specifying it within the context. The contextual markers suggesting a preaching of repentance are too strong on the other side. Therefore, if Peter had wanted to state something like View 3 (Christ proclaimed final condemnation to people in hell) or View 5 (Christ proclaimed final condemnation to angels in hell), he would have needed to say something like 'proclaimed condemnation' (*katakrima*) or 'proclaimed judgment' (*krisin*), otherwise his meaning would not have been understood by his readers.

Furthermore, if the preaching of condemnation is meant, it is difficult to explain in a satisfactory way why final condemnation was proclaimed only to these specific sinners (or fallen angels) rather than to all who were in hell. Why were only those who disobeyed during the building of the ark singled out? Of course they are viewed, both in biblical and extra-biblical literature, as especially ungodly sinners, yet this still does not explain why they alone receive this decisive condemnation at the time of the turning-point of all history, the death and resurrection of Christ.

It could be replied that they are mentioned by Peter as representative of all fallen angels (or all sinners). But if Peter had meant 'all', why did he just mention some? To know that he intended these to be representative of 'all', the reader would need some indication such as 'to all those like the spirits in prison who disobeyed when . . . (*etc.*)' or 'to the spirits in prison who formerly disobeyed . . . and to all like them who have sinned . . . (*etc.*)'. But since there is no such indication, it is better to understand Christ's preaching to be only to those specifically mentioned.

View 4, which holds that Christ proclaimed the completion of redemption to Old Testament believers, also does not do justice to the context. The mention of 'prison' and disobedience, as well as the waiting of the patience of God, and the comment that only eight were saved, all point to preaching directed to sinners who need repentance, not to righteous saints waiting to hear a glad cry of victory. Once again, with so many contextual indicators pointing in the other direction, had Peter meant that the preaching proclaimed Christ's victory, he would have had to specify the fact by writing 'proclaim victory' (*nikos* or some similar term); in the absence of such specification Peter's readers would not have inferred that sense for 'preached'. Furthermore, there is again no convincing reason why the proclamation of the completion of redemption should be made only to those spirits who disobeyed during the building of the ark, instead of to all Old Testament believers. Thus, the content of the proclamation is best understood to be a proclamation to sinners of their need to repent and trust in God.

This meaning is most suitable to the larger context of 1 Peter 3 as well. The entire section from 2:11 up to this point has been concerned with living as Christians in the midst of an unbelieving world, and Peter has frequently called attention to the need for a good witness to unbelievers who are hostile toward his Christian readers (see 2:12, 15; 3:1–2, 15–16). Especially relevant is the call to witness in 3:15–16 ('be ready always to give an answer', AV) which provides the immediately preceding context to 3:19–20.

III. WHEN DID CHRIST PREACH?

The previous discussion has concluded that the spirits in prison are people who disobeyed during the time of Noah, and that the preaching directed to them called them to repentance. These conclusions, if correct, rule out Views 3, 4, and 5, listed at the beginning of this discussion. However, they would nevertheless be consistent with both View 1 (Christ preached through Noah at the time the ark was being built) and View 2 (Christ preached between his death and resurrection, giving those who disobeyed before the flood a second chance for salvation). A decision in favour of one of these views can be taken if it is possible to establish the time at which the preaching took place.

A. THE CONNECTION BETWEEN VERSE 18 AND VERSE 19

The time of Christ's preaching in verse 19 can only be determined after understanding the last phrase of verse 18, *being put to death in the flesh but made alive in the spirit*, and, in the light of that, the sense of *in which* (*en ho*) at the beginning of verse 19.

Being put to death in the flesh indicates the fact that Jesus' 'flesh' or physical body was put to death (so NIV: 'He was put to death in the body'). Although 'flesh' (*sarx*) has a considerable range of meaning, whenever 'flesh' is contrasted to 'spirit' (*pneuma*), as here, the contrast is between physical, visible, transitory things which belong to this present world and invisible, eternal things which exist in the unseen 'spiritual' world of heaven or the age to come. An example of such a contrast occurs at 4:6: 'In order that though judged in the flesh like men [*i.e.* they died physically], they might live in the spirit like God [*i.e.* they might gain spiritual life in heaven].' (*Cf.* also Mt. 26:41; Mk. 14:38; Jn. 3:6; 6:63; Rom. 8:4–6, 9, 13; 1 Cor. 5:5; 2 Cor. 7:1, Gal. 3:3; 4:29; 5:16–17; 6:8; Col. 2:5; 1 Tim. 3:16, which is somewhat parallel in content to 1 Pet. 3:18; and Heb. 12:9, Gk. text.)

In the light of this contrast, *made alive in the spirit* must mean 'made alive in the eternal, spiritual realm, in the realm of the Spirit's activity'. Here it refers specifically to Christ's resurrection, because 'made alive' is the opposite of 'put to death' in the previous phrase. 'In the spiritual realm, the realm of the Holy Spirit's activity, Christ was raised from the dead.'

The NIV translation, 'but made alive by the Spirit' (similarly, AV), is also possible grammatically: there is no distinction in Greek between 'spirit' and 'Spirit', and the form of the term here (dative case) can be translated either 'in' or 'by'. It would, however, be somewhat unusual if the same grammatical structure used in parallel parts of the same sentence were meant to be understood differently (*i.e.* put to death *in* the body but made alive *by* the Spirit). Moreover, a different grammatical construction (*hypo* with genitive, as in 2 Pet. 1:21, 'moved by the Holy Spirit'; also in 1 Pet. 2:4; 2 Pet. 1:17; 3:2) would have been more normal – and certainly clearer – if Peter had wanted to say 'made alive *by* the Spirit'.

If this be the correct understanding of *put to death in the flesh but made alive in the spirit* in verse 18, the phrase 'in which' at the beginning of verse 19 should be understood to refer back to 'in the spirit' in verse 18[1] as meaning 'in which (spiritual) realm Christ preached to the spirits in prison'.

This does not necessarily mean 'in the resurrected body',[2] but rather 'in the realm of the Spirit's activity, the eternal, spiritual realm' (the realm in which Christ was raised from the dead, v. 18). It might be argued that *en ho* ('in which') in verse 19 means 'in the new eschatological age, the realm of the Holy Spirit's characteristic activity after Christ's resurrection'. This would be evident, one might say, from the fact that the New Testament authors often use *pneuma*, 'spirit', in this strongly eschatological sense.

However, while such a sense for *pneuma* is common in Paul, it is not clearly the case in Peter's writings. Non-eschatological uses of *pneuma* include 1:11 ('the Spirit of Christ' speaking in OT prophets) and 2 Peter 1:21 ('men moved by the Holy Spirit spoke from God'). And Peter's frequent emphasis on the reality of the unseen 'spiritual' realm (see 1:4, 8, 12; 2:5; 3:7, 12, 22; 4:14; 5:5, 8) makes it likely that 'in which' (spiritual realm) just means in the unseen dimension of existence, in the 'spiritual' world.

Selwyn (pp. 197, 315, 317) maintains that 'in which' (*en ho*) cannot refer to 'in the spirit' in verse 18 because there are no other instances in the New Testament where a relative pronoun has as its antecedent an 'adverbial dative'. He regards this grammatical difficulty as the 'most serious of all' (p. 317) the objections to the view that Christ was preaching through Noah before the flood. However, in spite of Selwyn's claim, there are several 'adverbial datives' in the New Testament which serve as antecedents to a relative pronoun:

[1]Reicke, pp. 110–111, understands *en ho* to mean not 'in which' but 'on which occasion' (on the basis of similar meaning in 2:12; 3:16, and, so he argues, elsewhere in 1 Peter). But the words and the phrase itself are so common that there is no reason to think that Peter only used it in one specialized way: relative pronouns should be understood to refer to whichever (grammatically correct) antecedent makes the most sense in each particular context. Here, 'spirit' is near at hand and makes good sense; it is the antecedent Peter's readers would have naturally understood.

[2]As argued by France, pp. 268–269. France rightly sees the contrast in v. 18 as between the 'natural human sphere of existence' and the 'eternal spiritual state of existence' (p. 267), but then (p. 268) overly restricts the 'eternal, spiritual sphere' to mean only the resurrected state of Christ. The 'flesh-spirit' contrast in v. 18 is rather between two spheres of activity,

Verse	Rel. pronoun	Adverbial dative antecedent
Acts 2:8	which (*hē*)[1]	in his own language (*tē idia dialektō*)
Eph. 2:2	which (*hais*)	in your trespasses and sins (*tois paraptōmasin kai tais hamartiais hymōn*)
Eph. 2:3	whom (*hois*)	in the sons of disobedience (*tois huiois tēs apeitheias*)
2 Pet. 1:4	which (*hōn*)	to his own glory and excellence (*idia doxē kai aretē*) (Sinaiticus, A, C, *etc.*)
2 Pet. 3:1	which (*hais*)	in all his letters (*pasais epistolais*)

Thus Selwyn's objection is not valid. However, it would be unpersuasive even without these examples, because it is exegetically illegitimate to demand parallel examples which are so narrowly specified that one would not expect to find many, if any, examples. (It would be similar to saying that *hōn*, 'of whom', in 3:3 cannot refer to 'wives' because there is no other example of a relative pronoun taking as its antecedent an articular feminine plural vocative – a claim that would be harder to disprove by examples than this one, in fact!) Nothing in the nature of New Testament Greek requires that relative pronouns only take antecedents that function in their own clauses in certain ways and not in others. Thus Selwyn has based his exegetical judgment on an artificial distinction which has no real significance in the actual use of the language.

We are now in a position to examine the two major interpretative possibilities as to when Christ preached to the spirits: sometime after his death (or resurrection), or during the time of Noah.

B. BETWEEN HIS DEATH AND RESURRECTION – OR AFTER HIS RESURRECTION

In favour of the view that the preaching occurred between Christ's death and resurrection, or perhaps even after his resur-

---

than between the two things mentioned in those spheres in v. 18, the pre- and post-resurrection states of Christ.

[1]See Gk. text or NASB, AV. The text is literally 'in his own language, in which he was born'.

rection, is the fact that Christ's death and resurrection are mentioned so specifically in verse 18, which immediately precedes this section. Peter seems to be connecting Christ's preaching to the spirits in prison quite closely in time with his being 'put to death in the flesh but made alive in the spirit' (v. 18).

However, this observation loses much of its force when one realizes that elsewhere in this letter Peter quite often uses a word or idea at the end of one section as a springboard to an entirely new section which has a distinctly different subject. He does this regularly by using a transitional relative pronoun ('who' or 'which'), sometimes with and sometimes without a preposition in front of it.

This is seen in the Greek in 1:6 ('in which you rejoice', marking a transition to the discussion of suffering); 1:8 ('whom having not seen', marking a transition to the discussion about present fellowship with Christ); 1:10 ('concerning which salvation', marking a transition to the discussion about OT prophets); 2:4 ('to whom coming', marking a transition to the discussion of the church as the new people of God); 2:22 ('who committed no sin', marking a transition to a discussion of Christ's sufferings and redemptive work); and 3:21 ('which also now saves you', marking a transition to a discussion of baptism). Note the same kind of transition, but to less distinct material, also in 1:12; 3:3; 3:6b; 4:4 and 5:9. This frequent stylistic device throughout 1 Peter means that one simply cannot argue that the phrase 'in which' at the beginning of verse 19 means that this verse must be continuing the same subject or the same line of thought (or the same chronological sequence) as verse 18 – Peter uses this literary device too frequently when changing to a distinct subject.

Furthermore, it is hard to see that the view that Christ proclaimed the message of salvation to the spirits in prison sometime after his death on the cross really suits the context. Peter is exhorting his readers to be faithful witnesses for Christ even if they should have to suffer. But if he then proceeds to tell them that even the worst sinners in all history, the generation of the flood, can be given another chance to repent after they have died, he would then be defeating his purpose in writing: what need would there be for believers to endure suffering now if those who refuse to become Christians now because of the cost involved can repent after death? And what point is there in enduring suffering as a Christian now if there is another chance to be saved after death?

Moreover, it is difficult to explain why only sinners who disobeyed during the building of the ark are given another opportunity to repent. Why not others as well, especially those who had no chance to hear the warnings to repent? Furthermore, the idea of a chance of salvation after death is difficult to reconcile with other parts of the New Testament (cf. Lk. 16:26; Heb. 9:27). It is unlikely that Peter's view on a matter of such importance would have differed fundamentally from that of the rest of the leadership of the early church.

These considerations leave us with View 1: the preaching to the spirits in prison was done at the time when Noah was building the ark.

C. AT THE TIME OF NOAH

1. Could Peter have thought this?

In consideration of View 1 (Christ preached through Noah when Noah was building the ark), one must ask if it was possible for Peter to conceive of Christ preaching through Noah. This certainly seems possible in the light of the fact that Peter calls Noah 'a herald (or, preacher) of righteousness' (2 Pet. 2:5), and in the light of the fact that Peter understands the 'spirit of Christ' to have been active during the Old Testament period, moving the prophets to predict 'the sufferings of Christ and the glories that were to follow' (1:11, NIV). In the light of this, although Peter does not specifically describe Noah as a prophet, it would not be difficult for him to think of the spirit of Christ as active in him as he preached to the flood generation.

2. Relationship to the larger context (especially 1 Peter 3:13–22)

a. Christ preaching through Noah
One objection which Dalton makes to View 1 is that it has no

clear link with its larger context. However, the opposite is actually the case. If we understand Peter here to be referring to Christ preaching through Noah, then the passage functions well in the immediate context of 3:13–22 and in the larger context of the whole letter. In fact, there are several remarkable parallels between the situation of Noah before the flood and the situation of Peter's readers.

(1) Noah was in a small minority of believers surrounded by a group of hostile unbelievers (who were perhaps even persecuting him). The readers are also a small minority and are surrounded by hostile unbelievers who make the threat of persecution very real (3:13–14; 4:4).

(2) Noah was righteous (Gn. 6:22; 7:5; 2 Pet. 2:5). Peter exhorts his readers to be righteous in a similarly difficult situation (3:10–12, 13, 16–17; 4:1–3).

(3) Noah witnessed boldly to the unbelievers around him, preaching repentance and warning of judgment soon to come (cf. 2 Pet. 2:5, 9). Similarly, Peter exhorts his readers not to fear (3:14) but to bear witness boldly (3:15–16), even in suffering if necessary (3:16; also 4:16), in order to bring others to God – just as Christ was willing to endure suffering in order to bring us to God (3:18). Peter also sounds a clear warning of judgment to come (4:5, 17–18; cf. 2 Pet. 3:10) which makes the reader's situation prior to judgment similar to that of Noah.

(4) Christ, though he was in an unseen 'spiritual realm', was preaching through Noah to the unbelievers around him (3:19–20). Similarly, Christ is working in an unseen spiritual way in the lives and hearts of Peter's readers (3:15; cf. 1:22; 4:11, 14). Thus, Peter by implication is reminding his readers that if Christ was preaching through Noah he certainly is also preaching through them as they bear witness to the unbelievers around them.

(5) In the time of Noah, God patiently awaited repentance from unbelievers, but finally did bring judgment. Similarly, at the time Peter is writing, God is patiently awaiting repentance from unbelievers (cf. 2 Pet. 3:9) but will certainly bring judgment on the unrepentant (4:5; cf. 2 Pet. 3:10).

(6) Finally, Noah was rescued with a few others (3:20). Similarly, Peter reminds his readers that they too will be saved,

even if their numbers are few, for Christ has certainly triumphed (3:22), and they will share in his triumph as well (4:13, 19; 5:10; *cf.* 2 Pet. 2:9).

The attractiveness of View 1 is thus enhanced by its clear compatibility with the context at several points. It fits well with Peter's purpose of encouraging suffering believers that they need not fear to be righteous and to bear faithful witness to the hostile unbelievers surrounding them, for Christ is at work in them as he was in Noah, and they, like Noah, will certainly be saved from the judgment to come.

In fact, it is the remarkable similarity between the situations of Noah and of Peter's readers which best explains why Peter, in reaching back to the Old Testament for an encouraging example, selects the incident of Noah preparing the ark. Far from being surprising or unusual, this example is contextually quite appropriate.

b. Contextual difficulties with Dalton's view

The appropriateness of this view in the context gives another argument for the superiority of View 1 over View 5 (Christ's proclaiming victory over fallen angels). For on the basis of View 5, the compatibility with context would not be nearly as great.

For the sake of argument, let us for the moment assume that Christ's preaching to the spirits in prison refers to his proclamation of condemnation to fallen angels, either between his death and resurrection or after his resurrection from the dead. And let us assume that the background in 1 Enoch claimed by Dalton and others is correct, so that Christ imitates and fulfils the pattern established by the preaching of condemnation to fallen angels by Enoch. The fact that Christ proclaimed his victory would then function, in a general way, as an encouragement to believers who were being persecuted. Thus, on Dalton's view, there is a connection with the larger context.

There are, however, several points at which the connection is imprecise or inconsistent. First, on Dalton's view Christ proclaims his triumph over fallen angels or evil spirits. Yet while Peter does mention the devil's opposition to believers (1 Pet. 5:8), the letter as a whole, and the immediate context, focus upon human, not demonic, sources of persecution

(3:13–16; 4:3–4; *etc.*). Moreover, in the one place where Peter does mention the devil's activities, he draws attention not to his past defeat, but to his present dangerous activity as he 'prowls around like a roaring lion' (5:8).

Second, the parallel to the readers' situation is not close since neither Christ nor Enoch (in 1 Enoch) are being persecuted any longer by those to whom they proclaimed final condemnation, unlike Peter's readers who, at the time of writing, are still being persecuted.

Third, although Enoch and Christ, according to this view, both went to declare condemnation to angels in hell, the readers would not find an example for imitation in that, for they certainly would not travel to hell and proclaim condemnation to sinful angels.

Fourth, witnessing to unbelievers, which is a major emphasis of Peter in this passage (3:14, 16–17; *cf.* 'bring us to God' in v. 18), is not really furthered; one does not encourage the preaching of repentance to sinful men by calling to mind two examples of the proclaiming of final condemnation to sinful angels!

3. *The translation 'when they formerly disobeyed'*

One final consideration in favour of View 1 is that it makes possible a grammatically preferable translation of 'formerly disobeyed' (*apeithesasin pote*) at the beginning of verse 20. The phrase is usually translated 'who formerly disobeyed', but there is no separate word for 'who' in the Greek text; this translation depends on understanding the participle *apeithesasin* as an adjectival participle modifying 'spirits' in the previous verse. The difficulty with understanding it this way turns on a technical point in Greek usage.

In order to make it clear that he wanted the phrase to be understood as an adjective modifying 'spirits' Peter should have written, according to the normal standards of Greek usage, *tois apeithesasin*, putting the definite article in front of the participle (and thus putting it in 'attributive position'). This is ordinarily necessary for adjectives (including participles) which modify articular nouns (nouns which have a definite article).

Thus, BDF, sec. 270, says,

An attributive adjective (participle) when used with an arthrous substantive must, as in classical, participate in the force of
the article by taking an intermediate position . . . or, if placed in
postposition (to which the participle with additional adjuncts is
especially susceptible), it *must* have its own article [italics mine].

BDF gives two types of exceptions to this rule:

(a) (BDF, sec. 269) A noun with two or more adjectives or
adjectival phrases need not have all of them between the definite
article and the noun (which may become awkward), and those
following the noun need not have the article, but only when
needed for emphasis or to avoid ambiguity.

One example of this is *genomenēn* in Acts 13:32. But note that in all
the examples given in BDF, there is little chance of ambiguity
because the adjective (or participle) immediately follows the noun
and is not separated by an intervening main verb as in 1 Peter 3:20.

(b) (BDF, sec. 416) Supplementary participles following verbs
of perception or cognition (knowing, seeing, hearing, *etc.*) do not
have the definite article. Examples are Mark 5:30; Luke 10:18;
2 Peter 1:18.

But apart from these categories where the absence of the
definite article is allowed there do not seem to be any clear
examples in the New Testament of anarthrous participles (participles which lack the definite article in front of them) which have
an arthrous antecedent (*i.e.* an antecedent with a definite article)
and which are adjectival (in that they modify the noun which is
their antecedent). Even among the examples which fall in the
categories of exceptions noted by BDF, in most cases the anarthrous adjectival participle will follow immediately after the noun it
modifies, and 2 Peter 1:18 (with the verb of perception 'we
heard') is the only example, even from those in the exceptional
categories, where I found the participle separated from its antecedent by the main verb of the sentence, as it is in 1 Peter 3:19–20.
Thus there may be no clearly parallel example anywhere else in
the New Testament which would justify the translation 'who
formerly disobeyed'.[1]

The difficulty of translating it this way is felt by at least one

---

[1]Lk. 2:5; 16:14; Acts 24:24; and 1 Pet. 4:12 all have participles which might be thought to be

grammar, which refers to the participle in 1 Peter 3:20 as 'unclassical' (MHT 3, p. 153), and 'not good Greek' (MHT 4, p. 129).

On the other hand, the usual way of translating anarthrous participles in the kind of construction found in 1 Peter 3:19–20 is to understand them adverbially (as modifying the verb in the sentence, rather than the noun which is their antecedent). Such adverbial participles may be translated in several different ways according to the context. Thus, if the context allowed it, a very proper grammatical translation of *apeithesasin pote* might be 'because they formerly disobeyed' or 'although they formerly disobeyed', or 'when they formerly disobeyed': in each case the phrase would modify the verbal idea 'preached'.

Such adverbial modification of a sentence by a participle is clearly possible even when the antecedent of the participle is a noun which is not the subject of the main verb (this is the case in 1 Pet. 3:20). The following examples are fairly close parallels to 1 Peter 3:20.

Mk. 16:10 (v.l.)	*penthousi*	temporal: 'while they mourned'
Jn. 1:36	*peripatounti*	circumstantial: 'as he walked'
Acts 7:2	*onti*	temporal: 'when he was in Mesopotamia'
Acts 7:26	*machomenois*	circumstantial: 'as they were quarrelling'
Acts 8:12	*euaggelizomenō*	temporal: 'when he preached'
Acts 11:17	*pisteusasin*	temporal: 'when we believed'
2 Cor. 5:14	*krinantas*	causal: 'because we are convinced'
Heb. 7:1	*hypostrephonti*	temporal: 'when he was returning'

These grammatical considerations open at least the possibility and perhaps the strong probability that we should translate

---

exceptions, but they are all actually adverbial (of attendant circumstance), even though they may be loosely translated in an adjectival way. 2 Corinthians 11:9 may be an exception, but here again the participle immediately follows the noun, unlike 1 Pet. 3:20; moreover, *elthontes* in 2 Cor. 11:9 may well be adverbial rather than adjectival (the NASB understands it adverbially: 'when the brethren came from Macedonia'); *cf.* P. Hughes, *Paul's Second Epistle to the Corinthians*, NIC (Grand Rapids: Eerdmans, 1962), p. 386.

apeithesasin pote in 1 Peter 3:20 adverbially – 'when they formerly disobeyed'.

Now in the light of the preceding discussion the translation 'when they formerly disobeyed' would fit the context well. And it must be said that it is not merely grammatically possible, but it is grammatically preferable to the translation 'who formerly disobeyed'.

It could be objected that it is unlikely that the participle has a temporal sense ('when') because the next phrase gives a further indication of time, namely, *when God's patience waited*. The presence of a further temporal clause would then make a temporal sense for *apeithesasin pote* unnecessary and perhaps even redundant.

However, against this, there are other instances of similar constructions which have two or more time references in succession. Examples are found in Colossians 3:7 (with a combination of aorist and imperfect tenses which parallels 1 Peter 3:19–20 quite closely); Philo, *On the Cherubim* 58; *On the Decalogue* 58; *On the Special Laws* 3.1; *cf.* Epistle of Barnabas 7.9 (manuscripts aleph, V read *pote*). In fact in 1 Peter 3:20 itself there is already more than one time reference: *when God's patience waited*, then *in the days of Noah*, then *during the building of the ark*. The addition of 'when they formerly disobeyed' to this sequence would not be awkward or difficult to understand. Moreover, 'formerly' (*pote*) is helpful in making Peter's meaning clear, for it immediately indicates to the reader that the 'disobeying' is not at the same time as Peter is writing but is at an earlier point in time, 'formerly'.

The translation 'when they formerly disobeyed' also answers the objection by Dalton (p. 148) that if Peter had meant to speak of spirits of persons who disobeyed he would have written *pneumasin tōn apeithēsantōn*, 'spirits of those who disobeyed'. If our understanding is correct, Peter wrote exactly what he meant to say, namely, that Christ preached to the spirits who are now in prison but he did so 'when they *formerly* disobeyed'.

4. Remaining objections

a. The verb poreutheis ('went')

There remain some other objections to this view. First, Dalton

(p. 35) objects that the verb *poreutheis* ('went') cannot be used to describe Christ's divine activity at the time of the Old Testament. But this objection is not a strong one, because the Old Testament often talks about a divine activity of God in terms of God's 'going' to a certain place (Gn. 3:8; 11:7; 18:21; *etc*; *cf*. 1 Cor. 10:4, which speaks of Christ following the people as they travelled through the wilderness). Moreover, the same verb (*poreuomai*) is used in 1 Peter 3:22 to speak of Christ's going into heaven. In fact, the use of *poreutheis* in 3:19 is necessary for Peter's purpose, for if Peter had just said that 'in the spiritual realm' Christ 'preached', it might suggest a distant activity of speaking out of heaven, whereas 'he went and preached' implies more personal involvement in going to the place of the hearers and therefore preaching through Noah.

b. The sequence death-resurrection-ascension

It might also be objected that the sequence *died . . . made alive . . . has gone into heaven* in 3:18–22 shows that the events coming between verse 18 and 22 must occur between Christ's resurrection and ascension.

Someone making such an objection might argue that three aorist participles show the structure of the passage: *thanatōtheis* ('died') and *zōopoiētheis* ('made alive') in 3:18, and *poreutheis* ('having gone') in 3:22. Therefore (one might conclude) the aorist participle *poreutheis* ('going' or 'having gone') in 3:19 must fit within this structure and must refer to some event between Christ's resurrection and ascension.

In response, we can certainly agree that there is a clear connection between *died* and *made alive* in 3:18; since both are aorist participles in adjacent phrases in the same sentence, and since their linkage is made explicit by the *men . . . de* ('on the one hand . . . on the other hand') construction in this part of the sentence.

It is quite another matter with *who has gone into heaven*, however. It comes not in an adjacent phrase but sixty words (or ten clauses) after *made alive in the spirit*. Ordinary readers (and listeners) would naturally settle on a sense for *poreutheis*, 'he went', which was suitable to its immediate context in 3:19 long before they reached 'having gone into heaven' in 3:22. And not every event between 3:18 and 3:22 occurred between Christ's resurrection and ascension on any account (note 'days of Noah' and 'baptism now saves you' as parenthetical items). Even in 3:22 itself such a suggested sequence is not followed, because *is at the right hand of God* is placed before *who has gone into heaven*, though in a chronological listing of Christ's activities the idea of going into heaven would come first, and being at God's right hand would come second.

So the idea of a sequence in the aorist participles should not be seen as a strong argument against the 'Christ preaching through Noah' view, but as an argument that may carry weight for readers who somehow 'see' the passage in that perspective. It must be said that such a structure is not made explicit by any clear contextual pointers, nor is it required by the context. Such a sequence may have been Peter's intention, but it probably was not. And even if it was, 3:19 can still be understood as a parenthetical statement outside the chronological sequence (just as 3:20–21).

Furthermore, the mention of Christ's ascension in 3:22 is probably better accounted for by the fact that it is the naturally sequential event to include after the mention of Christ's resurrection at the end of 3:21 (not the end of 3:18).

Lastly, Peter's frequent use of a relative pronoun to introduce a new subject (see above, p. 229) indicates that there is a strong possibility that there is no clear chronological sequence in this section. Certainly it must not be insisted upon if other factors in the context point in another direction.

c. Why did Peter not say that Christ preached 'through Noah'?

Finally, one might wonder why, if this was indeed Peter's meaning, he did not make it clearer by simply saying that Christ 'preached *through Noah* to the spirits in prison when they formerly disobeyed'. We cannot, of course, say with certainty why an author did not say something else. But we should realize at least that Peter's readers, with native-speaker ability in Greek, would have heard in his words the sense 'when they formerly disobeyed' much more readily than we do, especially since our minds are cluttered by English translations which say 'who formerly disobeyed'.

In addition to this grammatical factor, the abundance of extra-biblical testimony to Noah's preaching to rebellious unbelievers during the building of the ark would have made the sense proposed here much more readily understood. In fact, if we could have asked any first-century Jew or Christian the question, 'Who preached to those who disobeyed in the days of Noah, while the patience of God was waiting during the building of the ark?', there would certainly be only one answer: it was Noah who did this preaching.

To a group of Christians who had such an understanding of the biblical narrative, Peter then wrote that Christ preached to the disobedient people of Noah's time. It might not have been asking too much of his readers to expect them to realize that he meant that it was through Noah that Christ did this preaching. In short, the sentence may not have been as obscure to the original readers as it has long seemed to subsequent interpreters.

IV. CONCLUSION

Our conclusions on this passage may now be expressed in an extended paraphrase: 'In the spiritual realm of existence Christ went and preached through Noah to those who are now spirits in the prison of hell. This happened when they formerly disobeyed, when the patience of God was waiting in the days of Noah while the ark was being built.'

In its context, this passage thus functions (1) to encourage the readers to bear witness boldly in the midst of hostile unbelievers, just as Noah did; (2) to assure them that though they are few, God will surely save them; (3) to remind them of the certainty of final judgment and Christ's ultimate triumph over all the forces of evil which oppose them. This passage, similarly understood, can provide similar encouragement to Peter's readers today.[1]

---

[1]After completing this Appendix, I obtained a copy of John S. Feinberg's article, '1 Peter 3:18–20, Ancient Mythology, and the Intermediate State', *WTJ* 48 (1986), pp. 303–336. I am pleased to see that Dr Feinberg and I, working entirely independently and with widely differing methods of approaching this text, have reached very similar conclusions. His arguments on pp. 327–336 are especially forceful in showing several still-unresolved contextual and theological difficulties faced by any view which argues for a 'preaching of condemnation', whether to human beings or to angels (Views 3 and 5 above).